Freemasonry
AND ITS ETIQUETTE

Freemasonry
AND ITS ETIQUETTE

WILLIAM PRESTON
CAMPBELL-EVERDEN

Gramercy Books
New York

This 2001 edition is published by Gramercy Books™, an imprint of Random House Value Publishing, Inc. 280 Park Avenue, New York, N.Y. 10017.

Gramercy Books™ and design are trademarks of Random House Value Publishing, Inc.

Random House
New York • Toronto • London • Sydney • Auckland
http://www.randomhouse.com/

Printed and bound in the United States of America

Library of Congress Cataloging in Publication Data

Campbell-Everden, William Preston.
    Freemasonry and its etiquette.

1. Freemasons 2. Freemasons—Handbooks, manuals,
etc. I. An old past mater. II. Title.   III. Title:
The etiquette of freemasonry.

Hs395.C25   1978   366'.1   78-15432

ISBN 0-517-25914-1

8 7 6 5 4 3 2

CONTENTS

v

Contents

FOREWORD

MASONRY, or Freemasonry, is a 600-year-old fraternity with a 3,000-year-old tradition. The oldest, largest, and most widely known fraternal organization in the world, it is the prototype of most modern fraternal societies and service organizations.

Modern Freemasonry dates from the year 1717 when four very old Lodges met together in London to form the first Grand Lodge. Today there are over six million Masons in the world, and over half of these in the United States. The unit of organization is the Lodge, which may consist of a few dozen or several hundred members, and each Lodge belongs to a Grand Lodge. There are over 30,000 Lodges in the world, and more than 100 Grand Lodges. There is no central authority, and world recognition is maintained by a system of mutual fraternal recognition among Grand Lodges.

Freemasonry and Its Etiquette has long been the standard ready reference book for the individual Mason desirous of improving his knowledge of the fraternity, both the early history and the actual work that takes place within every regular and well-governed Lodge. Written by a member of a London Lodge, the Mother Grand Lodge of all Masonry, its carefully detailed and explicit suggestions are applicable to all English-speaking Lodges throughout the world.

Among the many facets of the fraternity covered are:

- Who are fit and proper persons to be made Masons?
- What is a Lodge of Freemasons?
- Ritual
- The Ceremonies
- The Lodge Officers and their duties
- Concordant Bodies.

Unlike the earlier exposés of the early Eighteenth Century, *Freemasonry and Its Etiquette* is a well-documented account of the details essential to the workings of the business of the Masonic Lodge.

Well written, in a lively and very read-

able manner, it is a valuable and necessary
addition to the working library of anyone
interested in the actual happenings within
a Lodge.

ALLAN BOUDREAU, Ph.D.
Grand Lodge Librarian
Grand Lodge Free and
Accepted Masons
of the State of New York
May 1978

FREEMASONRY

AND

ITS ETIQUETTE

INTRODUCTION

In introducing this treatise on Freemasonry and its Etiquette to the attention of the members of the Craft, it is desirable that a brief explanation should be given of the title selected for the work.

Obviously the word 'Freemasonry' conveys its own meaning and scope; but 'Etiquette' is intended to be understood, not only in its somewhat restricted signification —namely, 'The social observances required by good-breeding'—but also in its wider and more comprehensive meaning, as 'Regulations as to behaviour, dress, etc., to be observed by particular persons upon particular occasions; forms which are observed in particular places.'

In accordance with this wider interpretation of the word 'Etiquette,' many duties and details not provided for in the Book of Constitutions, or in the Ritual, will be fully considered; and, where necessary, will be discussed and explained in this work. It is also intended that the means and appliances, the technicalities and ceremonial observances (as distinct from the verbal portions of the Ceremonies), which are indispensably necessary for the decorous and harmonious working of the business of the Lodge, shall be detailed; and, where it may be needful, they will be fully explained.

It will readily be conceded that, in addition to the words of the several Ceremonies, there is need for instruction in the manner in which the Officers of the Lodge should perform certain portions of their respective duties. The Ritual contains directions here and there; but they are necessarily brief, and in some cases they may be misunderstood or wrongly interpreted. The saying is trite, but strictly true, that the Master of a Lodge—however perfect he may be himself—cannot achieve his best unless he be well supported and assisted by his Officers: whereas, if he be intelligently and zealously assisted by them, and the Ceremonies be well rendered by all concerned, the resultant effect upon the Candidate—almost to a certainty—will be, that he will form so favourable an opinion of the Institution, as to inspire him with a lasting love of the Craft, such as will cause him to become—in fact, and not in name only—'a true and faithful brother among us.'

On the other hand, if the duties of the subordinate Officers be performed in a perfunctory or slovenly manner, the beauty and the impressiveness of the several Ceremonies will be materially marred or altogether lost, so far as their effect upon the Candidate is concerned.

The experience of every thoughtful and intelligent Freemason, who attends his own Lodge with tolerable regularity, and who occasionally visits other Lodges, will fully confirm this assertion. He must have known instances wherein the want of attention to details, on the part of certain of the Officers, and the absence of the necessary preparation for the business to be transacted, have led to confusion and delay; and have in a great measure marred the effect of the Ceremonies. At a critical moment, in some important part of the Ceremony, which may have been led up to by a serious address, something—indispensable to the continuity of the work—was not at hand; perhaps the alms-dish, or the badge with which the Candidate in either degree was to be invested;

or the heavy M. in the Third Degree; or some other equally important detail.

In cases such as those mentioned, a certain degree of confusion was inevitable; whisperings, and hurried messages, and dartings hither and thither, to the great annoyance of all concerned, and to the certain distraction of the attention of the Candidate.

This work is commended to the attention of Officers of Lodges, of aspirants to office, and of all Freemasons who are lovers of order, in the earnest hope that the irregularities and inconveniences hereinbefore mentioned may, as far as is possible, be guarded against in their several Lodges.

* * * *

One of the objects of this work is to discuss 'the minor jurisprudence of the Craft.'

Jurisprudence is defined as 'the knowledge of the laws, customs, and rights of men in a state or a community.'

As far as we, as a community, are concerned, the Book of Constitutions may be taken as containing the major jurisprudence of the Order; but there are numberless small but far from unimportant matters not considered in the Constitutions, which form part of our System, and to which it is desir-

4

Introduction

able to call attention in a work of this character, dealing, as it is intended to do, with all the details, great and small, in any way connected with the Lodge, the Ceremonies, and the general business of the Craft, as far as private Lodges are concerned.

There is in every state and community the 'lex non scripta,' which, from precedent and immemorial usage, is held to be of equal force with statute law. Of this character are many of our ancient customs, upon which our Constitutions are silent, and upon which 'Freemasonry and its Etiquette' is expected to be an illuminating guide.

Some—probably many—of the subjects will be discussed, with more or less of elaboration of detail. It is hoped that the criticisms may not be considered to be unnecessary because they treat of things in constant use in every Lodge, or that more has been said than there is a positive necessity to say. If the thought should arise in the minds of any reader of these pages, 'All these requisites for a Lodge, and the mode of arrangement, etc., are to be found continually in the Lodge of which I am a member, and in the majority of those which I occasionally visit; then why this long repetition of detail of things with which I am perfectly familiar?' let such a Brother remember that there are many hundreds of Lodges lying beyond the sphere of his observation, and which, from various causes, are very far indeed from coming up to the standard of perfect equipment such as the proper performance of our Rites and Ceremonies demands.

Want of carefulness in details and in arrangement, and a deficiency in certain necessary things, ought not to occur in any Lodge of Freemasons; such a state of incompleteness is incompatible with the dignity of the Worshipful Master. It is the duty of the Director of Ceremonies, and, indeed, the duty of every Officer of the Lodge, to see 'that everything be done decently and in order.'

To sum up briefly, it may be said with entire truthfulness that a want of acquaintance with, or a great degree of disregard of, the 'Etiquette of Freemasonry' exists in too many of our Lodges; and that both in 'the forms which are observed in particular places' and in 'regulations as to behaviour, dress, etc., to be observed by particular persons upon particular occasions,' many of our Lodges and their members are more or less open to improvement.

It is with the view and in the hope of effecting corrections where they may be proved to be necessary that these pages have been written; not in any censorious or captious spirit, nor with any desire to promulgate fads or crotchets; nor, above all, 'to make innovation in the body of Freemasonry'; but in perfect singleness of mind and heart to give the results in plain language of the experience gained during a protracted and varied Masonic career, in the hope and trust that some instruction may be imparted, and possibly some improvements may be effected, where the need of improvement may be felt to exist.

So mote it be.

CHAPTER I

WHAT IS FREEMASONRY?

SPEAKING generally, Freemasonry is a Science which comprehends the principles, practices, and institutions of a secret brotherhood existing in all parts of the world, and known universally by the generic name of Freemasons.

The Fraternity is composed of a series of groups or communities known as Lodges, and these Private Lodges respectively own allegiance to one or other of the Grand Lodges or Grand Orients, according to the country in which they carry on their operations or according to the fundamental principles they profess.

Originally the one basic principle of them all, without exception, was an emphasized belief in the existence of a Supreme Being or Creator, in whose Name every Lodge was conducted; and subject to the confession of that belief, the follower of any theistic religion was, in that respect, acceptable as a member. In comparatively recent time the Grand Orient of France, in the development of what it considered liberty of conscience, discontinued its acknowledgment of the existence of a Supreme Being; and as a consequence, in 1878, relations were ruptured between the Grand Orient of France and Grand Lodge, which remained true to its original principle and reaffirmed that a belief in TGAOTU is the first and most important of the Ancient Landmarks (see Chapter II).

In 1898, for the same reason, Grand Lodge withdrew its recognition from the Grand Lodge of Peru, and again took occasion to reaffirm the Landmark.

This volume, 'Freemasonry and its Etiquette,' is specifically addressed to those Freemasons, wherever dispersed over the face of earth and water, who own allegiance to The United Grand Lodge of Ancient Free and Accepted Masons of England, which is hereinafter referred to as THE GRAND LODGE.

By the solemn Act of Union between the two Grand Lodges of Freemasons of England in December, 1813, it was 'declared and pronounced that pure Ancient Masonry consists of three degrees and no more—viz., those of the Entered Apprentice, the Fellow Craft, and the Master Mason, including the Supreme

Order of the Holy Royal Arch' (Chapter XXX).

Very early in our Masonic career we are taught that Freemasonry is a system of morality the peculiarities of which are veiled from the uninstructed and popular world by allegorical treaching and symbolical illustration.

Most of this teaching and illustration being oral, it is natural that diversities, small though numerous in their origin, should arise, and unless there exists some standard by which present practice may be brought continually into conformity with original precept, slight diversities beget other and larger diversities, and the result is sometimes interesting and sometimes disastrous, producing 'confusion worse confounded.'

The object of 'Freemasonry and its Etiquette' is to supply that standard, and the enable the Brethren to apply the Square and Compasses of certain duly recognized but often forgotten Principles to the incidents of their own everyday Masonic life, and with their aid to produce a Perfect Ashlar which may in turn be of service to less experienced Craftsmen as a faithful and reliable guide and model.

Freemasonry claims to have existed in

some form or other from the earliest period of time; but is more immediately derived from and based upon the secret organizations of the Operative Masons of the Middle Ages; and to distinguish it therefrom it is now termed Free and Accepted or Speculative Masonry.

The Masonic Lectures (see Chapter XXVII) thus refer to the two classes:—

'Masonry, according to the general acceptation of the term, is an Art founded on the principles of Geometry, and directed to the service and convenience of mankind. But Freemasonry, embracing a wider range, and having a more noble object in view—namely, the cultivation and improvement of the human mind—may with more propriety be called a Science, although its lessons for the most part are veiled in allegory and illustrated by symbols.'

The following sentences are taken from a brief sketch, entitled, 'Freemasonry: its Origin, History, and Design':

'The descendants of the Roman colleges of artificers established schools of architecture, and taught and practised the art of building among the newly enfranchised people. . . . From this school of Lombardian builders proceeded that society of architects who were known at that time by the appellation of Free Masons, and who from the tenth to the sixteenth century traversed the Continent of Europe, engaged almost exclusively in the construction of religious edifices, such as cathedrals, churches, and monasteries. The monastic orders formed an alliance with them, so that the convents frequently became their domiciles, and they instructed the monks in the secret principles of their art. The Popes took them under their protection, granted them charters of monopoly as ecclesiastical architects, and invested them with many important and exclusive privileges. Dissevering the ties which bound them to the monks, these Free Masons (so called to distinguish them from the rough masons, who were of an inferior grade, and not members of the corporation) subsequently established the guilds of stonemasons, which existed until the end of the seventeenth century in Germany, France, England, and Scotland.

'These stonemasons, or, as they continued to call themselves, Free Masons, had one peculiarity in their organization which is necessary to be considered if we would comprehend the relation that exists between them and the Freemasons of the present day, The society was necessarily an operative one, whose members were actually engaged in the manual labour of building, as well as in the more intellectual occupation of architectural designing. This, with the fact of their previous connection with the monks, who probably projected the plans which the Masons carried into execution, led to the admission among them of persons who were not operative Masons. These were high ecclesiastics, wealthy nobles, and men of science who were encouragers and patrons of the art. These, not competent to engage in the labour of building, were supposed to confine themselves to philosophic speculations on the principles of the art, and to symbolizing or spiritualizing its labour and its implements. Hence there resulted a division of the membership of the brotherhood into two classes, the practical and theoretical, or, as they are more commonly called, the operative and speculative, or "domatic" and "geomatic." The operative Masons always held the ascendancy in numbers until the seventeenth century, but the speculative Masons exerted a greater influence by their higher culture, their wealth, and their social position.

'In time there came a total and permanent disseverance of the two elements. At the beginning of the eighteenth century there were several Lodges in England, but

for a long time there had been no meeting
of a great assembly. In the year 1717,
Freemasonry was revived,* and the Grand
Lodge of England was established by four
of the Lodges which then existed in London.
This revival* took place through the influence and by the exertions of non-operative
or speculative Masons, and the Institution
has ever since mainly preserved that character. . . .

'Freemasonry of the present day is a
philosophic or speculative science, derived
from, and issuing out of, an operative art.
It is a science of symbolism.'

Freemasonry is founded on the purest
principles of piety and virtue; and the Grand
Principles on which the Order is founded are
Brotherly Love, Relief, and Truth.

It is natural, therefore, to find that upon
such foundations have been erected many
lasting monuments; and among the foremost of these may be mentioned the three
great Masonic Institutions, to which Chapter
XXVI is devoted.

But it may be as well to add here a few
words indicating what Freemasonry is NOT.
Freemasonry is *not*, and is not intended to
be, a benefit Society, from which in return
for certain calculated subscriptions, certain

* See Operative Masonry, Chapter XXXII.

calculated benefits are received by the subscriber; in other words, any person intending to be initiated should be solemnly warned against entertaining or being influenced by any mercenary or other unworthy motive as regards his own advantage in joining such an altruistic Society as Freemasonry claims to be. Its aims are to help others; and its noble gifts are intended for the benefit of others; and those who join it ought to be in such a position as will permit them, without detriment to themselves or their connections, to give freely of their substance for the maintenance of those truly masonic ornaments, Benevolence and Charity.

Freemasonry may be said to be the highest expression of those noble watchwords, 'Liberty, Equality, Fraternity,' and its true meaning has been happily described as 'the building of every part of a man into a spiritual house fit for the habitation of God.'

CHAPTER II

GRAND LODGES AND GRAND ORIENTS

THE Grand Lodge of England (1717) recognizes and is in fraternal relation with—

The Grand Lodge of Ireland (1730),

The Grand Lodge of Scotland (1736),

14 Foreign Grand Lodges and Grand Orients in the Eastern Hemisphere,

7 Colonial Grand Lodges,

9 Grand Lodges in the Dominion of Canada,

50 Grand Lodges in the United States of America, and about 12 other Grand Lodges and Grand Orients in the West Indies, Mexico, Central America and South America; and besides these there are

656 District and other Lodges abroad; so that the claim of Freemasonry to be 'Universal' would seem to be well supported.

The Grand Orient of France is not included in the above list, but on December 3, 1913, the Grand Secretary read to Grand Lodge the following message from the M.W. Grand Master:

'It is with deep satisfaction that I find myself able to signalize the auspicious occasion of the Centenary of the Union by an announcement which will, I am convinced, cause true rejoicing throughout the Craft.

'A body of Freemasons in France, confronted by a positive prohibition on the part of the Grand Orient to work in the name of the Great Architect of the Universe have, in fidelity to their Masonic pledges, resolved to uphold the true principles and tenets of the Craft, and have united several Lodges as the INDEPENDENT AND REGULAR NATIONAL GRAND LODGE OF FRANCE AND OF THE FRENCH COLONIES.

'This new body has approached me with the request that it may be recognized by the Grand Lodge of England, and, having received full assurance that it is pledged to adhere to those principles of Freemasonry which we regard as fundamental and essential, I have joyfully assented to the establishment of fraternal relations and the exchange of representatives.

'We are thus enabled to celebrate the hundredth anniversary of that Union which was the foundation of our solidarity and world-wide influence, by the consummation of a wish which has been ardently cherished by English Freemasons for many years past, and we are once more in the happy position of being able to enjoy Masonic intercourse with men of the great French nation.

'I trust that the bond thus established will strengthen and promote the good understanding which exists outside of the sphere of Freemasonry.'

It will be interesting to add that the obligations which will be imposed on all Lodges under this French Constitution are the following:

1. While the Lodge is at work the Bible will always be open.

2. The ceremonies will be conducted in strict conformity with the Ritual of the 'Régime Rectifié' which is followed by these Lodges, a Ritual which was drawn up in 1778 and sanctioned in 1782, and with which the Duke of Kent was initiated in 1792.

3. The Lodge will always be opened and closed with the invocation and in the name of the Great Architect of the Universe. All the summonses of the Order and of the Lodges will be printed with the symbols of the Great Architect of the Universe.

4. No religious or political discussion will be permitted in the Lodge.

5. The Lodge as such will never take part

officially in any political affair, but every individual Brother will preserve complete liberty of opinion and action.

6. Only those Brethren who are recognized as true Brethren by the Grand Lodge of England will be received in Lodge.

CHAPTER III

GRAND LODGES OF ENGLAND

[The history contained in this chapter was published in the *Freemason* on December 27, 1913, on the occasion of the Centenary of the Union (vol. liii, No. 2,338).

The historical account of the proceedings which took place on December 27, 1813, is based upon a report in William Preston's 'Illustrations of Masonry,' which has been amended by references to the late Brother W. J. Hughan's 'Memorials of the Masonic Union, 1813.']

FORMERLY England had four Grand Lodges. The oldest, and much the strongest, was founded at the Apple Tree Tavern, Charles Street, Covent Garden, London, in 1717. Members of it traced their origin to an assemblage of Freemasons by King Athelstan at York, in 926 A.D. The Scotch Lodges did not go back nearly so far. They were content to claim descent from those foreign Masons who came to their country in the twelfth century to build the abbeys of Melrose, Holyrood, and Kilwinning, and

there is abundant evidence that the Lodges
of York and Kilwinning were the parents of
many Lodges founded in various parts of
Great Britain. The Brethren of York,
conscious that their city was the Mecca of
Freemasonry, and believing that their Time
Immemorial Lodge was a direct descendant
of that which was existing in the fourteenth
century, determined that they would not
be behind those of London, and in 1725
formed the Grand Lodge of All England.
Despite its ambitious title, it had a very
chequered career down to the last decade
of the eighteenth century. About 1740 it,
as did also the private York Lodge, became
dormant. Both were revived in 1761, but
there is no evidence of their existence after
1792. That Grand Lodge confined its
activities within a limited area of 'All England.' Under its banner were two Lodges
in the City of York, one each in Scarborough,
Ripon, Knaresborough, Hovingham, Swain-
ton, and Rotherham, in Yorkshire; one in
Macclesfield, Cheshire; and one in Holling-
wood, Lancashire. The Grand Lodge of All
England also chartered at York the Grand
Lodge of England south of the River Trent
in 1799. It consisted of discontented members of the Time Immemorial Lodge of
Antiquity, of the Premier Grand Lodge (of

which Sir Christopher Wren* in his day was the Grand Master), and it granted warrants to only two Lodges, both in London. One was named Perfect Observance, the other Perseverance and Triumph. The career of this 'Mushroom Grand Lodge,' as the late Brother W. J. Hughan described it, was as inglorious as that of its parent.

The fourth Grand Lodge was the only real rival of the Premier Grand Lodge. It was constituted, on July 17, 1751, at the Turk's Head Tavern, Greek Street, Soho, London, as 'The Grand Lodge of England, according to the Old Institutions.' Its members were designated 'Ancients,' while those of the body from which it had seceded were known as 'Moderns.' The 'Ancients' were also spoken of as 'Athol Masons,' they having elected the third Duke of Athol as their first Grand Master in 1772, his son succeeding to the office at his death. Two reasons are offered for the founding of the new Grand Lodge. One is that the Regular Grand Lodge adopted severe measures against recalcitrant and impecunious Lodges.

* There is no real proof that Sir Christopher Wren was ever a Speculative Mason. The Minutes of the Worshipful Society of Free Masons (Operative) are said to show that their Grand Master, Sir Christopher Wren, was interred in St. Paul's with the proper ceremony of that Society.

The other is that it introduced innovations in the customs of the Craft which were particularly objected to by the operative section. 'The new body,' wrote the late Brother W. J. Hughan, 'became very popular, and in a few years was no mean competitor; its prototype and senior, but less pretentious organization, having also to contend against the introduction of the "Royal Arch," which was warmly supported, though not originated, by the "Ancients," who became known as the Grand Lodge of "Four Degrees," thus (for a time only) placing the parent society at a disadvantage.'

The 'Ancients' having established many Lodges and Provincial Lodges in England and in foreign countries, particularly in America, and having obtained the recognition of the Grand Lodges of Ireland and Scotland, and side almost unanimous support of the Grand Lodges of America, were eager to maintain their independence, and rejected all overtures tendered by the 'Moderns' for reunion; and in 1757 unanimously ordered:

'That if any Master, Wardens, or presiding officer, or any other person whose business it may be to admit members or visitors, shall admit or entertain in his or their Lodge during

Lodge hours or the time of transacting the proper business of Freemasonry, any Brother or visitor not strictly an Ancient Mason conformable to the Grand Lodge rules and order, such Lodge so transgressing shall forfeit its warrant, and the same may be disposed of by Grand Lodge.'

In 1801 the older Grand Lodge issued a counterblast. Some of its members were convicted of having patronized and acted as principal officers in 'an irregular society calling themselves Ancient Masons, in open violation of the laws of the Grand Lodge'; and it was determined that the laws should be enforced against these offending Brethren, unless they immediately abandoned such irregular meetings. These Brethren solicited the indulgence of the Grand Lodge for three months, hoping that during the interval they might be able to effect a union between the two societies. The indulgence was granted, and 'that no impediment might pervert so desirable an object, the charge against the offending Brethren was withdrawn, and a committee, consisting of Lord Moira and several other eminent characters, was appointed to pave the way for the intended union, and every means ordered to be used to bring the erring Brethren to a sense of their duty and allegiance.' Nothing came of this, for two years later the Grand Lodge was informed 'that the irregular Masons still continued refractory, and that so far from soliciting readmission among the Craft, they had not taken any steps to effect a union.' Their conduct was deemed highly censurable, and the laws of the Grand Lodge were ordered to be enforced against them. It was also unanimously resolved:

> 'That whenever it shall appear that any Masons under the English Constitution shall in future attend or countenance any Lodge or meeting of persons calling themselves Ancient Masons, under the sanction of any person claiming the title of Grand Master of England, who shall not have been duly elected in the Grand Lodge, the laws of the society shall not only be strictly enforced against them, but their names shall be erased from the list, and transmitted to all the regular Lodges under the Constitution of England.'

In 1806 Lord Moira reported to Grand Lodge that he had visited the Grand Lodge of Scotland and explained the position relating to the 'Modern' and 'Ancient' Masons in England, and that the Socttish Brethren had declared that they had been always led to think that the 'Moderns' were of very recent date and of no magnitude; and being convinced of their error, were desirous that the strictest union should subsist between the Grand Lodge of England and Scotland, and in proof thereof elected the Prince of Wales Grand Master of Scotland. Lord Moira further stated that, when the Scottish Brethren expressed a hope that the differences between the English Masons would be speedily settled, he replied that, after the rejection of the propositions of the Grand Lodge by the 'Ancients' three years before, it could not now, consistently with its honour, make any further advances; but would always be open to accept the mediation of the Grand Lodge of Scotland if it should think proper to interfere. Two years afterwards the Grand Lodge of Ireland approved the declaration of their Scottish Brethren, and pledged itself 'not to countenance or receive as a Brother any person standing under the interdict of the Grand Lodge of England for Masonic transgression.'

In April, 1809, the Grand Lodge agreed in opinion with the Committee of Charity that 'it is not necessary any longer for to continue in force those measures which were resorted to in or about the year 1789 respecting irregular Masons, and do therefore enjoin the several Lodges to revert to the ancient landmarks of the Society.' This was accepted as a step towards the much desired union. Still, more than four years elapsed before it was achieved; and then it came about as the result of the tactful intervention of three of the sons of George III. The Prince of Wales, who was initiated in 1787 at the Star and Garter Tavern, in Pall Mall, became Grand Master of the Premier Grand Lodge of England in 1790. When he accepted the Regency he vacated the office, and his brother, the Duke of Sussex, was elected to succeed him. The venerable and worthy head of the 'Ancients,' the Duke of Athol, was, says a contemporary record, 'soon convinced by the Royal Duke's arguments, strengthened by his own good sense and benevolent mind, how desirable must be an actual and cordial relation of the two societies under one head; for to pave the way for the Masons, his Grace in the handsomest measure resigned his seat of Grand Master.' He recommended as his successor the Duke of Kent, father of Queen Victoria, he having been initiated under the 'Ancient' constitution in the Union Lodge of Geneva. The Duke of Kent was acclaimed Grand Master in 1813. The two Royal Dukes, taking into counsel three distinguished Brethren belonging to each society, arranged Articles of Union between the two Grand Lodges of England (see Chapter IV), and these were ratified, confirmed, and sealed in each of those Lodges on December 1, 1813.

The same day a joint meeting of the Grand Lodges received the articles 'with Masonic acclamation,' and to carry them into effect constituted a Lodge of Reconciliation, consisting of equal members of the Old Institutions and the Constitution of England. Every care was taken that the parties to the union should be on a level of equality. As to the precedence of the Lodges, it was arranged that the two first Lodges under each Grand Lodge should draw lots for priority. The draw favoured the 'Ancients,' whose Grand Master's Lodge became No. 1 on the revised roll, the Lodge of Antiquity of the Regular Grand Lodge taking the second position, No. 2 of the 'Ancients' in the same order taking No. 3, and the second of the Time-Immemorial Lodges becoming No. 4. 'For two such old Lodges to accept lower positions in the united roll than their age entitled them to says much for the truly Masonic spirit of their members, who, to promote peace and harmony, consented to their juniors taking precedence of Lodges in existence prior to the formation of the Premier Grand Lodge.' Up to the time of the union 'Modern' Lodges placed on the roll numbered 1,085, while 'Ancient' Lodges warranted between 1751 and 1813 were 521.

The reunion of the two Grand Lodges of England was consummated with great solemnity on St. John's Day, December 27, 1813, in the Freemasons' Hall, London. The platform on the east was reserved for the Grand Masters, Grand Officers, and visitors. Masters, Wardens, and Past Masters, all dressed in black (except regimentals), with their respective insignia, and with white gloves, occupied the sides of the hall—the Masters in front, the Wardens behind, and the Past Masters on rising benches behind them. Care was taken that the Lodges were ranked so that the two Fraternities were completely intermixed. The two Fraternities had previously assembled in two adjoining rooms, and having opened two Grand Lodges, each according to its peculiar solemnities, they passed to the Assembly Hall in the following order:

Grand Usher, with his Staff.

Grand Usher, with his Staff.

The Duke of Kent's Band of Music, fifteen in number, all Masons, three and three.

Two Grand Stewards.

Two Grand Stewards.

A Cornucopia borne by a Master Mason.

A Cornucopia borne by a Master Mason.

Two Grand Stewards.

Two Grand Stewards.

Two Golden Ewers by Master Masons.

Two Golden Ewers by Master Masons.

The nine worthy and expert Masons, forming the Lodge of Reconciliation, in single file, rank to rank, with the emblems of Masonry.

The nine worthy and expert Masons, forming the Lodge of Reconciliation, in single file, rank to rank, with the emblems of Masonry.

The Grand Secretary, bearing the Book of Constitutions and Great Seal.

The Grand Secretary, bearing the Book of Constitutions and Great Seal.

The Grand Treasurer, with the Golden Key.

The Grand Treasurer, with the Golden Key.

The Corinthian Light.

The Corinthian Light.

The pillar of the Junior Grand Warden on a pedestal.

The pillar of the Junior Grand Warden on a pedestal.

The Junior Grand Warden, with his gavel.

The Junior Grand Warden, with his gavel.

The Deputy Grand Chaplain, with the Holy Bible.

The Grand Chaplain, with the Holy Bible.

The Grand Chaplain.

Past Grand Wardens.

Past Grand Wardens.

Provincial Grand Masters.

The Doric Light.

The Doric Light.

The pillar of the Senior Grand Warden on a pedestal.

The Senior Grand Warden, with his gavel.

Two Past Grand Masters.

The Deputy Grand Master.

The pillar of the Senior Grand Warden on a pedestal.

The Senior Grand Warden, with his gavel.

Acting Deputy Grand Master.

His Excellency the Count de Lagardje, the Swedish Ambassador, Grand Master of the first Lodge of the North, visitor.

The Royal Banner.

The Ionic Light.

The Grand Sword Bearer.

The Ionic Light.

The Grand Sword Bearer.

THE GRAND MASTER OF ENGLAND, THE DUKE OF KENT, WITH THE ACT OF UNION IN DUPLICATE.

Two Grand Stewards.

Grand Tyler.

THE GRAND MASTER OF ENGLAND, THE DUKE OF SUSSEX, WITH THE ACT OF UNION IN DUPLICATE.

Two Grand Stewards.

Grand Tyler.

Sir George Nayler, the Director of Ceremonies, having proclaimed silence, the Rev. Dr. Barry, Grand Chaplain to the Fraternity under the Duke of Kent, offered solemn prayer, and Sir George read the Act of Union. Then the Rev. Dr. Goghlan, after the sound of trumpet, proclaimed aloud: 'Hear ye: This is the Act of Union, engrossed, in confirmation of articles solemnly concluded between the two Grand Lodges of

Free and Accepted Masons of England, signed, sealed, and ratified by the two Grand Lodges respectively, by which they are to be hereafter and for ever known and acknowledged by the style and title of The United Grand Lodge of Ancient Freemasons of England. How say you, Brothers, representatives of the two Fraternities? Do you accept of, ratify, and confirm the same?' To which the assembly answered: 'We do accept, ratify, and confirm the same.' The Grand Chaplain then said: 'And may the Great Architect of the Universe make the Union perpetual.' To which all assembled replied: 'So mote it be.' Thereupon the two Grand Masters and the six Commissioners signed the deeds, and the Grand Masters affixed the great seals of their respective Grand Lodges to them. The trumpet again sounded, and the Rev. Dr. Barry, stepping forth, proclaimed: 'Be it known to all men that the Act of Union between the two Grand Lodges of Free and Accepted Masons of England is solemnly signed, sealed, ratified, and confirmed, and the two Fraternities are one, to be from henceforth known and acknowledged by the style and title of the United Grand Lodge of Ancient Freemasons of England, and may the Great Architect of the Universe make their union perpetual.' And the assembly said 'Amen.'

This was followed by a deeply impressive scene. 'The two Grand Masters, with their respective Deputies and Wardens,' says a contemporary record, 'advanced to the Ark of the Masonic Covenant, prepared under the direction of Brother John Soane, R.A., Grand Superintendent of Works, for the edifice of the Union, and in all time to come to be placed before the Throne. The Grand Masters standing in the East, with their Deputies on the right and left; the Grand Wardens in the West and South; the Square, the Plumb, the Level, and the Mallet were successively delivered to the Deputy Grand Masters, and by them presented to the two Grand Masters, who severally applied the Square to that part of the Ark which is square, the Plumb to the sides of the same, and the Level above it in three positions; and, lastly, they gave three knocks with the Mallet, saying, "May the Great Architect of the Universe enable us to uphold the Grand Edifice of Union, of which the Ark of the Covenant is the symbol, which shall contain within it the instrument of our brotherly love, and bear upon it the Holy Bible, Square, and Compass, as the light of our faith and the rule of our works. May

He dispose our hearts to make it perpetual."
And the Brethren said: "So mote it be."
The two Grand Masters placed the said Act
of Union in the interior of the said Ark.
The cornucopia, the wine, and oil were in
like manner presented to the Grand Masters,
who, according to ancient rite, poured forth
corn, wine, and oil on this said Ark, saying,
"As we pour forth corn, wine, and oil on
this Ark of the Masonic Covenant, may the
bountiful hand of heaven ever supply this
United Kingdom with abundance of corn,
wine, and oil, with all the necessaries and
comforts of life; and may He dispose our
hearts to be grateful for all His Gifts." And
the assembly said, "Amen." '

It having been found impracticable, from
the shortness of notice, for the sister Grand
Lodges of Scotland and Ireland to send
deputations to the assembly according to
the urgent request of the two Fraternities,
conferences had been held with the most
distinguished Grand Officers and enlightened
Masons resident in and near London, in order
to establish perfect agreement upon all the
essential points of Masonry, according to the
ancient traditions and general practice of
the Craft. The members of the Lodge of
Reconciliation, accompanied by Count de
Lagardje and Brother Dr. Van Hess, and

other distinguished Masons, withdrew to an adjoining room, where, being congregated and tyled, the result of all the previous conferences was made known. Returning to the Temple, Count de Lagardje declared that the forms agreed on and settled by the Lodge of Reconciliation were pure and correct. These forms were recognized as those 'to be alone observed and practised in the United Grand Lodge and all the Lodges dependent thereon until Time shall be no more.' Then, the Holy Bible spread open, with the Square and Compasses thereon, was laid on the Ark of the Covenant, and the two Grand Chaplains approached. The recognized obligation was then pronounced aloud by the Rev. Dr. Hemming, one of the Masters of the Lodge of Reconciliation, the whole of the Brethren repeating it after him, with joined hands, and declaring, 'By this solemn obligation we vow to abide, and the regulations of Ancient Freemasonry now recognized strictly to observe.'

The assembly next proceeded to constitute one Grand Lodge. All the Grand Officers of the two Fraternities having divested themselves of their insignia, and Past Grand Officers having taken the chairs, the Duke of Kent stated that when he took

upon himself the important office of Grand
Master of the Ancient Fraternity, his idea,
as declared at the time, was to facilitate
the important object of the Union, which
had that day been so happily concluded.
And he now proposed that his illustrious and
dear relative, the Duke of Sussex, should be
the Grand Master of the United Grand
Lodge of Ancient Freemasons of England
for the year ensuing. This having been
seconded by the Hon. Washington Shirley,
and carried unanimously and with Masonic
honours, His Royal · Highness was placed
on the Throne by the Duke of Kent and
Count de Lagardje, and solemnly obligated.
The Grand Master then nominated his
officers: Rev. S. Hemming, D.D., Senior
Grand. Warden; Isaac Lindo, Junior Grand
Warden; John Dent, Grand Treasurer;
William Meyrick, Grand Registrar; William
Henry White and Edward Harper, Grand
Secretaries; Rev. Edward Barry, D.D., and
Rev. Lucius Coghland, Grand Chaplains;
Rev. Isaac Knapp, Deputy Grand Chaplain;
John Soane, Grand Superintendent of
Works; Sir G. Nayler, Grand Director of
Ceremonies; Captain Jonathan Parker,
Grand Sword Bearer; Samuel Wesley, Grand
Organist; B. Aldhouse, Grand Usher; and
W. V. Salmon, Grand Tyler. It was then

solemnly proclaimed that the two Grand Lodges were incorporated and consolidated into one, and the Grand Master declared it to be open in due form according to ancient usage. The Grand Lodge was then called to refreshment, and from the cup of brotherly love the Grand Master drank to the Brethren, 'Peace, Goodwill, and Brotherly Love all over the World,' and then passed the cup. As it was going round, a choir sang a piece of music specially composed for the occasion (which is reproduced on another page of the same issue of the *Freemason*).

The Grand Lodge was recalled to labour, and as the first act of the United Fraternity, the Duke of Sussex moved:

'That an humble address be presented to H.R.H. the Prince Regent respectfully to acquaint him with the happy event of the reunion of the two great Grand Lodges of the Ancient Freemasons of England, an event which cannot fail to afford lively satisfaction to their Illustrious Patron, who presided for so many years over one of the Fraternities, and under whose auspices Freemasonry has risen to its present flourishing condition. That the unchangeable principles of the Institution are well known to His Royal Highness, and the great benefits and end of this reunion are to promote the influence and operation of these principles by more extensively inculcating loyalty and affection of their Sovereign, obedience to the laws and magistrates of their country, and the practice of all the religious and moral duties of life, objects which must be ever dear to His Royal Highness in the government of His Majesty's United Kingdom. That they humbly hope and pray for the continuance of the sanction of His Royal Highness's fraternal patronage; and that they beg leave to express their fervent gratitude for the many blessings which, in common with all their fellow-subjects, they derive from his benignant sway. That the Great Architect of the Universe may long secure these blessings to them and to their country by the preservation of His Royal Highness, their Illustrious Patron!'

Resolutions thanking the Dukes of Kent and Sussex for 'yielding to the prayer of the United Fraternities to take upon themselves the personal conduct of the negotiations for a reunion, which is this day, through their zeal, conciliation, and fraternal example so happily completed'; and commending the proceedings of the day to Grand Lodges of Scotland and Ireland, were also passed before the Lodge was closed 'in ample form and with solemn prayer.'

CHAPTER IV

ARTICLES OF UNION
BETWEEN THE TWO GRAND LODGES OF FREEMASONS OF ENGLAND

IN THE NAME OF THE GREAT ARCHITECT OF THE UNIVERSE—

The Most Worshipful His Royal Highness Prince Edward, Duke of Kent and Strathearn, Earl of Dublin, Knight Companion of the Most Noble Order of the Garter and of the Most Illustrious Order of Saint Patrick, Field-Marshal of His Majesty's Forces, Governor of Gibraltar, Colonel of the First or Royal Scots Regiment of Foot, and Grand Master of Free and Accepted Masons of England according to the Old Institutions; the Right Worshipful Thomas Harper, Deputy Grand Master; the Right Worshipful James Perry, Past Deputy

The Most Worshipful His Royal Highness Prince Augustus Frederick, Duke of Sussex, Earl of Inverness, Baron Arkton, Knight Companion of the Most Noble Order of the Garter, and Grand Master of the Society of Free and Accepted Masons under the Constitution of England; the Right Worshipful Waller Rodwell Wright, Provincial Grand Master of Masons in the Ionian Isles; the Right Worshipful Arthur Tegart, Past Grand Warden, and the Right Worshipful James Deans, Past Grand Warden; of the same

Grand Master; and the Right Worshipful James Agar, Past Deputy Grand Master; of the same Fraternity: for themselves and on behalf of the Grand Lodge of Freemasons of England, according to the Old Institutions: being thereto duly constituted and empowered: —on the one part,

Fraternity: for themselves and on behalf of the Grand Lodge of the Society of Freemasons under the Constitution of England: being thereto duly constituted and empowered:—on the other part,

HAVE AGREED AS FOLLOWS—

I. There shall be, from and after the day of the Festival of Saint John the Evangelist next ensuing, a full, perfect, and perpetual union of and between the two Fraternities of Free and Accepted Masons of England above described; so as that in all time hereafter they shall form and constitute but one Brotherhood, and that the said community shall be represented in one Grand Lodge, to be solemnly formed, constituted, and held, on the said day of the Festival of Saint John the Evangelist next ensuing, and from thenceforward for ever.

II. It is declared and pronounced, that pure Antient Masonry consists of three degrees, and no more; vizt. those of the Entered Apprentice, the Fellow Craft, and the Master Mason, including the Supreme

Order of the Holy Royal Arch. But this article is not intended to prevent any Lodge or Chapter from holding a meeting in any of the degrees of the Orders of Chivalry, according to the constitutions of the said Orders.

III. There shall be the most perfect unity of obligation, of discipline, of working the Lodges, of making, passing and raising, instructing and clothing Brothers; so that but one pure unsullied system, according to the genuine landmarks, laws, and traditions of the Craft, shall be maintained, upheld and practised, throughout the Masonic World, from the day and date of the said union until time shall be no more.

IV. To prevent all controversy or dispute as to the genuine and pure obligations, forms, rules and antient traditions of Masonry, and further to unite and bind the whole Fraternity of Masons in one indissoluble bond it is agreed that the obligations and forms that have, from time immemorial, been established, used, and practised, in the Craft, shall be recognized, accepted, and taken, by the members of both Fraternities, as the pure and genuine obligations and forms by which the incorporated Grand Lodge of England, and its dependent Lodges in every part of the World, shall be bound: and for the purpose of receiving and communicating due light and settling this uniformity of regulation and instruction (and particularly on matters which can neither be expressed nor described in writing), it is further agreed that brotherly application be made to the Grand Lodges of Scotland and Ireland to authorize, delegate and appoint, any two or more of their enlightened members to be present at the Grand Assembly on the solemn occasion of uniting the said Fraternities; and that the respective Grand Masters, Grand Officers, Masters, Past Masters, Wardens and Brothers, then and there present, shall solemnly engage to abide by the true forms and obligations (particularly in matters which can neither be described nor written), in the presence of the said Members of the Grand Lodges of Scotland and Ireland, that it may be declared, recognized, and known, that they all are bound by the same solemn pledge, and work under the same law.

V. For the purpose of establishing and securing this perfect uniformity in all the warranted Lodges, and also to prepare for this Grand Assembly, and to place all the Members of both Fraternities on the level

of equality on the day of Re-union, it is
agreed that as soon as these presents shall
have received the sanction of the respective
Grand Lodges, the two Grand Masters shall
appoint each nine worthy and expert Master
Masons, or Past Masters, of their respective
Fraternities, with Warrant and instructions
to meet together at some convenient central
place in London, when each party having
opened in a separate apartment a just and
perfect Lodge, agreeably to their peculiar
regulations they shall give and receive
mutually and reciprocally the obligations of
both Fraternities, deciding by lot which
shall take priority in giving and receiving
the same; and being thus all duly and
equally enlightened in both forms, they shall
be empowered and directed, either to hold
a Lodge under the warrant or dispensation
to be entrusted to them, and to be entitled
the Lodge of Reconciliation, or to visit the
several Lodges holding under both the
Grand Lodges for the purpose of obligating,
instructing and perfecting the Master, Past
Masters, Wardens, and Members, in both
the forms, and to make a return to the
Grand Secretaries of both the Grand Lodges
of the names of those whom they shall have
thus enlightened. And the said Grand
Secretaries shall be empowered to enrol

the names of all the Members thus remade in the Register of both the Grand Lodges, without fee or reward: it being ordered that no person shall be thus obligated and registered whom the Master and Wardens of his Lodge shall not certify by writing under their hands, that he is free on the books of his particular Lodge. Thus on the day of the Assembly of both Fraternities, the Grand Officers, Masters, Past Masters, and Wardens, who are alone to be present, shall all have taken the obligation by which each is bound, and be prepared, to make their solemn engagement, that they will thereafter abide by that which shall be recognized and declared to be the true and universally accepted obligation of the Master Mason.

VI. As soon as the Grand Masters, Grand Officers, and Members of the two present Grand Lodges, shall on the day of their Re-union have made the solemn declaration in the presence of the deputation of Grand or enlightened Masons from Scotland and Ireland, to abide and act by the universally recognized obligation of Master Mason, the Members shall forthwith proceed to the election of a Grand Master for the year ensuing; and to prevent delay, the Brother so elected shall forthwith be obligated, *pro tempore*, that the Grand Lodge may be formed. The said Grand Master shall then nominate and appoint his Deputy Grand Master, together with a Senior and Junior Grand Warden, Grand Secretary, or Secretaries, Grand Treasurer, Grand Chaplain, Grand Sword Bearer, Grand Usher, and Grand Tyler, who shall all be duly obligated and placed, and the Grand Incorporated Lodge shall then be opened, in due form, under the stile and title of the UNITED GRAND LODGE OF ANTIENT FREEMASONS OF ENGLAND.

The Grand Officers who held the several Offices before (unless such of them as may be re-appointed) shall take their places, as Past Grand Officers, in the respective degrees which they held before; and in case either, or both of the present Grand Secretaries, Ushers, and Tylers, should not be reappointed to their former situations, then annuities shall be paid to them during their respective lives out of the Grand Fund.

VII. THE UNITED GRAND LODGE OF ANTIENT FREEMASONS OF ENGLAND shall be composed, except on days of Festival, in the following manner, as a just and perfect representative of the whole Masonic Fraternity of England; that is to say, of—

The Grand Master,

Past Grand Masters,

Deputy Grand Master,

Past Deputy Grand Masters,

Grand Wardens,

Provincial Grand Masters,

Past Grand Wardens,

Past Provincial Grand Masters,

Grand Chaplain,

Grand Treasurer,

Joint Grand Secretary, or Grand Secretary if there be only one,

Grand Sword Bearer,

Twelve Grand Stewards, to be delegated by the Steward's Lodge from among their Members existing at the Union; it being understood and agreed that, from and after the Union, an annual appointment shall be made of the Stewards if necessary.

The actual Masters and Wardens of all Warranted Lodges,

Past Masters of Lodges, who have regularly served and passed the Chair before the day of Union, and who have continued without secession regular contributing Members of a Warranted Lodge. It being understood that of all Masters who, from and after the day of the said Union, shall regularly pass the chair of their respective Lodges, but one at a time, to be delegated by his Lodge, shall have a right to sit and vote in the said Grand Lodge; so that after the decease of all the regular Past Masters of any regular Lodge, who had attained that distinction at the time of the Union, the representation of such Lodge shall be by its actual Master, Wardens, and one Past Master only.

And all Grand Officers in the said respective Grand Lodges shall retain and hold their rank and privileges in the United Grand Lodge, as Past Grand Officers, including the present Provincial Grand Masters, the Grand Treasurers, Grand Secretaries, and Grand Chaplains, in their several degrees, according to the seniority of their respective appointments; and where such appointment shall have been contemporaneous, the seniority shall be determined by lot. In all other respects and above shall be the general order of Precedence in all time to come, with this express provision, that no Provincial Grand Master, hereafter to be appointed, shall be entitled to a seat in the Grand Lodge after he shall have retired from such situation, unless he shall have discharged the duties thereof for full five years.

VIII. The Representatives of the several Lodges shall sit under their respective banners according to seniority. The two first Lodges under each Grand Lodge to draw a lot in the first place for priority; and to which of the two the lot No. 1 shall fall, the other to rank as No. 2; and all the other Lodges shall fall in alternately, that is, the Lodge which is No. 2, of the Fraternity whose lot it shall be to draw No. 1, shall rank as No. 3, in the United Grand Lodge, and the other No. 2, shall rank as No. 4, and so on alternately through all the numbers respectively. And this shall for ever after be the order and rank of the Lodges in the Grand Lodge, and in Grand Processions, for which a plan and drawing shall be prepared previous to the Union. On the renewal of any of the Lodges now dormant, they shall take rank after all the Lodges existing at the Union, notwithstanding the numbers in which they may now stand on the respective rolls.

IX. The United Grand Lodge being now constituted, the first proceeding after solemn prayer shall be to read and proclaim the Act of Union, as previously executed and sealed with the great seals of the two Grand Lodges; after which the same shall be solemnly accepted by the Members present. A day shall then be appointed for the installation of the Grand Master and other Grand Officers with due solemnity; upon which occasion the Grand Master shall in open Lodge, with his own hand, affix the new great seal to the said instrument, which shall be deposited in the archives of the United Grand Lodge, and be the bond of union among the Masons of the Grand Lodge of England, and the Lodges dependant thereon, until time shall be no more. The said new great seal shall be made for the occasion, and shall be composed out of both the great seals now in use; after which the present two great seals shall be broken and defaced; and the new seal shall be alone used in all warrants, certificates, and other documents to be issued thereafter.

X. The regalia of the Grand Officers shall be, in addition to the white Gloves and apron, and the respective Jewels or emblems of distinction, garter blue and gold; and these shall alone belong to the Grand Officers present and past.

XI. Four Grand Lodges, representing the Craft, shall be held for quarterly communication in each year, on the first Wednesday in the Months of March, June, September, and December, on each of which occasions the Masters and Wardens of all the warranted Lodges shall deliver into the hands of the Grand Secretary and Grand Treasurer, a faithful list of all their contributing Members; and the warranted Lodges in and adjacent to London shall pay towards the grand fund one shilling per quarter for each Member, over and above the sum of half a guinea for each new-made Member, for the registry of his name, together with the sum of one shilling to the Grand Secretary as his fee for the same, and that this contribution of one shilling for each Member shall be made quarterly, and each quarter, in all time to come.

XII. It shall be in the power of the Grand Master, or in his absence of the Past Grand Masters, or in their absence of the Deputy Grand Master, or in his absence of the Past Deputy Grand Masters, or in their absence of the Grand Wardens, to summon and hold Grand Lodges of Emergency whenever the good of the Craft shall, in their judgment, require the same.

XIII. At the Grand Lodge to be held annually on the first Wednesday in September, the Grand Lodge shall elect a Grand Master for the year ensuing, (who shall nominate and appoint his own Deputy Grand Master, Grand Wardens, and Secretary), and they shall also nominate three fit and proper persons for each of the offices of Treasurer, Chaplain, and Sword Bearer, out of which the Grand Master shall, on the first Wednesday in the month of December, chuse and appoint one for each of the said offices; and on the Festival of St. John the Evangelist, then next ensuing, or on such other day as the said Grand Master shall appoint, there shall be held a Grand Lodge for the solemn installation of all the said Grand Officers, according to antient custom.

XIV. There may also be a Masonic Festival, annually, on the Anniversary of the Feast of St. John the Baptist, or of St. George, or such other day as the Grand Master shall appoint, which shall be dedicated alone to brotherly love and refreshment, and to which all regular Master Masons may have access, on providing themselves with tickets from the Grand Stewards appointed to conduct the same.

XV. After the day of the Re-union, as aforesaid, and when it shall be ascertained what are the obligations, forms, regulations, working, and instruction to be universally established, speedy and effectual steps shall be taken to obligate all the Members of each Lodge in all the degrees, according to the form taken and recognized by the Grand Master, Past Grand Masters, Grand Officers, and Representatives of Lodges, on the day of Re-union; and for this purpose the worthy and expert Master Masons appointed, as aforesaid, shall visit and attend the several Lodges, within the Bills of Mortality, in rotation, dividing themselves into quorums of not less than three each, for the greater expedition, and they shall assist the Master and Wardens to promulgate and enjoin the pure and unsullied system, that perfect reconciliation, unity of obligation, law, working, language, and dress, may be happily restored to the English Craft.

XVI. When the Master and Wardens of a warranted Lodge shall report to the Grand Master, to his satisfaction, that the Members of such Lodge have taken the proper enjoined obligation, and have conformed to the uniform working, cloathing, &c., then the Most Worshipful Grand Master shall direct the new Great Seal, to be affixed to their warrant, and the Lodge shall be adjudged to be regular, and entitled to all the privileges of the Craft: a certain term shall be allowed (to be fixed by the Grand Lodge) for establishing this uniformity; and all constitutional proceedings of any regular Lodge, which shall take place between the date of the union and the term so appointed, shall be deemed valid, on condition that such Lodge shall conform to the regulations of the Union within the time appointed, and means shall be taken to ascertain the regularity, and establish the uniformity of the Provincial Grand Lodges, Military Lodges, and Lodges holding of the two present Grand Lodges in distant parts, and it shall be in the power of the Grand Lodge to take the most effectual measures for the establishment of this unity of doctrine throughout the whole community of Masons, and to declare the Warrants to be forfeited, if the measures proposed shall be resisted or neglected.

XVII. The property of the said two Fraternities, whether freehold, leasehold, funded, real or personal, shall remain sacredly appropriate to the purposes for which it was created; it shall constitute one grand fund, by which the blessed object of Masonic benevolence may be more exten-

sively obtained. It shall either continue
under the trusts on which, whether freehold,
leasehold, or funded, the separate parts
thereof now stand; or it shall be in the
power of the said United Grand Lodge, at
any time hereafter, to add other names to
the said trusts; or, in case of the death of
any one Trustee, to nominate and appoint,
others for perpetuating the security of the
same; and in no event, and for no purpose,
shall the said united property be diverted
from its original purpose. It being understood and declared that, at any time after
the Union, it shall be in the power of the
Grand Lodge to incorporate the whole of
the said property and funds in one and the
same set of Trustees, who shall give bond
to hold the same in the name and on the
behalf of the United Fraternity. And it
is further agreed, that the Freemasons' Hall
shall be the place in which the United
Grand Lodge shall be held, with such additions made thereto as the increased numbers
of the Fraternity, thus to be united, may
require. And it is understood between the
parties, that, as there are now in the Hall
several whole length portraits of Past Grand
Masters, a portrait of the Most Worshipful
His Grace the Duke of Atholl, Past Grand
Master of Masons, according to the old

Institutions, shall be placed there in the same conspicuous manner.

XVIII. The fund, appropriate to the objects of Masonic benevolence, shall not be infringed on for any purpose, but shall be kept strictly and solely devoted to charity, and pains shall be taken to increase the same.

XIX. The distribution and application of this Charitable Fund shall be monthly, for which purpose a Committee, or Lodge of Benevolence, shall be held on the third Wednesday of every month, which Lodge shall consist of twelve Masters of Lodges (within the Bills of Mortality); and three Grand Officers, one of whom only (if more are present) shall act as President, and be entitled to vote. The said twelve Masters to be summoned by the choice and direction of the Grand Master, or his Deputy, not by any rule or rotation, but by discretion; so as that the Members, who are to judge of the cases that may come before them, shall not be subject to canvass, or to previous application, but shall have their minds free from prejudice, to decide on the merits of each case with the impartiality and purity of Masonic feeling: to which end it is declared that no Brother, being a Member of such Committee or Lodge, shall vote, upon the petition of any person to whom he is in any way related, or who is a Member of any Lodge or Masonic Society, to which he himself actually belongs, but such Brother may ask leave to be heard on the merits of such petition, and shall afterwards, during the discussion and voting thereon, withdraw.

XX. A plan, with rules and regulations, for the solemnity of the Union, shall be prepared by the Subscribers hereto, previous to the Festival of St. John, which shall be the form to be observed on that occasion.

XXI. A revision shall be made of the rules and regulations now established and in force in the two Fraternities, and a code of laws for the holding of the Grand Lodge, and of private Lodges; and, generally, for the whole conduct of the Craft, shall be forthwith prepared, and a new Book of Constitutions be composed and printed, under the superintendence of the Grand Officers, and with the sanction of the Grand Lodge.

Done at the Palace of Kensington, this 25th Day of November, in the Year of our Lord, 1813, and of Masonry, 5813.

EDWARD, G.M.
THOS. HARPER, D.G.M.
JA. PERRY, P.D.G.M.
JAS. AGAR, P.D.G.M.

Freemasonry and its Etiquette

In Grand Lodge, this first day of December, A.D. 1813, Ratified and Confirmed, and the Seal of the Grand Lodge affixed.

EDWARD, G.M.
ROBT. LESLIE, G.S.

In Grand Lodge, this first day of December, A.D. 1813, Ratified and Confirmed, and the Seal of the Grand Lodge affixed.

AUGUSTUS FREDERICK, G.M.
W. SHIRLEY, D.G.M., V.T.
WILLIAM H. WHITE, G.S.

In the presence of

JANO, PONTRISSON DE LAGARDJE,
G.M. of the Lodge of the North.

CHAPTER V

UNITED GRAND LODGE

THE United Grand Lodge of Antient Freemasons of England, or, as it is now styled in
the Book of Constitutions, the United Grand
Lodge of Antient Free and Accepted Masons
of England, came into existence, as narrated
in Chapter III, on St. John's Day, in
winter—viz., December 27, 1813—and now*
consists of the Masters, Past Masters, and
Wardens of all private Lodges on record,
together with the Grand Stewards of the
year and the present and past Grand
Officers, and the Grand Master at their head.

The Grand Lodge possesses the supreme
superintending authority, and alone has the
inherent power of enacting laws and regulations for the government of the Craft, and
of altering, repealing, and abrogating them,
always taking care that the antient Landmarks of the Order be preserved.

The Grand Lodge has also the power of
investigating, regulating, and deciding all
matters relative to the Craft, or to particular

* See Article VII.: Articles of Union.

Lodges, or to individual Brothers, which it may exercise either of itself or by such delegated authority as, in its wisdom and discretion, it may appoint; but the Grand Lodge alone has the power of erasing Lodges and expelling Brethren from the Craft, a power which it does not delegate to any subordinate authority in England.

Every Brother regularly elected and installed as Master of a Lodge, under the constitution of the Grand Lodge of England, who has filled that office for one year, so long as he continues a subscribing member of any such Lodge, is a member of the Grand Lodge; but having for twelve months ceased to be a subscribing member of any English Lodge, he no longer continues a member of the Grand Lodge, nor can he retain the right of membership of the Grand Lodge, as a Past Master, until he has again duly served the office of Master of such a Lodge.

Four Grand Lodges are held in London, for quarterly communication, in each year —viz., on the first Wednesday in the months of March, June, September, and December.

There is a Grand Masonic Festival annually, on the Wednesday next following St. George's Day, to which all regular Masons who provide themselves with tickets from the Grand Stewards of the year are admitted.

The Grand Master, according to antient usage, is nominated at the Grand Lodge in December in every year, and at the ensuing Grand Lodge in March the election takes place. The Grand Master, so elected, is regularly installed on the day of the Grand Masonic Festival.

No Brother can be a Grand Master unless he has been a Fellow Craft before his election, who is also to be nobly born, or a gentleman of the best fashion, or some eminent scholar, or other artist, descended of honest parents, and who is of singularly great merit in the opinion of the Lodges.

The Grand Master, if a Prince of the Blood Royal, appoints a Pro Grand Master, who must be a Peer of the Realm.

And for the better, and easier, and more honourable discharge of his office, the Grand Master has a power to choose his own Deputy Grand Master, who must then be, or have formerly been, the Master of a particular Lodge, and who has the privilege of acting whatever the Grand Master, his principal, should act, unless the said principal be present, or interpose his authority by letter.

These rulers and governors supreme and subordinate, of the antient Lodge, are to be obeyed in their respective stations by all the brethren, according to the old charges and regulations, with all humility, reverence, love, and alacrity.

* * * *

Nineteen Grand Stewards are annually appointed, for the regulation of the Grand Festival, under the directions of the Grand Master. They assist in conducting the arrangements made for the quarterly communications and other meetings of the Grand Lodge.

The Grand Stewards are appointed from nineteen different Lodges, each of which recommends one of its subscribing members, who must be a Master Mason, and presented by the former Grand Steward of that Lodge, for the approbation and appointment of the Grand Master; when so approved and appointed, he is entitled to wear the clothing of a Grand Steward (see p. 343).

* * * *

All members of the Grand Lodge may have papers of business and notices of special Grand Lodge meetings, together with all reports of the quarterly communications forwarded to them by post on registering their addresses and paying a fee of five shillings per annum in advance.

* * * *

United Grand Lodge

The Grand Lodge is declared to be opened in ample form when the Grand Master or Pro Grand Master is present; in due form when a Past Grand Master or the Deputy presides; at all other times, only in form, yet with the same authority (as prescribed by Rule 51 of the Book of Constitutions).

Grand Lodge is always considered to be opened for Master Masons only, and the correct Sn., when addressing the Chair, appears, by custom, to be that of the E.A.; and the correct method of employing it is explained on p. 178.

The Ceremonies of Opening and Closing Grand Lodge form the basis of, and are similar to, the Ceremonies, *mutatis mutandis*, of Opening and Closing Provincial or District Grand Lodges (see pp. 270 to 275).

* * * *

There will be found in the Book of Constitutions, in Grand Lodge Transactions, in the Ritual, and in Masonic writings and conversations generally frequent references to the Antient Landmarks of the Order.

The powers of Grand Lodge are circumscribed by these alone; and every Master Elect solemnly pledges himself to preserve them, and not to permit or suffer any deviation from them.

It will be well, therefore, for the reader to have some clear and accurate impression of the term.

The word Landmark in its ordinary sense is quite well understood to mean a conspicuous and immovable object (such as a mountain), or an object not easily moved or likely to be moved (such as a church), and so on, in descending scale, until we come down to pillars and posts of a more temporary and easily movable character.

A Land mark may thus be itself a boundary or a mark by which a boundary may be calculated and fixed, or by which a ship's course may be determined.

This is the expressive word which has been appropriated by our ancestors to indicate, metaphorically, the immutable character of the fundamental principles and customs of our Institution.

But while it is quite easy to understand what is meant by a Landmark, our difficulties commence when we attempt to apply the term in detail.

No official list of Landmarks has ever been complied. Writers of importance have prepared various enumerations of them; but these enumerations command more or less assent according to the individual judgment of the reader.

There is one, however, about which there is no question in the mind of any Free Mason, and Grand Lodge has on more than one occasion affirmed and reaffirmed it—viz., that "a belief in T.G.A.O.T.U. is the first and most important of the Antient Landmarks."

The relation of this Landmark to Freemasonry is as unalterable and undebatable as the relationship of the sun to the earth.

All the rest are dependent upon it and comprehended within it. In some of the others may be detected possibilities of change, gradual, involuntary, or deliberate.

The claim of a Landmark to be so regarded, must be tested, therefore, by its antiquity and by the degree in which it has resisted whatever mutability may be inherent therein.

By this gauge the reader may consider and determine for himself the respective rights and the relative importance of the following claimant which have been suggested and discussed by Dr. Mackey as additional Antient Landmarks of the Order:

> Modes of recognition.
> Division of Symbolic Masonry into three Degrees.
> The Legend of the third Degree.
> Government of Craft by a Grand Master.

Prerogative of Grand Master to preside;
to grant Dispensations; to make
Masons at sight.

Necessity of Lodge meetings.

Government of Lodge by a Master and
two Wardens.

Necessity of Lodge being duly Tyled.

Right of every Mason to be represented
in General Assembly; to appeal to
Grand Lodge; to visit any regular
Lodge without invitation.

Examination of visitors.

Equality and independence of Lodges,
inter se.

Subjection of every Mason to Masonic
Jurisdiction.

Qualifications and disqualifications of
Candidates.

Obligation on appropriate V.S.L.

Equality of all Masons.

Secrecy of the Institution.

Speculative Science founded on Operative Art.

Immutability of the Landmarks.

To the above may very fairly be added:

Uniformity of the Ritual,

as practised in each Jurisdiction.

(Art. XV of the Articles of Union, 1813.)

CHAPTER VI

PROVINCIAL AND DISTRICT GRAND LODGES

PROVINCIAL Grand Lodges emanate from the Provincial Grand Masters by virtue of the authority vested in them by their patents of appointment from the Grand Master. It therefore follows that Provincial Grand Lodges possess no other powers than those specified in the laws and regulations contained in the Book of Constitutions, and cannot meet but by the sanction of the Provincial Grand Master or his Deputy.

In Colonies and foreign parts the terms District Grand Master and District Grand Lodge are used to distinguish such Officers and Lodges from Provincial Grand Masters and Provincial Grand Lodges in England.

A Provincial or District Grand Lodge consists of the Provincial or District Grand Master, the present and past Provincial or District Grand Officers, the Provincial or District Grand Stewards for the year, the Master, Past Masters, and Wardens of all Lodges in the Province or District, and Past

Masters of any Lodge under the English Constitution, if members of Grand Lodge; but no Brother can be a member of a Provincial or District Grand Lodge unless he is a subscribing member of a Lodge within such Province or District.

Provincial and District Grand Officers must all be resident within the Province or District, unless by Dispensation from the Grand Master.

District Grand Lodges fix stated times for their regular meetings, not exceeding four times in the year; but the District Grand Master may summon and hold a special District Grand Lodge, whenever, in his judgment, it may be necessary.

Provincial and District Grand Officers do not take any rank out of their Province or District, but are entitled to wear the clothing at all Masonic meetings.

Provincial or District Grand Stewards do not take any rank out of their Province or District, and when out of Office are no longer members of the Provincial or District Grand Lodge unless otherwise qualified, but are entitled to wear the clothing at all Masonic meetings.

When the Provincial or District Grand Master presides, the Provincial or District Grand Lodge is to be declared open in *due form.* If the Deputy or any other Brother preside, in *form* only. (B. of C., 79.)

In many Provinces and Districts the Provincial or District Grand Lodge is invited by the different Lodges to hold its meetings one year in one locality and another year in another. In some Provinces two meetings are held in the year. The Lodge which is honoured by a visit is expected to make—under the direction of the Provincial Grand Secretary, assisted by the Prov. G. Director of Ceremonies—all arrangements for the proper reception and accommodation of the Provincial or District Grand Lodge, and for the members of the various Lodges.

The meetings being as a rule larger than could be accommodated in an ordinary Lodge-room, a room is engaged in some large building, sufficiently capacious for the general meeting, and some other rooms (preferably in the same building); one for the reception of the Provincial or District Grand Master (who requires a room for his exclusive use); another for Provincial or District Grand Officers; and a third for the Brethren generally.

The Brethren, not having present or past Provincial or District rank, enter the Lodge-room. The Worshipful Master and the Wardens of the Lodge visited occupy the three chairs, and open the Lodge in the three Degrees.

The Provincial Grand Director of Ceremonies marshals the Provincial or District Grand Officers in processional order, the Provincial or District Grand Master at the rear. Arrived at the door of the Lodge the report is given, the Provincial or District Grand Officers open out right and left, the Provincial or District Grand Master walks up the centre, the Senior Officers closing in; the others do the same, and in that inverted order they enter the Lodge. The Brethren all rise, and the Organist plays a march, or some appropriate composition, while the Provincial or District Grand Master and the Officers take their seats.

The Master of the Lodge and the Wardens back out of their respective places and hand in their Provincial or District successors.

*　　*　　*　　*

The Provincial or District Grand Lodge is then opened in due form, or in form according to No. 79 of the Book of Constitutions. The ceremonies of opening and closing Provincial or District Grand Lodge will be found on pp. 273-274.

*　　*　　*　　*

Provincial and District Grand Lodges

All Lodges held at a greater distance than ten miles from Freemasons' Hall, London, are Provincial or District Lodges, and are under the immediate superintendence of the Provincial or District Grand Master within whose jurisdiction they meet.

The Provincial or District Grand Master may preside in any Lodge he visits within his Province or District, his Deputy being placed on his right, and the Master of the Lodge on his left hand; his Wardens, if present, shall act as Wardens of the Lodge during the time he presides; but if they be absent, the Provincial or District Grand Master may direct the Wardens of the Lodge, or any Master Masons, to act as his Wardens *pro tempore*.

Unless the Provincial or District Grand Master be present, his Deputy may preside in any Lodge he may visit within his Province or District, the Master of the Lodge being placed on his right hand. The Provincial or District Grand Wardens, if present, are to act as Wardens of the Lodge during the time he presides.

* * * *

The reader's attention is invited to the remarks on the subject of the Charity Representative on pp. 359 and 362.

* * * *

Calendars are now published in many Provinces, containing the day, the hour, and the place of meeting of every Lodge within the Province; and many Lodges year by year send a copy to every subscribing member. The convenience of possessing such a Calendar is very great in many ways. A Brother is enabled on reference to his Calendar to make his engagements so that he may be free to attend his own Lodge, or to visit any other to which inclination or duty may lead him. The word 'duty' is used advisedly, because it is highly desirable that a kind and fraternal feeling should exist between neighbouring Lodges; and nothing tends so much to create and to foster this feeling as the interchange of visits between the several members of the Lodges in a district. The Principal Officers, especially, should consider it a part of their duty to set a good example in this respect. Something may be, and often is, gained in Masonic Knowledge by the interchange of such visits.

CHAPTER VII

GENERAL COMMITTEE

THE General Committee consists of the President of the Board of Benevolence, who, if present, acts as Chairman, the Present and Past Grand Officers, and the Master of every regular Lodge. It meets on the fourteenth day immediately preceding each quarterly communication.

Notices of such meetings are from time to time sent to the Secretaries of Lodges; the packet is marked 'to be forwarded,' and should be transmitted to the Worshipful Master without delay.

If the Master of any Lodge cannot attend the General Committee, the Immediate Past Master may supply his place; should that Brother be unable to attend, any other Past Master of such Lodge may act for him, but in every case the Past Master must be a subscribing member of that Lodge.

At this meeting all reports and representations from the Grand Master, or the Board of General Purposes, or any Board or Committee appointed by the Grand Lodge, are read.

In normal times the work of the General Committee is of a very perfunctory character; indeed, its very existence seems to be forgotten by most, except the *ex-officia* members of it, certain habitual attendants, and the permanent officials, whose duty it is to conduct its proceedings. From time to time, however, matters of importance are to be debated in Grand Lodge, and then the proceedings of the General Committee become more animated, as any member of the Grand Lodge intending to make motion therein, or to submit any matter to its consideration, must, at such General Committee, or by notice previously given or sent to the Grand Secretary, state, in writing, the nature of such intended motion or matter, that notice thereof may be printed on the paper of business.

No motion, or other matter, may be brought into discussion in the Grand Lodge, unless it shall have been previously communicated to the General Committee.

The General Committee may direct that any notice of motion which, in its judgment, is not within the cognizance of the Grand Lodge, shall be omitted from the list of business to be brought before the Grand Lodge.

All nominations for Boards or Committees must be given to the General Committee in writing, signed by a member of the Grand Lodge.

CHAPTER VIII

BOARD OF BENEVOLENCE

THE Board of Benevolence consists of a President, appointed by the Grand Master, two Vice-Presidents, elected at the Grand Lodge in December, and of all the present and past Grand Officers, and all actual Masters of Lodges, and twelve Past Masters of Lodges nominated at the General Committee annually in November, and elected by the Grand Lodge in December, in the same manner as the elected members of the Board of General Purposes.

No Past Master is eligible to be re-elected who neglects to attend the Board of Benevolence at six meetings.

If the actual Master of the year of any Lodge cannot attend, the Immediate Past Master may supply his place: should that Brother be unable to attend, any other Past Master of such Lodge may act for him; but in every case the Past Master must be a subscribing member of the Lodge.

The Board meets on the last Wednesday but one of every month, to administer the

Fund of Benevolence. This Fund was established in 1727, and is applied to relieving Masons and their families.

Article XVIII of the Act of Union provides: The Fund, appropriate to the objects of Masonic benevolence, shall not be infringed on for any purpose, but shall be kept strictly and solely devoted to charity, and pains shall be taken to increase the same.

The Fund is at present derived partly from Interest on Investments, partly from Fees of Honour, partly from Dispensation Fees, and partly from a capitation fee from each member of the private Lodges (4s. per head in London, 2s. in country), known as Quarterage.

The sum so produced is considerable, totalling £22,000 in the year 1913; and the grants made are generous, especially in any exceptionally deserving case, or in cases where the Brother in question is shown to have been active in charitable affairs when in a position to have been so.

Members who are to judge of the cases that may come before them may not be subject to canvass, or to previous application; but must have their minds free from prejudice, to decide on the merits of each case with the impartiality and purity of Masonic feeling: to which end it is declared that no Brother, being a Member of such Committee or Lodge, may vote, upon the petition of any person to whom he is in any way related, or who is a Member of any Lodge or Masonic Society, to which he himself actually belongs; but such Brother may ask leave to be heard on the merits of such petition, and must afterwards, during the discussion and voting thereon, withdraw.

No Brother can claim relief 'as of right.' The fund of Benevolence is not a Benefit Society.

No Mason registered under the constitution of the Grand Lodge of England can receive the benefit of the Fund of Benevolence unless he has paid the full Initiation or Joining fee, continued a subscribing member to a contributing Lodge for at least five years, and during that period paid his quarterly dues to the Fund of Benevolence. The limitation of five years, however, does not apply to the cases of shipwreck, capture at sea, loss by fire, or blindness, or serious accident, fully attested and proved. Any Brother who has ceased subscribing for the immediate past twenty years is not eligible to petition the Board unless he has previously subscribed to his Lodge for fifteen years or upwards.

A Brother who has been relieved cannot petition a second time within one year. A widow who has been relieved cannot petition again.

It is a matter of considerable thought to the Board that claims are arising in greater numbers from Masons of short standing, thus indicating that not enough care is taken to see that Initiates are in sufficiently assured circumstances to warrant their admission to a Society of which the basis is assistance to others (see p. 15).

CHAPTER IX

BOARD OF GENERAL PURPOSES

THE Board of General Purposes consists of the Grand Master, Pro Grand Master, Deputy Grand Master, the Grand Wardens of the year, the Grand Treasurer, the Grand Registrar, the Deputy Grand Registrar, a President, Past Presidents, the President of the Board of Benevolence, the Grand Director of Ceremonies, and twenty-four other members.

The President and six of such 'other members' are annually appointed by the Grand Master, at the quarterly Grand Lodge in June; and the Grand Lodge, on the same day, elects by ballot from among the actual Masters and Past Masters of Lodges as many as may be required to make up the remaining eighteen members. A Master and Past Master or more than one Past Master of the same Lodge cannot be elected as such on the same Board; but this does not disqualify any Past Master, being a subscribing member and Master of another Lodge, from being elected for and representing such other Lodge as Master.

One-third at least of the members must

go out of office annually, but are eligible for re-election.

The Board meets on the third Tuesday in every month at four o'clock precisely. It may also be convened at other times by command of the Grand Master, or by the authority of the President.

Five members constitute a Board and proceed to business, except in the decision of Masonic complaints, for which purpose at least seven members must be present.

The Board has full power to inspect all books and papers relating to the accounts of the Grand Lodge, and to give orders for the correct arrangement of them; and to summon the Grand Treasurer, Grand Registrar, Grand Secretary, or other Brother having possession of any books, papers, documents, or accounts belonging to the Grand Lodge, and to give such directions as may be necessary.

Except when otherwise specially directed by resolution of the Grand Lodge, the Board has the direction of everything relating to the buildings and furniture of the Grand Lodge.

The Board may recommend to the Grand Lodge whatever it shall deem necessary or advantageous to the welfare and good government of the Craft, and may originate plans for the better regulation of the Grand

Lodge and the arrangement of its general transactions, but no recommendations or reports of the Board or of any Committee appointed by the Board may be issued for the consideration of or be voted upon by the Craft until they have been discussed by the Members of Grand Lodge in regular or especial meeting assembled.

The Board has likewise the care and regulation of all the concerns of the Grand Lodge, and conducts the correspondence between the Grand Lodge and its subordinate Lodges and Brethren, and communications with sister Grand Lodges and Brethren of eminence and distinction throughout the world.

The Board has authority to hear and determine all subjects of Masonic complaint or irregularity respecting Lodges or individual Masons, when regularly brought before it, and generally to take cognizance of all matters relating to the Craft.

The Board may proceed to admonition, fine, or suspension, according to the laws; and its decision is final, unless an appeal be made to the Grand Lodge.

The Board may summon the Officers of any Lodge to attend it and to produce the warrant, books, papers, and accounts of the Lodge, or may summon any Brother to attend it and produce his certificate.

CHAPTER X

WHO ARE FIT AND PROPER PERSONS
TO BE MADE MASONS?

THIS is a most important question, and one which lies at the foundation of the Masonic edifice. It should be carefully considered *before* the initiation of a Candidate, as it is too late to discuss it afterwards. Indeed, it should be carefully considered before the Candidate is proposed in Lodge, and great responsibility attaches to those who seek to introduce members from the uninstructed and popular world.

One excellent test to be applied is this: Is the proposed Candidate one whom we would unhesitatingly admit to our own home, and introduce to our own family circle with confidence?

The Book of Constitutions warns us against the great discredit and injury likely to be brought upon our antient and honourable Fraternity by the admission of undesirable members, and enjoins strict inquiry into the characters and qualifications of persons wishful to become members; and in order that this injunction may be properly obeyed there should be a written proposal and recommendation from both proposer and seconder. It is an excellent custom in many Lodges to refer to a Standing Committee every such notice of intention to propose a person for initiation. That Standing Committee is responsible to the Lodge for a personal interview with and a proper inquiry into, and report upon, the merits of the Candidate; who must be of good report (see Proposition Form, Appendix (D), p. 429). There is no ambiguity about the necessary qualifications. The answer to the question above propounded is authoritatively stated to be—just, upright, and free men of mature age, sound judgment, and strict morals; and at the time of initiation every Candidate should be in reputable circumstances (see pp. 15 and 101) and of sufficient education (see p. 101).

He ought to be free born, but it is conceded under the present Constitution [1847] that if a man be free, although he may not have been free born, he is eligible to be made a Mason.

He must profess, and should earnestly hold, a sincere belief in the Great Creator and Ruler of the Universe.

The Antient Charges instruct us that a Mason is obliged, by his tenure, to obey

the moral law; and if he rightly understand
the art, he will never be a stupid atheist nor
an irreligious libertine. He, of all men,
should best understand that God seeth
not as man seeth; for man looketh at the
outward appearance, but God looketh to
the heart. A Mason is, therefore, particularly bound never to act against the
dictates of his conscience. Let a man's
religion or mode of worship be what it may,
he is not excluded from the Order, provided
he believe in the glorious Architect of
heaven and earth, and practise the sacred
duties of morality. Masons unite with the
virtuous of every persuasion in the firm and
pleasing bond of fraternal love: they are
taught to view the errors of mankind with
compassion, and to strive, by the purity of
their own conduct, to demonstrate the
superior excellence of the faith they may
profess. Thus Masonry is the centre of
union between good men and true, and the
happy means of conciliating friendship
amongst those who must otherwise have
remained at a perpetual distance.

A Mason is a peaceable subject to the civil
powers, wherever he resides or works, and is
never to be concerned in plots and conspiracies
against the peace and welfare of the nation,
nor to behave himself undutifully to inferior

magistrates. He is cheerfully to conform to every lawful authority; to uphold, on every occasion, the interest of the community, and zealously promote the prosperity of his own country. Masonry has ever flourished in times of peace, and been always injured by war, bloodshed, and confusion; so that kings and princes in every age have been much disposed to encourage the Craftsmen on account of their peaceableness and loyalty, whereby they practically answer the cavils of their adversaries and promote the honour of the fraternity. Craftsmen are bound by peculiar ties to promote peace, cultivate harmony, and live in concord and brotherly love.

The persons made Masons or admitted members of a Lodge must be good and true men, free born, and of mature and discreet age and sound judgment; no bondmen, no women, no immoral or scandalous men, but of good report.

Candidates may, nevertheless, know that no master should take an apprentice, unless he has sufficient employment for him; and, unless he be a perfect youth, having no maim or defect* in his body that may render

* In 1875, the Board of General Purposes issued a circular intimating that so long as physical deformity did not prevent a candidate from exercising Masonic functions—presumably from making the signs—it is not a disqualification.

him incapable of learning the art, of serving his master's lord, and of being made a Brother, and then a Fellow Craft in due time, after he has served such a term of years as the custom of the country directs; and that he should be descended of honest parents; that so, when otherwise qualified, he may arrive to the honour of being the Warden, and then the Master of the Lodge, the Grand Warden, and at length the Grand Master of all the Lodges according to his merit.

* * * *

It may be convenient to state here that for all practical purposes the terms Free Masonry, Freemasonry, and Masonry; Free-Mason, Freemason, and Mason are synonymous and interchangeable—that is to say, that the words Masonry and Mason in the mouth of a Freemason mean Freemasonry and Freemason.

In ancient documents persons are recorded as Free Man and Free Mason; this gradually shortened into Free Man and Mason; and finally Free Mason.

About 1717 period, Dr. Anderson appears to have made the two words into one, Freemason.

No confusion is likely to arise in these

days by employing either, whether at will or by accident. The correct style of a Freemason is equally a Free and Accepted Mason, or an Ancient Freemason. Masonry in its operative sense is the parent of Masonry in its speculative sense. The greater includes the lesser, and the true Mason will see nothing but Honour, Grace, and Dignity in the beautiful mechanical Art of Masonry which gave birth to the Speculative Craft now called Free Masonry.

The Articles of Union, than which there can be no better guide or authority, speak (Article I) of the two Fraternities of Free and Accepted Masons, to be hereafter and for ever known and acknowledged by the style and title of Ancient Freemasons; Article II defines pure Antient Masonry; Articles VI and VII speak of Freemasons; and throughout there seems to be no attempt to establish any distinction of differentiation in the terms.

CHAPTER XI

WHAT IS A LODGE OF FREEMASONS?

A LODGE is an assemblage of Brethren met to expatiate on the mysteries of the Craft, or, in the language of the Antient Charge, a Lodge is a place where Freemasons assemble to work and to instruct and improve themselves in the mysteries of the antient science. In an extended sense it applies to persons as well as to place; hence every regular assembly or duly organized meeting of Masons is called a 'Lodge.'

Every brother ought to belong to some Lodge, and be subject to its by-laws and the General Regulations of the Craft.

A Lodge may be either general or particular, as will be best understood by attending it, and there a knowledge of the established usages and customs of the Craft is alone to be acquired.

From antient times no Master or Fellow could be absent from his Lodge, especially when warned to appear at it, without incurring a severe censure, unless it appeared to the Master and Wardens that pure necessity hindered him.

What is a Lodge of Freemasons?

'In the Lodge while constituted you are not to hold private committees, or separate conversation, without leave from the Master, nor to talk of anything impertinently or unseemly, nor interrupt the Master or Wardens, or any Brother speaking to the Master; nor behave yourself ludicrously or jestingly while the Lodge is engaged in what is serious and solemn, nor use any unbecoming language upon any pretence whatsoever; but to pay due reverence to your Master, Wardens, and Fellows, and put them to worship.'

No private piques or quarrels must be brought within the door of the Lodge, far less any quarrels about religion, or nations, or State policy, we being only, as Masons, of the universal religion above mentioned; we are also of all nations, tongues, kindreds, and languages, and are resolved against all politics, as what never yet conduced to the welfare of the Lodge, nor ever will.

CHAPTER XII

'PARTICULAR' OR PRIVATE LODGES

No Lodge may be held without a Charter or Warrant of constitution from the Grand Master. Every Lodge must be regularly constituted and consecrated; and no countenance ought to be given to any irregular Lodge.

Lodges rank in precedence in the order of their numbers as registered in the books of the Grand Lodge.

The Grand Steward's Lodge does not have a number, but is registered in the books of the Grand Lodge; and placed in the printed list, at the head of all other Lodges, and ranks accordingly.

The Warrant of the Lodge is specially entrusted to the Master for the time being at his installation. He is responsible for its safe custody, and must produce it at every meeting of the Lodge. The Lodge of Antiquity, No. 2, and the Royal Somerset House and Inverness Lodge, No. 4, act under immemorial constitutions.

If a warrant be lost, the Lodge must

suspend its meetings until a warrant of confirmation has been applied for and granted by the Grand Master.

Every Lodge is distinguished by a name or title, as well as a number.

The regular Officers of a Lodge consist of the Master and his two Wardens, a Treasurer, a Secretary, two Deacons, an Inner Guard, and a Tyler.

The Master may also appoint a Chaplain, a Director of Ceremonies, an Assistant Director of Ceremonies, an Almoner, an Organist, an Assistant Secretary, and Stewards.

No Brother can hold more than one *regular* office in the Lodge at one and the same time.

In cases where Officers other than Regular Officers are appointed, the order of appointment is as follows: Worshipful Master, Senior Warden, Junior Warden, Chaplain, Treasurer, Secretary, Senior Deacon, Junior Deacon, Director of Ceremonies, Assistant Director of Ceremonies, Almoner, Organist, Assistant Secretary, Inner Guard, Stewards, Tyler.

As 'all preferment among Masons is grounded upon real worth and personal merit only,' the foregoing order of appointment and investiture give no Brother the right to claim advancement by rotation, 'that so the lords may be well served, the brethren not put to shame, nor the Royal Craft despised.' The appointment of all Officers except the Treasurer and Tyler is in the sole discretion and power of the Worshipful Master.

Every Lodge must, annually, on the day named by its by-laws for that purpose, elect its Master by ballot.

'Mo Master is chosen by seniority, but for his merit.'

At the next regular meeting, immediately after the confirmation of the Minutes, he is duly installed.

No Master Elect may assume the Chair until he has been regularly installed.

No Warden can be installed as Master of a Lodge (except by Dispensation from the Grand Master) unless he has served the office as an Invested Warden for a full year—that is to say, from one regular Installation Meeting until the next regular Installation Meeting. (See p. 320.)

No Installing Master may proceed unless satisfied of such service or Dispensation.

Every Master Elect, before being placed in the chair, must solemnly pledge himself to preserve the Landmarks* of the Order; to

* See pp. 63, 64, 65, 66, 67.

observe its ancient usages and established customs; and strictly to enforce them within his own Lodge.

The Master is responsible for the due observance of the laws by the Lodge over which he presides.

No Brother may be Master of more than one Lodge at the same time, without a Dispensation.

No Brother may continue Master for more than two years in succession, unless by a Dispensation.

No Brother can be a Grand Warden until he has been Master of a Lodge.

N.B.—In antient times no Brother, however skilled in the Craft, was called a Master-Mason until he had been elected into the Chair of a Lodge.

Upon his installation the Master appoints and invests his Wardens and other Officers, and invests the Treasurer.

No Brother can be a Warden until he has passed the part of a Fellow Craft.

No Warden is chosen by seniority, but for his merit.

The Treasurer is annually elected by ballot on the regular day of election of Master.

The Tyler is to be chosen by show of hands.

No proprietor or manager of the tavern or house at which the Lodge meets may hold any office in the Lodge without a Dispensation from the Grand Master or the Provincial or District Grand Master.

Should the Master be dissatisfied with the conduct of any of the Officers, he may lay the cause of complaint before the Lodge at a regular meeting (seven days' notice thereof in writing having been previously sent to the Brother complained of), and if it appears to the majority of the Brethren present that the complaint is well founded, the Master has power to displace such Officer, and to appoint another.

If a vacancy occurs in any office other than that of Treasurer or Tyler, the Master appoints a Brother to serve such office for the remainder of the year; and if the vacancy be in the office of Treasurer or Tyler the Lodge may, after due notice in the summons, elect a successor for the remainder of the year.

If the Master dies, is removed, or is rendered incapable of discharging the duties of his office, the Senior Warden, and in the absence of the Senior Warden, the Junior Warden, and in the absence of both Wardens, the Immediate Past Master, or in his absence the Senior Past Master, acts as

Master in summoning the Lodge, until the next installation of Master.

In the Master's absence, the Immediate Past Master, or, if he be absent, the Senior Past Master of the Lodge present, or if no Past Master of the Lodge be present, then the Senior Past Master who is a subscribing member of the Lodge takes the chair. And if no Past Master who is a member of the Lodge be present, then the Senior Warden, or in his absence the Junior Warden, rules the Lodge. When a Warden rules the Lodge, he may not occupy the Master's chair; nor can initiations take place or degrees be conferred unless the chair be occupied by a Brother who is a Master or Past Master in the Craft.

The Master and Wardens of a Lodge are enjoined to visit other Lodges as often as they conveniently can, in order that the same usages and customs may be observed throughout the Craft, and a good understanding cultivated amongst Freemasons.

No visitor may be admitted into a Lodge unless he be personally known to, or well vouched for, after due examination, by one of the Brethren present, or until he has produced the certificate of the Grand Lodge to which he claims to belong, and has given satisfactory proof that he is the Brother named in the certificate, or other proper vouchers of his having been initiated in a regular Lodge. Every visitor during his presence in the Lodge is subject to its by-laws. (See p. 308.)

No Brother who has ceased to be a subscribing member of a Lodge is permitted to visit any one Lodge more than once until he again becomes a subscribing member of some Lodge, but this does not apply to the visits of a Brother to any Lodge of which he has been elected a non-subscribing or honorary member.

All Lodges held within ten miles of Freemasons' Hall, London, are London Lodges.

Every Lodge has the power of framing by-laws for its government, provided they are not inconsistent with the regulations of the Grand Lodge. The by-laws must be submitted to the Grand Secretary for the approval of the Grand Master. When finally approved, a printed copy must be sent to the Grand Secretary; and when any alteration is made, such alteration must, in like manner, be submitted. No law or alteration is valid until so submitted and approved. The by-laws of the Lodge must be printed, and a copy delivered to the Master on his installation, who by his acceptance thereof is deemed to solemnly pledge himself to observe and enforce them.

Every Brother must be supplied with a printed copy of the by-laws of the Lodge when he becomes a member, and his acceptance thereof is deemed to be declaration of his submission to them.

The regular days of meeting of the Lodge and its place of meeting are specified in the by-laws, and no meeting of the Lodge may be held elsewhere, except by Dispensation. The by-laws also specify the regular meeting for the election of the Master, Treasurer, and Tyler.

A Lodge of Emergency may at any time be called by the authority of the Master, or in his absence, of the Senior Warden, or, in his absence, of the Junior Warden, but on no pretence without such authority. The business to be transacted at such Lodge of Emergency must be expressed in the summons, and no other business may be entered upon.

The jewels and furniture of every Lodge belong to, and are the property of, the Master and Wardens for the time being, in trust for the members of the Lodge.

Every Lodge must keep a minute-book, in which the Master, or the Brother appointed by him as Secretary, must regularly enter from time to time—

First—The names of all persons initiated, passed, or raised in the Lodge, or who shall become members thereof, with the dates of their proposal, initiation, passing, and raising or admission respectively, together with their ages, addresses, titles, professions, or occupations.

Secondly—The names of all members present at each meeting of the Lodge, together with those of all visiting Brethren, with their Lodges and Masonic rank.

Thirdly—Minutes of all such transactions of the Lodge as are proper to be written.

The minutes can only be confirmed at a subsequent regular meeting of the Lodge.

Secretaries who, by the by-laws of their Lodges, are exempted from the payment of subscription, shall be considered in all respects as regular subscribing members of their Lodges, their services being equivalent to subscription, provided their dues to the Grand Lodge have been paid.

All money received, or paid for, or on account of a Lodge, must be from time to time regularly entered in proper books, which are the property of the Lodge. The accounts of the Lodge must be audited, at least once in every year, by a committee appointed by the Lodge.

The majority of the members present at

any Lodge duly summoned have an undoubted right to regulate their own proceedings, provided that they are consistent with the general laws and regulations of the Craft; no member, therefore, is permitted to enter in the minute-book of his Lodge a protest against any resolution or proceeding which may have taken place, except on the ground of its being contrary to the laws and usages of the Craft, and for the purpose of complaining or appealing to a higher Masonic authority.

Whenever it happens that the votes are equal upon any question to be decided by a majority, either by ballot or otherwise, the Master in the chair is entitled to give a second or casting vote.

Great discredit and injury having been brought upon our antient and honourable Fraternity from admitting members and receiving candidates without due notice being given or inquiry made into their characters and qualifications, and from passing and raising Masons without due instruction* in the respective degrees, it is declared to be specially incumbent on all members of Lodges to see that particular attention be paid to these several points.

No person may be made a Mason without

* See Lodges of Instruction, Chapter XIII.

having been proposed and seconded at one regular Lodge, and balloted for at the next regular Lodge.

No person may be made a Mason under the age of twenty-one years, unless by Dispensation.

A Lewis is entitled to the 'privilege' of being made a Freemason *in precedence* of his fellow Candidates. Thus, his name stands first upon the Summons, and is the first mentioned at the door of the Lodge, and he is the foremost in the perambulation. The privilege of a Lewis has this extent—no more.

On the occasion of the Initiation of one of the sons of H.R.H. the Grand Master, a short account of the event was given in one of the London daily papers. The writer of that description, evidently a Freemason, added: 'The young Prince had not availed himself of the privilege which, as a Lewis (*i.e.*, the eldest son of a Freemason), he might have claimed, that of being made a Freemason before he had attained the full age of twenty-one years.'

This is a wrong idea altogether: no Lewis, be he Prince or peasant, can successfully claim such a privilege. Rule 157 in the Book of Constitutions is clear and emphatic upon the subject. Only by dispensation can any person be made a Freemason under the age of twenty-one years. The whole extent of the 'privilege' of a Lewis is, that it gives him precedence at his Initiation 'over any other person, however dignified by rank or fortune.'

Every candidate must be a free man, and at the time of initiation in reputable circumstances.

Previously to his initiation, every candidate must subscribe his name at full length to a declaration. (See p. 430.)

N.B.—A person who cannot write is consequently ineligible to be admitted into the Order.

No Brother may be admitted a joining member of a Lodge without being proposed and seconded in open Lodge at a regular meeting. (See p. 333.)

No person may be made a Mason in, or admitted a member of, a Lodge, if, on the ballot, three black balls appear against him.

No Lodge may initiate into Masonry more than two persons on the same day, unless by a Dispensation.

No person may be made a Mason for less than five guineas, in England.

No Lodge may confer a higher degree on any Brother at a less interval than four weeks from his receiving a previous degree, nor until he has passed an examination* in open Lodge in that degree.

No Brother may appear clothed in any of the jewels, collars, or badges of the Craft, in any procession, or at any funeral, ball, theatre, public assembly, or meeting, or at any place of public resort, unless the Grand Master, Provincial Grand Master, or District Grand Master, as the case may be, shall have previously given a dispensation for Brethren to be there present in Masonic clothing.

Should a Lodge fail to meet for one year it is liable to be erased.

When a Lodge can prove an uninterrupted working existence of one hundred years, it may, by Petition, and on payment of the prescribed Fee, obtain from the M.W. Grand Master a Centenary Warrant. (See p. 189.)

* See Lodges of Instruction, Chapter XIII.

CHAPTER XIII

LODGES OF INSTRUCTION

'A YOUNGER Brother shall be instructed in working, to prevent spoiling the materials for want of judgment; and for increasing and continuing of brotherly love.'

No Lodge of Instruction may be holden unless under the sanction of a regular warranted Lodge, or by the special licence and authority of the Grand Master.

This special licence has never been granted. There is only one instance of its having been applied for, and it was then refused (1830), on the ground that the licence ought to be given only in cases of a very special nature where the application of an extraordinary remedy had become requisite.

The Lodge giving its sanction, and the Brethren to whom such licence is granted, must be answerable for the proceedings, and responsible that the mode of working adopted has received the sanction of the Grand Lodge.

The object of this Law is that Grand

Lodge may have a known responsible party in the event of irregularity; and the refusal of the special licence mentioned above was based on this important principle.

If a Lodge which has given its sanction for a Lodge of Instruction being held under its warrant shall see fit, it may at any regular meeting withdraw that sanction by a resolution of the Lodge, to be communicated to the Lodge of Instruction; provided notice of the intention to withdraw the sanction be inserted in the summons for that meeting.

Lodges of Instruction should be constituted as formally as Regular Lodges, and should meet with as much regularity, but more frequently.

Notice of the times and places of meeting of Lodges of Instruction within the London district must be submitted for approval to the Grand Secretary, otherwise to the Provincial or District Grand Secretaries respectively.

Lodges of Instruction should, for continuity of management and policy, be governed by a Committee, including one or more competent Preceptors; and all the Officers, permanent and rotational, should be elected and appointed, with as much regularity and formality as in Regular Lodges.

Lodges of Instruction

Lodges of Instruction must keep minutes recording the names of all Brethren present at each meeting and of Brethren appointed to hold office, and such minutes must be produced when called for by the Grand Master, the Provincial or District Grand Master, Board of General Purposes, or the Lodge granting the sanction.

The Furniture, Working Tools, and Appointments should be as complete as possible.

'All the tools used in working shall be approved by the Grand Lodge.'

The Officers should all wear Masonic clothing during the performance of their duties.

All the 'proceedings' should be carried out in such a methodical way as to be a careful, elaborate, and complete education, not only in the ceremonies, but in all those matters which the Mason will encounter in Regular Lodges; in fact, all the proceedings should be object-lessons in Masonic Etiquette.

Everything should be watched with much more strictness than in Regular Lodges, as a mistake uncorrected in a Lodge of Instruction is more likely to create a precedent of evil, than the same error in a Regular Lodge.

In Lodges of Instruction the Preceptor's word is Law; and there must be no questioning of his ruling or discussion about the Ritual while Lodges of Instruction are open for Masonic business.

Prompt obedience to all 'signs' is the motto for workers in Lodges of Instruction.

It is quite permissible, and, indeed, desirable, that from time to time, in addition to the ordinary routine work of Ceremonies and Lectures, miscellaneous instruction should be afforded to members upon all matters which interest them, care being taken to distinguish between those points which are matters of Law and those which are matters of individual taste and discretion.

Needless to say, there should be complete unanimity and uniformity among the Preceptors as to the mode of working.

Brethren, able and willing to conform to these conditions, are not too numerous. Those who are capable are often unwilling, and those who are willing are often unable.

Educational enthusiasm, however, is spreading, and educational facilities are increasing. The true standard is becoming more and more widely recognized. The desirability—indeed, the necessity—for conformity is more readily accepted.

Brethren nowadays are more desirous of 'doing the work,' and in doing it the desire of doing it well is engendered and fostered.

The Masonic Year Book gives a list of 221 Lodges of Instruction meeting under sanction in London, and 345 Lodges of Instruction meeting under sanction in the Provinces.

No doubt there are others which have not complied with the prescribed rules, and are therefore not mentioned in the Year Book; while there are, of course, various unauthorized clubs meeting on Sundays the existence of which is officially ignored.

In June, 1874, certain Brethren were summoned to Grand Lodge and reprimanded for holding a 'Club of Instruction,' without due authority, in an Inn, and advertising the same in the public journals.

A great responsibility is cast by Grand Lodge upon those 'answerable for the proceedings' of Lodges of Instruction; and it is to be feared that this responsibility is insufficiently realized in many quarters.

Many Lodges of Instruction meet by force of circumstances, on Licensed Premises, where the use of a room is granted for a nominal sum in the expectation of further

profit resulting from the sale of drinks
and smokes to be consumed in the Lodge
Room!

Nothing more derogatory to the dignity
of the proceedings can well be conceived,
and the repetition of the beautiful phrases
of the Ritual in such an atmosphere amounts
to a desecration of it. On the practical side
of the question, nothing could be more con-
ducive to an imperfect rehearsal than the
petty interruptions caused (say) by lighting
a pipe in the middle of a ceremony. Very
little self-denial would be needed to dispense
with these indulgences until the 'call off,'
while the profit of 'the house' would not be
less—it might even be more—by postponing
the slaking of thirst for a brief season.

What says the 'Antient Charge' on this
point? 'After the Lodge is over you may
enjoy yourselves with innocent mirth, treating one another according to ability.'

But, apart from and above 'the proceedings' of the Lodge of Instruction, there is
the far more important responsibility 'that
the mode of working adopted has received
the sanction of the Grand Lodge'; and this
is a matter about which much argument
often arises, argument which for the most
part arises from want of knowledge of cer-

tain cardinal facts. Indeed, it may often be said with truth, the more vehement the argument, the less the foundation for it.

It is an excellent rule in cases of doubt to go to the fountain-head in search of knowledge; and, to apply this rule to the case in point, if a Preceptor of a Lodge of Instruction wishes to discharge his responsibility, and wishes to be sure that 'the mode of working adopted has received the sanction of the Grand Lodge,' the surest and most direct method for him is obviously to ascertain 'whether Grand Lodge sanctions any particular "mode of working" or form of Ritual, and, if so, what it is, and where it can be obtained.'

This is the course recently followed by the writer, who is a Preceptor of a Lodge of Instruction, and the important and convincing reply of the Grand Secretary will be found on pp. 118-119.

The subject of 'mode of working' or Ritual is so important that it will be treated at length in the next chapter.

CHAPTER XIV

RITUAL

NEXT in importance to 'the foundation on which Freemasonry rests—the practice of every moral and social virtue'—the solemn ceremonies by which every Mason is made acquainted with 'the mysteries and privileges of Freemasonry' undoubtedly must take a prominent position in the thoughts of every earnest member of our great Fraternity.

Every Mason remembers the deep impression made upon his mind by the first touching experiences of his novitiate, and in after-years it becomes his valued and responsible privilege to assist in creating those sacred impressions upon the minds of his Brethren in the early stages of their Masonic education.

These ceremonies are comprehensively described as 'Ritual.'

Our ancient Brethren viewed the question of 'Ritual' very seriously, and almost the first act of the United Grand Lodge in 1813 was to constitute the Lodge of Reconciliation, composed (in conformity with the Articles of Union) of an equal number of representatives of the two previous Grand Lodges, for the express purpose of *settling the Ritual once and for all*; and Grand Lodge approved, sanctioned, and confirmed that Ritual on June 5, 1816.

Article XV of the Act of Union (*q.v.*) provides:—

'For this purpose the worthy and expert Master Masons, appointed as aforesaid, shall visit and attend the several Lodges, . . . and they shall assist the Master and Wardens to promulgate and enjoin *the pure and unsullied system*, that perfect reconciliation, unity of obligation, law, working, language and dress, may be happily restored to the English Craft.'

Article XVI reads:

'It shall be in the power of the Grand Lodge to take the most effectual measures for the establishment of this *unity of doctrine* throughout the whole community of Masons, and to declare the Warrants to be forfeited, if the measures proposed shall be resisted.'

Ignorance of these cardinal facts breeds in the minds of some an idea that the Ritual can follow the deviations of personal idiosyncrasies, individual and collective.

It is not so. *No Mason has a right to*

tamper with a comma of it. Only Grand Lodge could do that (*vide* Article 4 of Book of Constitutions).

'The Grand Lodge possesses the supreme superintending authority, and alone has the inherent power of enacting laws and regulations for the government of the Craft; and of altering, repealing, and abrogating them; always taking care that the antient Landmarks of the Order be preserved.'

'It is not in the power of any man or body of men to make innovation in the body of Masonry,' and any attempt to introduce or perpetuate *any deviation* is a breach of that Law of Obedience to which a Mason's attention has been 'peculiarly and forcibly directed.'

It may be freely, if sorrowfully, admitted that there are, unfortunately, many errors and discrepancies, and even misstatements of fact, in the Ritual submitted by the Lodge of Reconciliation and approved by Grand Lodge in 1816; but it is difficult to conceive with what *authority* any subordinate Mason or body of Masons, can imagine himself or themselves to be clothed, which would warrant him or them in even deliberating upon the subject of the Ritual with a view to alter it after it has once been sanctioned and confirmed by the United Grand Lodge.

Ritual

Every Worshipful Master is under a special obligation 'not to permit or suffer *any deviation* from the established Land-marks of the Order.'

If Grand Lodge in 1813 treated the question of Ritual as of such primary importance, there can be no excuse for us to treat it lightly or irreverently in these days; and as in civil matters, *ignorantia legis neminem excusat*, so in Masonic matters it is inexcusable to blunder as a consequence of failure 'to make a daily advancement in Masonic knowledge,' and it becomes our bounden duty to assure ourselves that we are rightly discharging our responsibility in this connection.

This, however, is a busy world, and many causes conspire to make us treat our Masonry more as a social relaxation than an earnest probing of 'the hidden mysteries of Nature and Science'; and we are, often perforce, more content to remain in the category of those whose duty it is to 'submit and obey' than to qualify ourselves by study and research to occupy fitly the position of those whose function it becomes to 'rule and teach.'

The subject, however, is of primary importance, and the following collated facts will enable the reader to arrive at a sound conclusion upon a serious and vexed question:

The constant desire of Grand Lodge to insure Uniformity of Working is evidenced by the measures it has taken from time to time for the purpose of supervising and co-ordinating the 'Working' of subordinate Lodges.

That this desire is by no means of modern growth may be learned from official records of the ancient régime. So far back as September 2, 1752, it was resolved: 'That this Grand Committee shall be formed immediately into a working Lodge of Master Masons, in order to hear a Lecture from the Grand Secretary. The Lodge was opened in antient form, and every part of real Freemasonry was traced and explained, except the Royal Arch.'

In the year 1792 the Nine Excellent Masters, familiarly known as 'The Nine Worthies,' were instituted by the Grand Committee. These Brethren were elected annually to assist Grand officers in visiting Lodges, in order 'that the general uniformity of Ancient Masonry may be preserved and handed down unchanged to posterity.'

The Lodge of Promulgation was instituted by Warrant, dated October 28, 1809, from the Grand Master of the Grand Lodge of

England, *'authorizing certain distinguished Brethren to hold a special Lodge for the purpose of ascertaining and promulgating the Ancient Land-Marks of the Craft.'*

In the case of the Lodge of Promulgation, '. . . the object to be attained was to make the Lodges of the Moderns fall into line with those of the Antients as regards their Land-Marks and esoteric practices.'

'There can be no possible doubt that the Grand Lodge of the Moderns gave in on all points where their Ceremonies differed from those of the Antients.'

The Articles of Union, November 25, 1813, themselves lay especial stress on the point of Uniformity.

Articles III, IV, and V refer to '. . . the purpose of establishing and securing Uniformity of Working.'

Article XV provides '. . . that perfect reconciliation, Unity of obligation, law, working, language, and dress, may be happily restored to the English Craft.'

Article XVI enacts that '. . . Grand Lodge may declare the Warrants to be forfeited if the measures proposed shall be resisted.'

The Lodge of Reconciliation was constituted December 7, 1813, '. . . with power to meet, unite, and incorporate themselves with a Lodge of equal numbers . . . according to the Old Institutions contained and set forth in Articles 4 and 15 of a certain instrument bearing date November 25 last entitled "Articles of Union" between the two Grand Lodges of England. . . .'

The Lodge of Reconciliation worked for over two years at its important task.

On May 20, 1816, the Ceremonies of the three degrees were rehearsed for the approval of the United Grand Lodge.

On June 5, 1816, alterations on two points* in the Third Degree having been resolved upon, the several Ceremonies recommended were approved, sanctioned, and confirmed.

On August 6, 1818, the Grand Secretary (E. Harper), in reply to an inquiry concerning the correct Ritual, wrote that 'Bro. Peter W. Gilkes would instruct "in the *correct* method adopted since the Union."

'Bro. Peter W. Gilkes was officially acknowledged as the most perfect exponent of the Ceremonies and Ritual of the Craft.

'He was in a manner something Johnsonian in regard to Masonry. No advantage could be taken of him in Lodge; *he would not allow the slightest deviation in word, or manner, or matter.* . . .'

In 1823 Emulation Lodge of Improvement was formed to teach this approved

* See Appendix: Master's Light.

'Mode of Working,' and did so under the leadership of Bro. Peter W. Gilkes from 1825 until his death in 1833.

The Board of Installed Masters was Warranted February 6, 1827, in these words: '. . . And feeling how important it is that all Rites and Ceremonies in the Craft should be conducted with Uniformity and correctness, and with a view, therefore, to produce such Uniformity, we have thought it proper to appoint, and do accordingly nominate and appoint . . . to make known to all who may be entitled to participate in such knowledge, the Rites and Ceremonies of Installation as the same have already been approved by us. . . .'

In 1827 this Board of Installed Masters held three meetings at Freemasons' Hall, which were very numerously attended by Masters and Past Masters, who 'expressed themselves highly satisfied with the ceremonies and explanations which were then afforded them.'

In 1833 Bro. Stephen Barton Wilson (afterwards P.G.D.) succeeded Bro. Peter W. Gilkes as Leading Member of the Emulation Lodge of Improvement.

On September 6, 1843, the Grand Secretary (W. H. White) wrote, in reply to an inquiry whether any alteration had been made in the Ceremonies, that no alteration had 'been made since the Grand Lodge formally approved and decided on them in the year 1816. Bro. Gilkes was fully Master of all the Ceremonies, and, I believe, most strictly observed them.'

Bro. S. B. Wilson remained in command until his death, April 25, 1866.

Bro. Thomas Fenn (afterwards P.B.G.P.) succeeded Bro. S. B. Wilson, and remained in charge until 1894, when

Bro. R. Clay Sudlow (afterwards P.G.D.) took up that position, and retained it until his death in 1914.

There has thus been an uninterrupted chain of communication from the Lodge of Reconciliation down to the present day, and at this point the following letter finds an appropriate place:

'UNITED GRAND LODGE OF ENGLAND,
'FREEMASONS' HALL
'GREAT QUEEN STREET,
LONDON, W.C.
'*November 22, 1912.*

'DEAR SIR AND BROTHER,

'I am in receipt of your letter of the 20th instant, and am pleased to learn that a correct rendering of the Ritual is a subject of concern to the members of your Lodge.

'While it is true that no *edict* has ever

been issued by Grand Lodge as to any particular working being accepted, nor is it considered compulsory that Lodges should conform to what is termed the "Emulation" system of ritual, on the other hand it is an historical fact that Grand Lodge in 1816 definitely adopted and gave its approval to the system of working submitted to it by the Lodge of Reconciliation, and it is also a fact that this is the system which the "Emulation" Lodge of Improvement was founded in 1823 to teach, and which is taught by that Lodge to-day.

'The late Bro. Thomas Fenn, who was considered the most able exponent of Masonic Ritual of his day, always held the opinion that the "Emulation" working was authorized, and that opinion is also held by Bro. Sudlow, his successor in the teaching of that system. Certainly no other system or ritual has received at any time the official approval of Grand Lodge.

'I am,

Yours fraternally,

'E. LETCHWORTH, G.S.

'W. Bro. W. P. Cambell-Everden, L.R.,
    Lodge No. 19, London.'

It must be admitted by all unbiased minds that, having regard to the great and extraordinary care which Emulation Lodge of Improvement has, fortunately, always taken to preserve its own rigid and absolute conformity with the original 'Mode of Working' adopted by the Lodge of Reconciliation in 1816, while no other Lodge has had the inclination or the means to take such measures, it would redound to the credit of Freemasonry in general if every Lodge were now to revert to, and in the future adhere to, that standard of accuracy and strict conformity with—

1. The 'Mode of Working' and Ancient Ceremonies of Initiation, Passing, and Raising, as approved, sanctioned, and confirmed by the United Grand Lodge on June 5, 1816; and

2. The Ceremony of Installation as agreed by the Board of Installed Masters and sanctioned and approved by the Grand Master in 1827; and

3. The Lectures corresponding with the said Ceremonies and the ancient usages and established customs of the Order.

Ne Varientur.

CHAPTER XV

EMULATION LODGE OF IMPROVEMENT

No work embracing Lodges of Instruction and Ritual would be complete without a reference to the Emulation Lodge of Improvement.

Those who wish to know all about it cannot do better than read Bro. Sadler's 'Illustrated History of the Emulation Lodge of Improvement' (published by Spencer and Co.); and their 'desire of knowledge' may be gently stimulated by a perusal of a pleasant little pamphlet by Bro. F. Bebbington Goodacre (published by Hutton and Co., Ormskirk, Lancs.).

'Emulation Lodge of Improvement,' which meets every Friday evening at six o'clock at Freemasons' Hall from October to June inclusive (Good Friday excepted), was founded in 1823 to work the precise form of Ritual settled by the Lodge of Reconciliation, as approved, sanctioned, and confirmed by the Grand Lodge on June 5, 1816, and as recorded on the Minutes of Grand Lodge.

The fundamental principle of 'Emulation,' its absolute *raison d'être*, is the conviction that <u>*no one has any right to alter one word*</u> of that Ritual, or to tamper with it in any way.

Its claim is that it works now, always has worked, and always will work (without variation, and even without the possibility of variation, of a letter, character, or figure), <u>that</u> Ritual and <u>that</u> alone.

It takes its stand upon the simple idea that whatever the Ritual was settled to be by Grand Lodge in 1816, so it must remain, word for word and letter for letter, until (if ever) Grand Lodge should see fit to alter it.

It is unable to conceive with what authority any subordinate Mason, or body of Masons, can imagine himself or themselves to be clothed, which would warrant him or them in even deliberating upon the subject of Ritual, with a view to alter it, after it has once been sanctioned and confirmed by United Grand Lodge.

Consequently it has no sympathy with those who desire to 'correct' or 'improve' the Ritual, or to render it more 'consistent,' 'harmonious,' or 'logical,' or more 'historically accurate,' to introduce words into it, or to round off phrases, or to make it 'more grammatical,' 'more dignified,' or to 'bring it up to date'—in other words, to 'tinker' with it.

It is from the erroneous idea that any neophyte may exercise his prancing fancy upon the sacred ground of our ancient and honourable institution, and rush in where angels fear to tread, that the existing diversities of practice have unfortunately emanated.

Many causes have contributed to this idea, and among them may be mentioned:

1. Apathy of Masons generally on the subject.

2. Want of knowledge or remembrance of past history.

3. Failure to instruct incomers.

4. Bad advice on the subject.

5. Modesty on the part of 'Emulation.'

By the wonderful expansion of Freemasonry, thousands and thousands of Masons have been brought into being; and, as during the last eighty years there has been unfortunately no Official, no Authorized Preceptor* charged with the duty of keeping

* Several attempts have, from time to time, been made to induce Grand Lodge to appoint a Committee for the purpose of securing and insuring Uniformity of Ritual. On December 1, 1869, a motion for the appointment of such a Committee was carried unanimously in Grand Lodge, but on June 1, 1870, it was agreed to postpone the appointment *sine die*.

Masons within due bounds as to Ritual, many Lodges, from want of knowledge, or from indifference, have, in the most haphazard fashion, dropped into a little system of their own or followed local ideas.

Some 'Clubs,' indeed, have started with the *avowed* object of constructing a Ritual of their own, not perceiving that *ipso facto* they are transgressing their elementary vows of Obedience.

The consequence has been that many variations of the Ritual have arisen; and, not having been officially stamped out, they have flourished like weeds, become numerically considerable, and have audaciously developed themselves into 'Workings.'

These 'Workings' are, of course, utterly unauthorized.

The only Ritual which has ever been authorized is the Ritual which was settled once and for all by the Lodge of Reconciliation in 1813 to 1816.

The Grand Secretary writes on the subject:

'This is the system which the Emulation Lodge of Improvement was founded in 1823 to teach, and which is taught by that Lodge to-day' (see Letter, *in extenso*, pp. 118 and 119).

The corroborative evidence of this invariability is manifold.

In the first place there is the uninterrupted

descent of the Emulation Ritual from Peter William Gilkes, who was officially acknowledged by Grand Lodge as the exponent of the Ritual of the Lodge of Reconciliation.

Peter William Gilkes personally taught that Ritual to Stephen Barton Wilson, who personally taught it to Thomas Fenn, who personally taught it to R. Clay Sudlow.

Then there is the evidence on which they all base themselves as to the extraordinary care which has always been taken to safeguard its accuracy, amounting to an impossibility of alteration, all of which will be found in Bro. Sadler's 'History.'

The reverent spirit in which this care is exercised is apparent in the following extract from a speech by Bro. R. Clay Sudlow (February 23, 1894):

'. . . We look upon the Trust delivered to us by those Brethren as very important indeed—a very sacred one—and speaking for myself, and I am sure speaking in the name of my colleagues, I may say that that Trust shall be most faithfully, most honourably, and most religiously preserved.'

Finally, there is one most convincing test which is available to-day, and that is: Let anyone working there try to make a tiny little variation in the course of his work and see what happens!

Every Mason should visit the Emulation Lodge of Improvement, even if only to see what it is like.

No one can judge without facts in evidence.

The beauty of the work as it is performed there, the absolute accuracy, the unvarying system, the attention to detail, will enable the observant Mason to realize that here, at any rate, is a wonderful model.

But when to that admiration is added the conviction that it is the only authorized version, the intending student must come to the conclusion that he ought not to learn any other. It is simply waste of time to do so.

But Emulation Lodge of Improvement is not in the ordinary sense a Lodge of Instruction. It is rather a Lodge of Demonstration to which Masons, from all parts of the world, come with the object of seeing how the work ought to be done.

Therefore anyone undertaking to work there is expected to be a qualified exponent of the work of the office he undertakes.

To meet this difficulty and to permit the gradual development of the system, Emulation Lodge of Improvement has of late years recognized a series of Emulation-Working Lodges of Instruction, in which the Emulation system is strictly adhered to, and in which the earnest Mason may thoroughly learn the various Ceremonies, and so qualify himself to work at Headquarters. Obviously he can the more readily do this if he has not already filled his mind with the vagaries of various unrecognized 'Workings.'

Every Mason, therefore, should join one or more of these Emulation-Working Lodges of Instruction* in order to learn, and perfect himself in, the one and only Ritual ever authorized by Grand Lodge.

He should make a practice also of attending Emulation Lodge of Improvement on Friday nights to familiarize himself with every detail.

Then when his turn comes to take up regular Office in his own Lodge, he will not only have confidence that he will be able to do the right thing in the right way, but he will doubtless feel it to be his privilege and duty to assist the good work by leading the footsteps of his younger brethren in the straight and narrow path he himself has trodden.

*　　*　　*　　*

A few words are added, by request, with reference to that which is sometimes accus-

* A List of Lodges of Instruction recognized by the Committee of the Emulation Lodge of Improvement may be had by application to the Secretary direct.

ingly spoken of as the Intolerance of Emulation.

The form of the answer greatly depends upon the spirit in which the accusation is made; but, assuming it to be made *academically*, let us freely admit—nay, *claim*—that Emulation is, and always will be, intolerant to the last degree of—wilful error, or intentional deviation from the Ritual of the Lodge of Reconciliation which, and which alone, Emulation recognizes and teaches.

Let us also admit and claim that, in its moments of teaching and demonstration, Emulation is also intolerant of the slightest accidental error, or unintentional deviation from the absolute accuracy which is its basic and fundamental principle.

The I.P.M., assisted by brother committeemen, sits earnestly watchful for the slightest lapse, so that it may be corrected on the instant.

This *educational intolerance of error in the Emulation Lodge of Improvement* is the greatest—indeed, the only possible—safeguard for the pure and unsullied transmission of the Ritual of the Lodge of Reconciliation from generation to generation; and, in the minds of the thinking Masons who support the Emulation Lodge of Improvement, constitutes one of the principal claims to their gratitude and praise.

But the *intolerance of Emulation is limited to its educational aspect*, and any suggestion of intolerance, in any other than an educational sense, can only emanate from some among those (and unfortunately they are many) who do not know Emulation as it really is, and are not on visiting terms with it.

Obviously the primary object of Emulation is that the only Ritual ever authorized should, in consequence of previous instruction, be worked in the Regular Lodges with ease and accuracy and uniformity, but Emulation does not claim that its *authority* should penetrate into the Regular Lodge, and overshadow the functions of the Master.

In the Regular Lodge the Worshipful Master is supreme, and the principal object of solicitude is the Candidate; and all Forms, Ceremonies, and Ritual are, uninterruptedly, subservient to that object, and in that spirit.

In the Lodge of Instruction the Preceptor as I.P.M. is, *de facto*, supreme, and the principal object of solicitude is the absolute accuracy of every detail; and all Forms, Ceremonies, and Ritual are, interruptedly, subservient to that object.

The occasions being unlike, the circumstances do not admit of comparison.

Emulationists recognize to the full that purity of Ritual is not the *sum total* of Freemasonry—that it is not even of the *essence* of Freemasonry.

It is the beautiful goblet from which the good wine of Freemasonry is poured; but if the *quality* of the Nectar offered to the Candidate be inferior, in vain will be the artistic *beauty* of the vessel.

Emulationists fully recognize that the Mysteries and Privileges of Freemasonry may be taught, and often are taught, in phrases which do not correspond with any known form of Ritual; they recognize also that Brethren who give proof in their conduct from day to day that the Grand Principles on which the Order is founded are in their *hearts* are better exemplars of Masonry than those who possess merely the literal and verbal accuracy of its teachings.

But Emulationists also recognize that it is possible to have *both sincerity and accuracy,* and they desire to have both.

Hence the self-sacrificing labours of those who have devoted their time and energy, and practically their lives, to the achievement of the high object they have in view.

CHAPTER XVI

A LODGE AND ITS FURNITURE

IT may not be unprofitable for us to consider in some detail the Lodge and its Ornaments, Furniture, and Jewels.

The jewels and furniture of every Lodge belong to, and are the property of, the Master and Wardens for the time being, in trust for the members of the Lodge.

With regard to the Furniture, we shall discuss it, not only in the technical and restricted sense of the word, as it is described in the Explanation of the Tracing Board, and in the Lectures (that is, as consisting of the Volume of the Sacred Law, the Compasses, and the Square), but also in the more general acceptation of the term, including everything that is necessary for the decorous performance of the Ceremonies, and for the reasonable comfort and convenience of the Officers and the Brethren.

When 'the good man of the house' calls together 'his friends and his neighbours,' he makes all necessary arrangements for their reception, in order that they may derive the fullest enjoyment from his hospitality. This is the etiquette of private life. It should be with us also a matter of etiquette that our Lodge should be fitly arranged; that nothing be wanting; that all the means and appliances should be good of their kind; not mean or sordid, and, so far, unworthy of our Order; and especially that we should fulfil the conditions of the old adage, 'A place for everything, and everything in its place'; because, without a proper arrangement of everything that may be used, or to which attention may be directed, in the course of the several Ceremonies, the solemnity and the impressiveness of those Ceremonies may be considerably lessened, or altogether destroyed.

Unless the established order be strictly observed in the arrangement of the Lodge, and its Ornaments, Furniture, and Jewels, the Lodge cannot be said to be properly prepared; or to be 'just, perfect, and regular,' in the ordinary acceptation of the term; and the 'etiquette of Freemasonry' cannot be strictly maintained.

We will discuss these subjects consecutively, in the order in which they stand in the Explanation of the Tracing Board of the First Degree and in the First Lecture.

The form of the Lodge is said to be a parallelopipedon; and its situation is described as being 'due east and west.' For the latter proposition full and sufficient reasons are given in the Explanation.

It is highly desirable that these two conditions should be literally fulfilled whenever and wherever it may be possible. Too often, however, from circumstances which are beyond the control of the members of a Lodge, a literal fulfilment of the prescribed form and situation is impossible.

Very many Lodges are compelled to hold their meetings in hotels or public rooms, the shape or the position, and often both, of which do not agree with the model or ideal Lodge. Frequently there is no alternative room in the locality, and nothing can be done but to make the best of existing circumstances, and to hold, in practice, that the Master's chair denotes the East, and the Senior Warden's the West, of the Lodge.

It is very desirable, indeed necessary, that the door of entrance should be in the west, or quasi-west, and on the left of the Senior Warden's chair. In this position there are several advantages. The Junior Deacon on the one side of the Senior Warden and the Inner Guard on the other, balance each other, as it were. The Junior Warden and the Inner Guard are within clear view of each other; and members of the Lodge and visitors are, immediately on their entrance into the Lodge, brought under the direct notice of the Junior Warden. This is highly necessary, because he is responsible for all who enter, notwithstanding that all announcements of the names of both members and visitors are made by the Inner Guard to the Worshipful Master, who directs their admission. If the Candidate be admitted on the left of the Senior Warden, he is at once in the proper position for all that is to follow; from that starting-point he is enabled to make the complete perambulation of the Lodge, and on his return to the same place he is presented.

On the other hand, if he must enter on the right he must pass behind the Senior Warden's chair.

In cases where the door is on the right hand of the Senior Warden, and no change is possible, the tact of the Deacons and of the Director of Ceremonies must be exercised in order to minimize the awkwardness of the position.

The Ornaments of the Lodge are the Mosaic Pavement, the Indented or Tessellated Border, and the Blazing Star or Glory in the centre. One sometimes sees in a Lodge a carpet of some conventional pattern upon the floor; this is highly objectionable, and forms a direct contradiction to the description given in the Explanation of the Tracing Board previously quoted. It is happily becoming more and more rare in practice.

A carpet woven in the pattern of the Mosaic Pavement in black and white, or printed on felted drugget, is easily procurable—the latter at a small cost. A carpet the full size of the room, with a wide border, both of the prescribed pattern and colours, is highly desirable. In any case, 'the Blazing Star or Glory in the centre' should not be omitted.

'The furniture of the Lodge' comprises 'the Volume of the Sacred Law, the Compasses, and Square.' It is sad to find in some Lodges (probably few in number) that these indispensable furnishings of the Lodge are more or less mean and sordid in character—the Bible small, old, and dilapidated, and the Compasses and Square an ill-assorted couple: the Square of some common wood, the Compasses of brass, cheap and objectionable.

These things should not be. They show, first, a want of proper and becoming respect to the Volume of the Sacred Law, 'which is given as the rule and guide of our faith';

secondly, to the Compasses, the distinguishing Jewel of the Grand Master of our Order; and thirdly, to the Square, the time-honoured emblem and cognizance of the Craft, which teaches us to regulate our lives and actions.

A handsomely-bound Bible of moderate size, and the Square and Compasses *in silver*, will scarcely be beyond the means of any Lodge. They are often presented by zealous and liberal Brethren to their respective Lodges, and in such cases the gifts are almost invariably worthy of the givers and of the recipients.

The Jewels comprise 'three movable and three immovable.' 'The movable jewels are the Square, Level, and Plumb-rule.' 'They are called movable jewels, because they are worn by the Master, and his Wardens' (during the period of their tenure of their several offices), 'and are transferable to their successors on nights of installation.' The collars bearing these several jewels should be placed upon the chairs, respectively, of the Master and his Wardens, previously to the opening of the Lodge.

The Jewels of the Officers of private Lodges are prescribed as follow:

Masters: The square.

Past Masters: The square and the diagram of the 47th prop. First Book of

Euclid engraven on a silver plate, pendent within it.

Senior Warden: The level.

Junior Warden: The plumb rule.

Chaplain: A book within a triangle surmounting a glory.

Treasurer: A key.

Secretary: Two pens in saltire, tied by a ribbon.

Deacons: Dove and olive branch (p. 338).

Director of Ceremonies: Two rods in saltire, tied by a ribbon.

Assistant Director of Ceremonies: Two rods in saltire, tied by a ribbon, surmounted by a bar, bearing the word 'Assistant.'

Almoner: A Scrip Purse, upon which is a heart.

Organist: A lyre.

Assistant Secretary: Two pens in saltire, tied by a ribbon, surmounted by a bar bearing the word 'Assistant.'

Inner Guard: Two swords in saltire.

Stewards: A cornucopia between the legs of a pair of compasses extended.

Tyler: A sword.

The above jewels to be in silver, except those of the Officers of the Lodge of Antiquity, No. 2, and of the British Lodge, No. 8, which are golden or gilt.

'The immovable jewels are the Tracing

Board, and the Rough and Perfect Ashlars.'
'They are called immovable jewels because
they lie open and immovable in the Lodge,
for the Brethren to moralize on.'

Tracing Boards are doubtless derived from
the Operative Free Masons' Trestle Boards
which are placed in each stoneyard (or
degree), and upon which the actual tools and
other requisites are placed.

With regard to the position of the Tracing
Boards, there is much difference in practice
in different Lodges. In some old Lodges
they are simply the canvases not framed;
this is objectionable chiefly in consequence
of the difficulty experienced by the Junior
Deacon in handling them rapidly, and the
consequent damage and defacement likely
to ensue, as he lays and relays them upon
the floor according to the Degree in which
the Lodge is working.

In other Lodges the three Tracing Boards
are framed and are hung upon the walls of
the Lodge room. By this arrangement they
are better secured from damage; but it is
objectionable because it not infrequently
happens that the whole of the three are left
upon the walls, irrespective of the Ceremony
which is being performed. Clearly, during
an Initiation the Tracing Boards of the
Second and Third Degrees should not be

exposed to view, and similarly during the Ceremony of Passing the Tracing Boards of the First and Third Degree should be kept concealed.

Probably the best plan is to have the Tracing Boards painted on wooden panels and laid, according to the degree in which the Lodge is open, either upon the floor of the Lodge or against the Junior Warden's Pedestal, so that all may be reminded (and especially incoming Brethren) of the degree in which the Lodge is at that moment working. It is the duty of the Junior Deacon to attend to these changes.

A regards Biblical, and even traditional, accuracy, the present Tracing Boards leave much to be desired, especially the Second and the Third. A criticism of their inconsistencies and anachronisms will be found in the Appendix.

The proper place for the Rough Ashlar is on the Junior Warden's pedestal; it is there in full view. The stone should not be quite 'rough-hewn, as taken from the quarry' by the Quarrymen, Rough Masons, or Cowans. This is intended 'for the Entered Apprentice to work, mark, and indent on.' It should show evidence of having been so worked, marked, and indented; it should be as though a succession of E. As. had tried their ' 'prentice hand' upon it; had indeed *rough-dressed* it with the Gavel, and had knocked off some at least of the 'superfluous knobs and excrescences.'

Indications might also be shown of some rudimentary work with the Chisel, this working tool being presented to the Entered Apprentice in order that he may with it 'further smooth and prepare the stone and render it fit for the hands of the more expert Workman.'

After the stone has been 'rough-dressed' by First Degree men, and made one-sixteenth of an inch larger than the required size in each direction, it is passed on to the second stoneyard, where the Fellows of the Craft bring it to the exact size required, and polish it if so ordered. It is then a Perfect Ashlar.

The Perfect Ashlar is 'a stone of a true die or square.' The severest test to which the skill of an operative Mason can be submitted is the production of a perfect cube. It has even been asserted that a *perfect* cube has never yet been produced.

Its position should be on the Senior Warden's pedestal, properly suspended, with the Lewis inserted in the centre. The explanation of the Lewis, as it is given in the 'Explanation of the First Tracing Board,' runs thus: 'It is depicted by certain pieces of metal, dovetailed into a stone forming a cramp; and when in combination with some of the mechanical powers, such as a system of pulleys, it enables the Operative Mason to raise great weights to certain heights with little encumbrance, and to fix them on their proper bases.'

This may be seen in operation during the erection of any edifice which is being built wholly or partially of stone, and notably in the case of the laying of a foundation or chief corner-stone, at which some Masonic or other ceremony of a public character is observed.

It will readily be seen that a chain or rope passed *round* the stone, and especially the keystone of an arch, would prevent its being properly bedded in its place. Nothing could answer the purpose more effectually than the Lewis, which, with slight—if, indeed, any—modification in its form, has been for many centuries an indispensable implement in Operative Masonry; while in Speculative Masonry it has from time immemorial been one of the most interesting and expressive of the Symbols of our Order.

In some old Lodges one may sometimes see a curious and complicated structure, consisting of a crane with a windlass, on a platform (a cumbrous affair, generally broken or otherwise out of order), for the purpose of suspending the Perfect Ashlar. It may be interesting from its age, but it takes up too much room, and is altogether inconvenient wherever it may be placed in the Lodge.

A very simple plan of construction is to have three quasi-scaffold-poles, with their bases fixed to a flat triangle, and with a 'tackle and fall,' and a 'cleet' to which the end of the cord is made fast; the poles are tapered, and, of course, are brought together at the top. This plan is neat, inexpensive, and efficient, and at the same time it has the merit of being a model, in miniature, of that which is in constant use in Operative Masonry in laying foundation-stones, etc.

The three great Pillars which support a Freemasons' Lodge are called Wisdom, Strength, and Beauty, and find expression in the Ionic, Doric, and Corinthian Columns which are respectively attributed to Solomon, King of Israel; Hiram, King of Tyre; and Hiram Abiph, and are now assigned to the Worshipful Master and the Senior and Junior Wardens.

The Columns of the Senior and Junior Wardens are symbolically brought into service in the ceremonies of opening and closing the Lodge. The Master's Column is always stationary.

A Lodge and its Furniture

The three lesser Lights, which represent the Sun, Moon, and Master of the Lodge, are placed in candlesticks, which correspond, as regards Orders of Architecture, with the respective columns above mentioned.

The pedestals of the Worshipful Master, and of the Senior and Junior Warden, should be of sufficient size to accord with the rank of those Officers. Each should bear on the front the Working Tool by which each Officer is specially distinguished—namely, the Square for the Master, the Level for the Senior Warden, and the Plumb-rule for the Junior Warden. These may be really working tools, of the size and make of those in use in the Second Degree, securely fixed in the centre of the front of the pedestal. The effect of this is bolder and better than when the emblem is merely painted or gilt on the pedestal.

The top of each pedestal and the plinth should be in the usual form—a rectangular oblong.

The three chairs should be large and grandiose in character, made each in strict accordance with the Order in Architecture assigned to each of the three principal Officers. They should be spacious, well proportioned, and very handsome. The pedestals should also correspond to the three

Orders—that is, they should have each two
columns, the bases, the shafts, and the
capitals of each pair of columns being perfectly true to each of the three Orders.

Each of the Wardens' chairs should stand
upon a platform (7 to 8 inches high).
All the three pedestals should stand upon
the floor; consequently, they should be of
sufficient height to allow for the elevation
of the platform, and in the case of the
Master's pedestal for the platform and the
daïs combined. It is by no means uncommon *in outlying districts* to see tall
pedestals and the Wardens' chairs standing
on the floor—that is, without a platform—
the result being that those officers partially
disappear when they sit down.

Of the Working Tools of the Entered
Apprentice Degree little mention need be
made of the 24-inch Gauge or the Chisel.
The most important is the Gavel. This is
presented to the Worshipful Master when
he is installed into the Chair, as the Gavel
is an emblem of power; yet one sees occasionally in the Lodge the Master and the
Wardens each with, not a Gavel, but a light
Mall (a miniature copy of the heavy Mall of
the Third Degree)—that is, a small mallet
with a turned head—whereas the Gavel has
a slightly elongated head, with one end *flat-*

faced like a hammer, the other end having a blunt axe-edge.

This shape is admirably adapted to the work which it is represented as being designed to perform—namely, 'to knock off all superfluous knobs and excrescences.' An actual working tool of the operative mason of the present day is really a Gavel, with the head longer than that which we use. It is called a 'Walling Hammer.'

It is highly desirable that the regulation Gavels should be used in every Lodge. They are supplied in sets of three, bearing respectively the emblem of the Master, and of the Senior and the Junior Warden. They can be procured at a small cost from those who supply Lodge furniture.

Incidentally, it may be mentioned that some provision should be made for the protection of the tops of the Pedestals from the result of the strokes of the Gavel, and the Wardens should understand that heavy gavelling is unnecessary, and painful to nerves.

In the First Degree there are other and indispensable requisites, among which may be mentioned in their proper sequence the Bfd. and C.T. required by the T. before the admission of the Candidate; the Pd. required by the Inner Guard on the entrance of the

Candidate; the K.S. in the W. for his use
immediately after his entrance; the K.S. at
the Master's Pedestal for use during the
Ob.; the Cs. during the Ob.; the C.T.
during the Address; the Lambskin for the
investiture of the Candidate by the Senior
Warden; the Almsdish, or Charity Box,
which should be the real thing and suitable,
not a part of the Ballot Box; the Charter
or Warrant, for the inspection of the Candidate; a Book of Constitutions, and a
copy of the By-laws of the Lodge, both of
which latter should be presented to the Candidate, to remain in his own possession for
his future serious perusal. This is an essential custom. The newly-admitted Brother
naturally is desirous to gain all the knowledge
that is possible to him of the nature and the
Constitution of the Fraternity of which he
has become a member. He can take them to
his home, and at his ease he can read them
with the attention and carefulness which
have been recommended to him by the
Worshipful Master; and the zeal, born of
his recent Initiation, will lead him to follow
literally, and with profit to himself, the way
of 'Masonic knowledge,' in which, in the
Charge, he is told that he is to make 'daily
advancement.' The desirability of every
member of the Craft possessing a copy of

the Book of Constitutions led to its being produced in the first instance at the low price of one shilling and sixpence, and the Constitutions require (Section 138) that every member of a Lodge shall be supplied with a printed copy of its By-laws, as his acceptance thereof is deemed to be a declaration of his submission to them.

In addition to the Working Tools of the Second Degree, two additional Ss. will be required; one by the Inner Guard on the entrance of the Candidate, and one by the Junior Deacon at the Master's Pedestal.

The P.R. is to try and adjust uprights while fixing them upon their proper bases.

In erecting stone great care must be taken that each stone must be placed upon its 'proper basis'; that is, upon its 'natural bed,' and to prevent error every ashlar stone must be marked with the 'proper basis' or 'bed-mark.'

In addition to the Working Tools of the Third Degree, an extra pair of Cs. will be needed by the Inner Guard on the entrance of the Candidate.

Among the requisites indispensable in the furnishing of a Lodge in the Third Degree are the heavy M., the Sheet, and the Emblems of Mortality.

All sorts of devices are resorted to, to represent *that* over which the Candidate has to pass, in advancing from West to East. In one Lodge, the Tyler was brought in, and was made to take the necessary position, and was covered up. In a very great number of Lodges at the present time, a canvas painted to represent a C. of the modern shape is used. This utterly fails to represent the thing signified, which is an O. G.; besides being at variance with the custom of the East.

A Tracing Board for the Third Degree giving a representation of an O. G., with *something*, dim and indistinct, lying in it, would be the beau-ideal of a Third Tracing Board; an accurate presentment of the event commemorated, as distinguished from the picture, which does duty for a Tracing Board in the vast majority of Lodges— a travesty of the scene which is the central object of the Third Degree.

Inexpensive substitutes may easily be found; the least costly, perhaps, is a piece of black cloth or linen (a parallelogram, of course, as a G. would be) about six feet by two; a white or light-grey border round it, in order to define its limits, is desirable, considering the state of the Lodge at the time.

A Lodge and its Furniture

The Working Tools of the various Degrees
are nowadays, with rare exceptions, generally appropriate, and in order. In newly-
formed Lodges it may be said that they
are invariably so, having been generally
purchased in sets complete; but in some old
Lodges we find notable exceptions, such as
a nondescript Level or Compasses, and far
too often a common *lead pencil* instead of
the port-crayon.

A criticism of the Third Tracing Board will
be found in the Appendix.

* * * *

An organ or harmonium is happily now
considered to be an indispensable item in
the furniture of a Lodge.

* * * *

See Masonic Mourning, p. 268.

CHAPTER XVII

ETIQUETTE WITHIN THE LODGE

PROCESSIONAL ENTRY

IT is customary in some Lodges for the Worshipful Master, Past Masters, and Wardens to make a formal entry into the Lodge Room. If this be intended, the Brethren should assemble in the Lodge Room, and the Procession should be formed up in the Ante-Room, and when ready the Organist should perform a suitable accompaniment, and the Procession should enter in the following order:

The Tyler, with drawn sword; and I. G.
The Dir. of Ceremonies (with A.D.C.).
The Deacons.
The Wardens.
The Worshipful Master.
The Past Masters.

On arriving near the Master's Pedestal, the Brethren preceding him open out to right and left, and the Worshipful Master passes through to his Chair. The Senior Deacon remains with him, at, or near to, his right.

The procession passes on, leaving the Past

Masters when they arrive at their appointed place in the S.E. on the left of the Master's Chair.

On arriving near the Junior Warden's Chair, the preceding Brethren again open out as before, and the Junior Warden passes through to his seat.

Similarly, on arriving near the Senior Warden's Chair, where the Junior Deacon remains.

The Tyler, I. G., and D. C. pass on.

The I. G. takes his place on the left of the S. W.; the Tyler passes out of the Lodge, and closes the door, which the I. G. locks, and the D. C. or D. Cs. take their places.

In taking their places in their respective chairs, the Worshipful Master and the Wardens should invariably follow the course of the Sun—that is, the Master should enter on the North side. The Senior Warden should enter on the South side, and the Junior Warden should enter on the East side.

ARRANGEMENT OF SEATS

On the RIGHT of the W.M.

The Prov. G.M. and/or Dep. Prov. G.M.

Grand Officers next to Dep. Prov. G.M.

Prov. G. Officers (or London Rank).

Distinguished Visitors.
Senior Deacon.
Ordinary Visitors.

On the LEFT of the W.M.
Immediate Past Master.
Chaplain.
Past Masters in Rank and Seniority.
Brethren generally.

Every visiting Brother who is a Master of
a Lodge or a Past Master should, immediately
upon his entrance into the Lodge, be conducted by the Director of Ceremonies (or,
in his absence, should be invited by the
Worshipful Master) to the daïs or to a seat
on the right of the Worshipful Master. (The
daïs is out of date nowadays in most London
Lodges.) If all the seats there are occupied,
it will be in accordance with etiquette—
and, indeed, with ordinary politeness—that
a member of the Lodge shall give place in
favour of the visiting Brother. (See p. 319.)

OPENING ODE

When the formal entry has been completed, as above, or (in cases where there is
no formal entry) when the Brethren are
assembled, the opening Ode may be sung.

This is a well-known Ode, commencing, 'Hail Eternal!' (see p. 238).

In the third verse there is a reference to the Badge and mystic Sign. Certain ingenious Brethren make certain motions when these words are sung, but it is quite improper to do so—as, for one reason, the Lodge is not yet open; and no masonic Sign should ever be given except in open Lodge.

The opening Ode should always be sung *before* the Lodge is opened, and *not after* (see p. 294).

WARRANT

'No Lodge can meet without a Warrant'; and the Worshipful Master is responsible for its safe custody and for its production at every meeting of the Lodge.

Care should therefore be taken to see that the Warrant is in evidence before proceedings are commenced.

OPENING, FIRST DEGREE

The Lodge is then opened in the First Degree.

When the W. M. addresses the J. W., the J. W. should not make any Sn. When directed to do so by the J. W., the I. G. 'sees' that the L. is P. T. by giving the E. A. Ks. He does not open the door to do so.

These Ks. being answered by the T., and reported by the I. G. to the J. W., the J. W. gives ━▌ and reports to the W. M. (Ks. only; no Sn.).

In doing this, the J. W. should not turn his body towards the W. M., only his head.

When the W. M. addresses the S. W., the S. W. should not make any Sn.

When the Brethren are called to order, they should all simultaneously take Sp., and then give Sn. of E. A., looking (not turning) to the E., so that they may presently keep time accurately with the W. M.

All Sps. and Sns. should be silently done.

Care should be taken that the Sn. should be perfect and uniform and square. There is much slovenliness with regard to this.

The Sn. should commence where it rests. There should not be a preliminary motion, or point.

One point connected with the opening (and closing) of the Lodge arises in this place—namely, Is it etiquette for one or more or the whole of the Brethren present to pronounce the words 'So mote it be' at the conclusion of the prayer by the Worshipful Master? Opinions and practice differ upon the subject. It is held in Emulation Working Lodges that the Immediate Past Master *alone* should use the words; in others, that the right belongs to all the Past Masters, and to none below that rank. The practice in many Lodges is for all the Brethren to join in the repetition of the words; and in many Lodges the words are sung to the accompaniment of the organ.

There is no authoritative pronouncement upon the subject, therefore we must expect to find differences in practice in different Lodges.

The Sn. should be maintained until the word 'open' is pronounced by the W. M., when the Sn. should be dis. with perfect uniformity, hand remaining open.

W. M. ➤ S. W. ➤; and Col.

J. W. ➤ and Col.

I. G. ks., and T. replies.

J. D. adjusts T. B.—I. P. M. opens V. S. I. (2 Chron. vi), and adjusts S. and C.

All sit when W. M. sits—not before.

Minutes

By direction of the W. M. (no ➤), the Secretary reads all unconfirmed Minutes of all preceding Meetings; Regular and Emergency. The Minutes should always be read in the First Degree, as every Initiate is entitled to hear them and vote on them.

The W. M. then puts the Minutes—

separately, if of more than one Meeting. (No ➤.)

The Confirmation of the Minutes is usually a perfunctory proceeding, and in ordinary circumstances can only relate to the accuracy of the record or the propriety of recording the item.

The single exception is in relation to the election of Master, who is not deemed to be elected until the Minutes, so far at least as relates to his election, have been confirmed (Const. 105). (See note on p. 318.)

Votes at one meeting which, by their nature or according to the By-laws, require confirmation at a subsequent meeting —*e.g.*, votes relating to grants of money— cannot be properly dealt with on the motion for confirming the Minutes.

They should be the subject of a separate motion, on due notice printed on the summons, "that . . . . be confirmed."

In other words, if in the interval between one meeting and another other counsels prevail and that which was done at the previous meeting does not meet with the approval of those assembled at the next meeting, then, if the vote in question is one which requires confirmation, the alteration must be effected by voting against the motion to confirm the previous resolution as mentioned in the preceding paragraph. But if the matter complained of is already complete (*i.e.*, does not require a confirmatory vote), then in that case any alteration can only be effected by a substantive motion, on due notice given, to rescind the previous resolution.

In June, 1905, Grand Lodge decided that due notice must be given of any intended motion for non-confirmation of Minutes, so that it may appear on the printed Agenda.

In September, 1911, Grand Lodge upheld the ruling of a District Grand Master that a proposition of non-confirmation could not be made for the purpose of a revision of opinion, nor for the purpose of allowing second thoughts to prevail; the only question involved being accuracy of record.

Further, a motion to rescind a previous resolution would, if carried, have more force than an inoperative refusal to confirm the Minutes of the previous meeting.

On the other hand, the confirmation of the Minutes does not legalize that which was illegal *ab initio*.

As to signing Minutes, see p. 339.

ADMISSIONS AFTER OPENING

The correct manner of saluting the Worshipful Master by Brethren who enter or leave the Lodge after it has been opened follows well-defined rules according to the circumstances of the moment—*i.e.*, whether the Lodge is in the First, the Second, or the Third Degree.

There is no law upon the subject, but the custom is sufficiently established to enable us to dogmatize upon it.

On Entering

1. If the Lodge is in the First Degree, the entering Brother should take Sp. and give Sn. of E. A.

2. If the Lodge is in the Second Degree, the entrant should take Sp. and give Sn. of E. A.; then take Sp. and give the three Sns. of F. C. in consecutive order.

3. If the Lodge is in the Third Degree, the entrant should take Sp. and give Sn. of E. A.; then take Sp. and give the first two Sns. of F. C.; and (instead of giving third Sn. of F. C.) he should take Sp. and convert F. C. position into Sn. of H.; then give S. of S., and P. S. of third.

On Leaving

4. In whatever degree the Lodge is open, the exeant should take Sp. and give the P. S. of that degree.

On Re-entering

5. Exactly the same as 4. (See p. 340.)

The only exception to these rules is in relation to the Candidate, who salutes according to the special instructions given to him at the time by the Deacon.

The body should be erect while Sns. are given. Even in the S. of S. it is only the head which is bent. There should be no ceremonial bowing to the W. M. On the contrary, there should rather be a military stiffening.

The Worshipful Master, upon the admission of a visitor from another Lodge, may say: 'I greet you well, Brother A.B.' This form of greeting would appear to be of ancient date; it has a good old Masonic flavour about it; it is courteous to a visitor as distinguished from a Member of the Lodge. It is a form of welcome quite distinct from anything one hears in the outer world. This, or some other equally courteous greeting to visitors, is worthy of observance in Lodges generally.

When a Member of the Lodge enters or leaves the Lodge, and salutes according to the then Degree, it is a simple act of courtesy for the Worshipful Master to bow an acknowledgment. It is unnecessary for the Master to utter any words of welcome to a member of the Lodge; that form of greeting being reserved for visitors only.

It is, perhaps, unnecessary to mention that in the case of a Brother of Grand Rank, or Provincial or District Grand Rank or London Rank, visiting a Lodge other than his own, the Brethren should all rise, and remain standing until their visitor has taken his seat.

The correct salutes to Grand Officers within the Lodge are as follow:

M.W.G.M. and M. W. Pro. G.M. .. 11
R.W.D.G.M. 9
R.W. Brethren 7
V.W. Brethren 5
Other Grand Officers 3

Provincial Grand Officers:
R. W. Prov. G.M. 7
W. Dep. Prov. G.M. (in their own Province) 5
W.Asst. Prov. G.M. (in their own Province) 5
Other Prov. Grand Officers (in their own Province) 3
Prov. Grand Officers (on investment) 3
G. or R.Sns. (given only in 3rd Deg.)

On the occasion of a report after the Lodge is opened, the Inner Guard announces it to the Junior Warden, who by a single knock directs the I.G. to ascertain who wants admission. The I.G. then announces the claimant for admission to the Worshipful Master, who directs the I.G. to admit him.

This authority of the J.W. relates to ordinary *reports* only. When a Candidate is announced in either Degree, the Junior Warden, after receiving notice thereof from the Inner Guard, conveys the announcement to the Worshipful Master in the proper form, who replies as prescribed in the Ritual.

The difference of procedure pointed out in the two preceding paragraphs will show the indispensable necessity of the Tyler and of the Inner Guard being thoroughly conversant with the proper knocks in each Degree, because any mistake or confusion between the two must inevitably lead to confusion in the Lodge (see pp. 305-307).

In some Country Lodges there is a distinction made between a 'Report' and an 'Alarm.' There is considerable force in the argument which supports this course of procedure, but the fact remains that the only recognized ks. are those detailed on pp. 306-307.

When two or more Brethren are announced it is not necessary to give the names of all; on the other hand, it is not right to omit the mention of any name, as one too often hears, in this way: 'Several Brethren seek admission.' The correct form is for the Tyler to say to the Inner Guard: 'Brother A. B. and other Brethren'; and the Inner Guard will say: 'Worshipful Master, Brother A. B. and other Brethren.' If a visitor or visitors happen to be of the group, he or they should be allowed to go first, and, as a matter of course, his name or their names would be announced. In the case of a visitor it is customary for the Tyler and Inner Guard to add: 'Vouched for by Brother . . . .' (the member inviting him). (See p. 95.)

The Worshipful Master's reply to the announcement is: 'Admit him' or 'them,' as the case may be.

The use of additional words subserves no useful end or purpose; redundant forms of expression have crept into the working of Lodges, no one knows whence, or how, or why. Masters of Lodges and Directors of Ceremonies should always be especially careful to nip in the bud the first introduction of all superfluous and meaningless phrases and forms of expression, even as, with the Gavel, the Entered Apprentice is taught 'to knock off all superfluous knobs and excrescences.'

In connection with the Gavel we may mention that it is desirable that the Wardens should be always ready to answer the ▬▮ of the Worshipful Master. When laid again upon the pedestal the Gavel should be replaced silently, so that no other sound is heard than the actual ks.

Much unnecessary energy is too often displayed in the use of the Gavel. One sometimes hears a succession of sounding blows that would not discredit Thor himself, emitting sounds that may be heard far beyond the Lodge room. This is objectionable, for more than one obvious reason. A moderately sharp *tap*, and not a heavy blow, is all that is required upon any occasion.

A very useful precaution for securing the top of the pedestal from injury is to provide (for each pedestal) a flat piece of wood—presumably oak, like the pedestal—say 5 or 6 inches square and $\frac{3}{4}$ inch thick, the underside covered with cloth. This will receive the indentations inevitably consequent upon the repeated taps, or, worse, the blows of the Gavel.

JOINING MEMBERS

If there is a proposal duly made on the summons to admit a joining member, it is well to take the ballot as soon as possible after the confirmation of the Minutes. The proposer and seconder should be called on to state their case in full, vouching for the proposed member and explaining the reasons which lead them to suppose he will be an acquisition to the Lodge. It is assumed that the proposal will have been already approved by the Standing Committee (see pp. 83 and 439).

Assuming the result of the ballot to be favourable, and the Brother in attendance, he should be escorted to the W. M. by the Director of Ceremonies and formally introduced. The W. M. should make a suitable speech to the joining member, bidding him welcome in his own name and on behalf of the Lodge.

At the subsequent post-prandial proceedings a special toast should be given in his honour (see p. 351).

A Past Master of an English Lodge joining another English Lodge becomes a Past Master *in* the Lodge he joins, and takes rank and precedence immediately after the Immediate Past Master of the year in which he joins, and before the Worshipful Master of the year in which he joins.

As a Past Master he immediately becomes eligible for office as Worshipful Master; but it is to be assumed that in ordinary course he would, *cæteris paribus*, rank for office immediately after the last initiate or joining member, according to date.

CANDIDATE

If there is a Candidate duly proposed on the Summons, a Ballot should be taken.

A proposal must be made and seconded on the printed summons, and this proposal should have been already the subject of investigation by the Standing Committee (see p. 83). But that is not all. When that item of the Agenda is reached, the proposer and seconder should make the proposal in open Lodge and *viva voce*, so that the tongue of good report may be heard in favour of the candidate.

The Ballot is a most important proceeding, and should be effected in an impressive manner. When the Worshipful Master directs it to be taken, the Junior Deacon distributes the balls, commencing with the Immediate Past Master, and finishing at the Worshipful Master; and the Senior

Deacon collects them in the Ballot Box in the same order.

Several candidates may be balloted for at the same time; any adverse vote involving a separate ballot for each.

The Ballot is intended to be absolutely secret, so as to give absolute freedom from fear of consequences. A black ball is quite as legal as a white one, and any brother who votes according to his conscience has a right to be protected.

Abstention from voting is permissible, and does not count against the candidate.

The result of the Ballot should be forthwith notified by the Inner Guard to the Tyler, in order that the Candidate may be prepared without delay.

INITIATION

The Ceremony of Initiation may then be taken (see p. 200).

PRAYERS

During the prayers in the various ceremonies, when the attitude of reverence is adopted, the th. is not visible. At the close the h. is 'dropped,' not 'drawn.'

*　　*　　*　　*

Obn.

It should be remembered the Sn. during the E. A. Obn. should be the P. S. of an E. A.

Questions before Passing

If the Ceremony of Passing is to be done, the necessary Questions should be put, and the Candidate entrusted (see p. 210).

Opening, Second Degree

All E. As. having been directed to retire, the Lodge may be opened in the Second Degree.

The preliminary points are to be observed as before.

When the Brethren, by direction of the J. W., prove themselves Cn., they should look to the East, and should take their time from the I. P. M. The object is to get the Brethren to make every movement in silence and in unison. This can be done only by taking the time from one man.

―――――

Perhaps the best example of discipline in this respect is to be found in military Lodges. The perfection of accuracy and precision of movement and of time are, of course, to be expected from these drilled and trained men;

these qualities, however, are not difficult in practice in private Lodges: the habit is easily acquired, but, unfortunately, so many of the Brethren do not strive after combined and simultaneous action. Every Brother should visit a military Lodge if one such happen to be held 'within the length of his cable-tow,' and he will see how charming and instructive such a visit will be; 'profit and pleasure will be the result,' to a certainty.

They should, thus, in silence and in unison dis. E. A., take Sp., place r. h. before placing l. h. When, however, the W. M. declares 'the Lodge duly open on the S.,' the order is reversed: the l. h. is d. at the word 'open,' and then at the word 'S.' the third portion of the threefold Sn. is given with the r. h. in two distinct motions.

W. M. —◀ S. W. —◀ J. W. —◀.
I. G. ks., and T. replies.

N.B.—If a Candidate is outside, the gavels give gentle ks., and the I.G. does not communicate the ks. to T. He stands in his place and gives ks. on his cuff. This is so done whether in 'opening' or 'resuming.'

J. D. adjusts T. B.
I. P. M. adjusts S. and C.
All sit when W. M. sits—not before.

Etiquette within the Lodge

PASSING

The Ceremony of Passing may now be taken (see p. 212).

OBN.

It should be remembered that the Sn. during the F. C. Obn. is the P. S. of a F. C.

QUESTIONS BEFORE RAISING

If the Ceremony of Raising is to be done, the necessary Questions should be put and the Candidate entrusted (see p. 221).

OPENING, THIRD DEGREE

All F. Cs. having been directed to retire, the Lodge may be opened in the Third Degree.

The preliminary points are to be observed as before.

When the Brethren, by direction of the J. W., prove themselves M. Ms. by Sns., they should, in silence, and in unison, take Sp.; convert F. C. into S. of H.; S. of S.; P. S. from extreme left, and 'recover.' The hand should lie quite flat on the same plane as the floor; not with drooping fingers.

There is no evolution in the whole range of ceremonial observance in the Lodge, in which so many and so wide divergences from the correct forms are to be seen, as in the making of these three Ss., more especially in the first. This Sn. cannot, of course, be described; we can only suggest that in all the movements the body should be quite erect, and the motions should be made with freedom of action, and should be carefully developed, but at the same time with no exaggeration of gesture. The proper movements and positions, once acquired, are perfectly easy, and are never forgotten.

The last answer in the opening in the Third Degree, made by the Senior Warden—'That being a point from which a Master Mason cannot err'—is a very curious one: it is explained at length in the sixth section of the first Lecture, and is referred to in Esotery.

When the W. M. reaches the word 'open,' all draw sharply; when C. is pronounced, all drop in unison, without 'recovery.'

This is the only occasion on which there is no 'recovery.'

W. M. ━┫ S. W. ━┫ J. W. ━┫.
I. G. ks., and T. replies.

N.B.—If a Candidate is outside, the gavels give gentle ks., and the I.G. does not communicate the ks. to T. He stands in his place and gives ks. on his cuff. This is so done whether in 'opening' or 'resuming.'

J. D. adjusts T. B.

I. P. M. adjusts S. and C.

G. or R. S. all simultaneously.

All sit when W. M. sits—not before.

*　　*　　*　　*

(*In some Country Lodges the Worshipful Master alone first gives the G. or R. S., next the Worshipful Master and Senior Warden, and thirdly the Worshipful Master, the Wardens, and the whole of the Brethren. The words accompany the s. . . . in each case—that is, they are spoken first by the Worshipful Master alone, then by the Worshipful Master and the Senior Warden together, and thirdly by all together.*)

This is mentioned as the survival of a curious custom; not as an example to be followed.

*　　*　　*　　*

RAISING

The Ceremony of Raising may now be taken (see p. 330).

The Sheet must be fully spread, and never folded either at the commencement or subsequently.

The Master's Light must never be extinguished while the Lodge is open; neither may it by any means be shaded or obscured;

nor may any Lantern or other device, with or without a Star, be permitted.

An official communication on this important point will be found in the Appendix (pp. 420-422).

In this connection reference may be made to an ingenious 'deviation' which has crept into some Lodges in which the electric switch plays a disconcerting part at the Master's solemn allusion to the Morning Star.

The slightest reflection will show the modernity of this undignified innovation.

The proper point at which to restore Ls. and remove the sheet is after the retirement of the Candidate 'to restore,' etc.

Obn.

It should be remembered that the Sn. during the M. M. Obn. is the P.S. of a M. M.

*   *   *   *

Order of Business

As a general rule, it will be found convenient to commence by opening the Lodge in all the Degrees in which there is work to be done, and the Worshipful Master to 'resume' up and down as occasion requires. This enables the programme to be varied and carried out in any order without confusion. (See p. 337.)

Etiquette within the Lodge

A good rule is observed in many—perhaps the majority of—Lodges, in the order in which the ceremonies are performed. If Initiations, Passings, and Raisings have to be performed at any one meeting, the Raisings are taken first, the Passings next, and the Initiations last. Good reasons can be assigned for this regulation: *inter alia*, the number of Brethren present is, as a rule, greater towards the end of the meeting than at the beginning, and consequently the Lodge is at its best in point of appearance; therefore it is calculated to make a better impression upon the mind of the Candidates.

*   *   *   *

When from any cause either of the Principal Officers leaves his chair for any appreciable period of time, another Brother should take his place. In such cases a good custom prevails in probably the majority of Lodges—namely, the Officer who is leaving his chair takes the right hand of the Brother who is to take his place, and as it were inducts him into the chair which he himself has vacated. If and when the proper Officer returns, his *locum tenens* offers his right hand, and assists the officer back into his chair in the same manner. This is true politeness, and therefore true etiquette. It has in it a grace and dignity worthy of our Ancient and Illustrious Order.

The reason why the Principal Officers should always enter and leave their several chairs in the manner thus described is the same as that which prescribes that the Candidates in each Degree should be led 'up the North, past the Worshipful Master in the East, down the South, and be conducted to the Senior Warden in the West'—namely, that we follow 'the due course of the Sun, which rises in the East, gains its meridian lustre in the South, and sets in the West.' (*Vide* Lecture in the First Degree.)

* * * *

'SQUARING' THE LODGE

This should only be done ceremonially and when prescribed in the Ritual.

In the ordinary peregrinations of the members or officers in the execution of their non-ceremonial duties the attempt to 'square' the Lodge is distinctly a superfluous knob or excrescence which should be knocked off by the gavel.

* * * *

CALLING OFF AND ON

If the programme of business be a long one, it is desirable to make a break at about 'half time.' A definite short period for refreshment is better than the constant disturbance and interruption caused by Brethren retiring and returning in twos and threes.

* * * *

At the conclusion of all ceremonial work the Lodge should be resumed in the Third Degree (if not then working in that degree), and then closed in the Third Degree.

CLOSING THIRD DEGREE

In the closings the L. is proved close tyled.

The com. of the S. Ss. demands considerable care.

The Ws. leave their places by the left side, and stand to order, r.f. in h. of l.

The J. W. takes Sp., gives P. G. leading from 2 to 3, elevates hs., and under them whs. P. W.; recovers, takes Sp., gives S. of H.; S. of S.; P. S.; 5 Ps. of F.; and whs. W. of M. M.; recovers, salutes, and returns to his place the right side.

The S. W. takes up position facing W. M., and asks the W. M. to receive the S. Ss.

The W. M. descends from Ped. by the S. E. side, and take up position immediately in front of it, r.f. in h. of l.

The S. W. then repeats what J. W. has

already done; with the exception that the Ws. are audible.

They both return to places. They should, on resuming their several positions, re-enter their respective places on the side opposite to that by which they left them.

The W. M. confirms S. Ss., and eventually directs the S. W. to close the L.

The W. M. ━▪ with L. H., still standing to order with P. S. of M. M.

The S. W. closes the L.; all dis. Sn. and recover in unison; gives ▬▪.

The J. W. repeats ━▪.

The I. G. ks.; T. replies.

The J. D. attends to T. B. The I. P. M. attends to S. and Cs.

All sit if, and when, W. M. sits, not before.

Closing Second Degree

Usually without pause, the L. is proved close tyled.

The discovery of the S. S. in the C. of the Bdg. is announced, and after prayer by the W. M. the S. W. is directed to close the L.; the W. M. ━▪ with L. H. still standing to order as a F. C.

The S. W. closes L. and gives ▬▪.

The J. W. gives ━▪.

The I. G. gives ks.; T. replies.

All sit when W. M. sits, not before.

MOTIONS PURSUANT TO NOTICE

The Lodge being now in the First Degree, if there is any motion of which notice has been given, it may now be discussed.

The discussion must follow strictly the ordered lines of regulated debate (p. 330).

The Worshipful Master is the supreme ruler, and when he has decided points of order or other matters of graver importance, he must on no account permit any appeal to the Lodge from his decision.

The only possible appeal from the decision of the Master is to Provincial Grand Lodge or to Grand Lodge, as the case may be.

FIRST RISING

After the conclusion of all ceremonial work and masonic business (if any), and while the Lodge is still open in the First Degree, the Worshipful Master gives one ▬▬, which is followed by the Wardens; he then rises and says: 'Brethren! I rise for the first time to ask if any Brother has aught to propose for the good of Freemasonry in general, or of this (naming it) Lodge in particular.'

On this occasion or 'first rising' initiates and joining members are proposed, and Notices of Motion (other than financial) are given.

It is generally understood that notice of any motion of *more than minor importance* should be given at a regular meeting of the Lodge, and that the motion itself should be set forth in the Summons convoking the meeting at which it is to be brought forward. It is obvious that Brethren who were not present when the notice was given have a clear right to be duly notified by circular of the terms and scope of the motion, and of the meeting at which it is to be discussed.

*   *   *   *

When speaking to the Worshipful Master on occasions other than those prescribed in the Ceremonies, the correct method on commencing to speak is to salute and dis. the Sn. of the degree in which the Lodge is then working; and on finishing to do similarly. It looks awkward, besides being inconvenient, to keep the Sn. up during a speech.

Initial letters, representing the names of the Officers, as, for example, W. M., S. W., J. W., and so on to I. G., are only used in order to save space in printing. No abbreviations of any kind should be used in the Lodge at any time, upon any occasion. The Worshipful Master should never be addressed as 'W. M.,' either during the Ceremonies or at any other period during the meeting. One sometimes hears the Master addressed as 'Worshipful.' This is altogether inexcusable, being totally devoid of the respect due to the high position which the Master holds.

Past Masters may sometimes be heard to address the Worshipful Master as 'Worshipful Sir,' thus implying (we presume) the perfect equality of themselves with the Master. This is a mistaken idea altogether. The Worshipful Master, during the period of his tenure of that Office, is paramount over all, over every member of the Lodge, be he Past Master or Entered Apprentice; there is no exception to this rule.

Unfortunately, habits of this kind are contagious, and we hear occasionally a Junior Warden (not being a Past Master) reply, 'I am, Worshipful Sir'; and others below the rank even of Junior Warden are apt to follow the bad example. All such deviations from established rule and order, and from the etiquette of the Lodge, should be strictly guarded against and repressed, whoever may be the offender in this respect, and whatever may be his status in the Lodge.

In the case of one Past Master addressing another, 'Worshipful Brother' would be a better term. 'Sir' belongs to the outer world; it has no flavour of Freemasonry about it; it is better to leave it behind when we enter the Lodge. In the not improbable case of one Past Master acting as Master *pro tempore*, and another Past Master acting as an officer, in any capacity, if from any cause the officer should have to address the Acting Master, he should address him as 'Worshipful Master.' Although not the reigning W. M., he is, for the time being, the Master of the Lodge, and thereby invested with plenary powers, and fully entitled to the honours due to the actual Worshipful Master.

* * * *

SECOND RISING

After an interval of time the ━┫ are given as before, and the question is repeated, substituting the words 'for the second time.' On the 'second rising' financial matters are disposed of, and notice of motion relating to finance are given.

* * * *

THIRD RISING

Again, after an interval, the ━┫ and the question are repeated 'for the third time.'

It is specially to be noted that the Master asks these questions only when the Lodge is opened in the First Degree, and for a very sufficient reason. In the discussion of any motion, or of any subject that may come up during the meeting of the Lodge, an Entered Apprentice, who is a subscribing member, has as clear a right to vote upon the matter under discussion as any other member of the Lodge. For this reason the questions mentioned in the preceding paragraph are generally reserved until after the ceremonial business of the Lodge has been disposed of.

Another advantage is gained by delaying discussions, and the proposition of Candidates, or of joining members, until the latter portion of the sitting—namely, that Brethren, whose 'public or private avocations' have precluded the possibility of an early attendance at the Lodge, will probably have arrived, and they may then be enabled to make any proposition, or to take a part in any deliberation or discussion having for its object 'the good of Freemasonry in general, or of their own Lodge in particular.'

On the 'third rising,' 'hearty good wishes' are given to the W. M.

Some correspondence appeared in 1890 in the *Freemason* upon the question of the right of visitors to tender to the Lodge in which they are guests 'hearty good wishes' from the Lodges of which they are severally members. Most of the letters were of an inquiring character; the respective writers wanted to know if they had or had not been rightly informed as to Grand Lodge having expressed an opinion 'unfavourable to the continuance of the custom.' Grand Lodge has expressed no opinion favourable or otherwise upon the subject.

The opinion of the late Grand Registrar of the Order was taken upon the question, and he gave it to the effect 'that no Brother has the right to convey the good wishes, hearty or otherwise, of his own Lodge to any other Lodge without the permission of his own Worshipful Master.' Nevertheless, it is an ancient custom, kindly, genial, fraternal, harmless in itself if used in moderation, and genuinely Masonic; it existed before we were born, it will endure long after we are buried.

In the meantime we may safely go on in the old way, giving and receiving 'hearty good wishes,' as the custom has been 'from a time of which the memory of man runneth not to the contrary.'

CLOSING THE LODGE

The Lodge is proved close tyled. The S. W. is interrogated as to his constant place in the Lodge, and after solemn prayer by the W. M., the S. W. is directed to close the L.; the W. M. ➡ with L. H. still standing to order as E. A.

The S. W. closes the L. and gives ➡.

The J. W. announces the next meeting, and gives ➡. J. D. adjusts T. B.

The I. G. gives ks., and the T. replies.

The Lodge must be 'closed.' There is no power to 'adjourn' it.

The I. P. M. calls on the Brethren to lock up the Ss. in a safe repository, uniting in the act F. F. F.

Sometimes the Brethren join in a pious ejaculation: 'May God preserve the Craft,' but it is unorthodox and quite redundant, seeing that the W. M. in the final prayer has already besought the G. A. O. T. U. to preserve the Order by cementing and adorning it with every moral and social virtue.

The Lodge being closed, the customary closing Masonic Ode (see p. 251) may be sung.

PROCESSION

At the conclusion of the Ode the Director of Ceremonies calls on the Brethren to remain standing while the W. M., Wardens, Grand Officers, Members of London Rank, and distinguished Visitors leave the Lodge.

The procession is formed in the following

manner; the Organist, meanwhile, furnishing suitable instrumental accompaniment:

The D. C. signals the J. D. to proceed. The J. D. 'squares' the L. and picks up the S. D. They proceed in company to the left of the J. W.'s Pedestal. He descends and follows them to the left of the S. W.'s Pedestal. The S. W. descends, and the quartet advance to the left of the W. M.'s Pedestal. The W. M. descends and follows the Wardens. The P. Ms. fall in behind, and the Grand Officers, Members of London Rank, and Visitors of high degree join in their order of precedence (juniors first *inter se*), and so all march out; ordinary Visitors and the Brethren of the Lodge following at the end.

CHAPTER XVIII

DRESS, JEWELS, AND PUNCTUALITY

IN discussing 'Freemasonry and its Etiquette,' the question of dress naturally suggests itself for consideration. We may briefly state the conclusions at which the consensus of opinion and of practice, in the great majority of cases, would appear to have arrived.

In Lodges where the members dine together after the business of the Lodge is concluded, evening dress is the rule. This is, indeed, so general that it may almost be said to be invariable and universal.

In other Lodges, where a supper or some moderate refreshment is provided, evening dress is not universal. Still, in some even of these the Brethren make it a rule to wear full evening dress both at their own meetings and when visiting other Lodges. The difficulty in the way of this graceful custom is that the interval between the cessation of the professional or business avocations of many of the members and the hour for the meeting of the Lodge will not allow time sufficient for an entire change of dress.

In cities and large towns, where in the Lodges the Initiations are more or less frequent, there are often two, and occasionally three, Ceremonies to be performed on the same evening, and necessarily the hour for meeting must be comparatively early. This will probably account for the fact that some members have acquired the doubtful habit of attending the Lodge in the habiliments of ordinary every-day life. In this respect each Lodge is, as a rule, governed by its own custom and usage; but the members should strive, where it is necessary, rather to attain to a higher standard of propriety in the matter of dress than to degenerate to a lower level.

In certain Lodges the summons states 'Evening Dress.' This, at least, may be expected of every member, whatever be his circumstances in life, and every effort should be made by those in authority in the Lodge to promote uniformity in this respect, as far as may be done without wounding the susceptibilities of any individual member who from any cause may deviate from the general rule.

If morning dress be allowed, it should be black, or very dark in colour; black boots, not brown; and for all outside occasions of ceremony silk hats are *de rigueur*.

Dress, Jewels, and Punctuality

In cases of Lodges of Emergency, Lodges of Instruction, and, indeed, on all Masonic occasions where morning dress is worn, the Apron should be worn outside the coat.

While we are discussing that branch of our subject which relates to 'dress,' a few words may be said about the Jewels which may or may not be worn in the Lodge. Few of our members are ignorant of the rule which strictly forbids the wearing in a Craft Lodge of a Jewel belonging to any Degree which is not recognized by, and is not under the authority of, the Grand Lodge. To this rule there is positively no exception. It is therefore a breach not only of etiquette but of the constitutions, to enter the Lodge wearing the Jewel of the Mark, or some other by-degree, such as that of the Knights-Templar.

It is true that H.R.H. the Grand Master is a member of these Degrees, and has Past Rank in both; and such membership is constitutionally regular (see Act of Union); but although he is at the head of one of them, Grand Lodge does not recognize them, nor exercise jurisdiction over them in any way; therefore the Jewels of those Degrees are not allowed to be worn in a Craft Lodge.

The case of Royal Arch Jewels is entirely

different from these. The degree of the
Master Mason includes the Supreme Order of
the Holy Royal Arch (Art. 1, Book of Constitutions). H.R.H. the Duke of Connaught
is First Grand Principal of the Order, and
the Grand Secretary in the Craft is always
Grand Scribe E. in the Grand Chapter of
Royal Arch Masons, consequently all the
Jewels of the Royal Arch Order may be
worn in a Craft Lodge.

The Jewels issued to Stewards of the Institutions are by courtesy worn for twelve
months—*i.e.*, until the next festival.

The Jewels issued at the Centenary
Festivals of the Girls' and Boys' Institutions
have been declared Life Jewels, and may be
worn permanently.

The Jewels which may with perfect propriety be worn in a Craft Lodge (and in a
Royal Arch Chapter also) are those of the
Master or Past Master; Permanent Charity
Jewels and Clasps; Present Stewards of either
or all of the Institutions; Founders'; Centenary; Quatuor Coronati; and the Jewel com-
memorating the Jubilee of Her late Majesty,
the late Patroness of our Order; also the
Jewels of the Royal Arch Order, whether
of ordinary Royal Arch Masons, or of
Present or Past First Principals, or Present
or Past Grand, or Provincial, or District

Grand Principals, and some others which need not be specified, with this special reservation, that they must belong to either the Craft or the Royal Arch Order, and no other. Miniature Jewels, each being a facsimile in design of the full-size Jewels, are now very frequently worn by Brethren who have become entitled to wear a considerable number of these honourable badges of distinction.

Many of these Jewels have been presented to the wearers, and are the memorials of the gratitude of their several Lodges for eminent and often long-continued services, and which the recipients may well feel pleasure and pride in wearing. They are something more than mere personal adornments; they subserve an excellent purpose by inciting younger Brethren to increased zeal and energy in the work of the Lodge. 'The hope of reward sweetens labour'; and when work is sweetened by hope and lightened by zeal, it becomes a labour of love; and 'profit' to the Lodge and 'pleasure' to the worker 'will be the result.'

Application by a Lodge for permission for its members to wear a Centenary Jewel must be by petition to the Grand Master, in which petition the necessary particulars as to the origin of the Lodge are to be given, as well as proof of its uninterrupted existence for one hundred years.

When permission has been granted to a Lodge for its members to wear a Centenary Jewel, the privilege of wearing the Jewel is restricted to actual *bona fide* subscribing members, being Master Masons; and for so long only as they pay the stipulated subscription to the Lodge and are returned to the Grand Lodge.

The design for a conventional Centenary Jewel has now been approved by the Grand Master, but about forty ancient Lodges have their own designs, which are, of course, very interesting by reason of their antiquity.

A Brother having served the office of Steward to any two of the Institutions has the privilege of wearing the Charity Jewel, provided he, at each time of so serving, personally subscribed ten guineas at the least.

A Brother entitled to wear the Charity Jewel, and who may have served the office of Steward to any of the Institutions a second time, may wear a clasp attached to the ribbon, and an additional clasp for each occasion of having served the office of Steward if he personally subscribed a like amount.

A Vice-President may wear a rosette attached to the ribbon immediately above the Jewel.

Dress, Jewels, and Punctuality

A vice-Patron may wear the Jewel suspended from a ribbon around his neck.

With regard to the wearing of Grand or London Rank or Provincial Grand clothing, much difference of opinion and of practice exists. Many—probably the majority of—Brethren have undress aprons and collars, which they always wear at the ordinary meetings of their own Lodge. Some even of these wear full dress if visiting a Lodge other than their own, even if it be a regular meeting of the Lodge which they are visiting. Upon Festivals or other occasions out of the ordinary way they would, as a matter of course, wear full-dress clothing, with all proper insignia appertaining thereto, either in their own or in any other Lodge. Instances are not wanting of Brethren considering it to be their duty to wear the full-dress clothing upon every occasion during the year of their tenure of Grand or Provincial Grand Office. No reason can be urged against their doing so. There is no hard-and-fast rule upon the subject. Customs vary in different districts, and individual taste seems to be the chief guide in this matter.

At all the regular meetings of Grand Lodge, and of Provincial, and of District Grand Lodges, full-dress clothing is invariably worn. On all occasions when full-dress

clothing is worn, the traditional white tie
and gloves should be worn—a comparatively recent fashion of wearing black ties
for full dress, to the contrary, notwithstanding. The black tie is not 'in accordance
with the ancient usage and established custom of the Order' in this respect.

At meetings of Provincial or of District
Lodges, upon special occasions other than
the regular meetings, Provincial or District
Grand Masters often allow undress clothing
to be worn.

In Short, we should show—in so far as
outward observance can show—our estima-
tion of and our respect for Freemasonry by
always being fitly attired in the Lodge. The
advice of Polonius to his son Laertes is of
very wide application; it suits the case in
question:

> 'Costly thy habit as thy purse can buy,
> But not expressed in fancy; rich, not gaudy;
> For the apparel oft proclaims the man.'

As regards Masonic Mourning dress, see
p. 268.

*   *   *   *

Very little needs to be said upon the subject of punctuality in attendance on the part
of both Officers and Brethren, but it can

hardly be passed over without notice In these days of railway locomotion and of high pressure generally in business matters, sharp time is as a rule obliged to be observed by all sorts and conditions of men in the affairs of the outer world. The same rule should, by every possible means, be applied to the meetings of the Lodge. The Master should open the Lodge upon every occasion punctually at the hour stated in the summons. He should be supported in this by his Officers. He and they should always be clothed and in their seats *before the time*, and as the hour strikes the Master's gavel should sound. Certainly the general attendance would be far more punctual and not less numerous.

The time stated upon the summons should be understood to mean that time, and not half an hour or an hour later. In the address to the Wardens after their investiture and their induction into their respective chairs the following sentence occurs: 'You ought to be examples of good order and *regularity*.' Regularity in this sense cannot be separated from punctuality, and the precept applies with equal force to all the Officers of the Lodge. Their acceptance of their several Offices should be taken virtually as a pledge that, with the honour, they also acknowledge their responsibility for a faithful and *punctual* performance of their several duties to the best of their skill and ability.

Unpunctuality, to which is due the frequent paucity in numbers when the Lodge is opened, and even during a Ceremony which may be performed at the earlier portion of the meeting, is not only a bad compliment and a great discouragement to the Worshipful Master: it also produces a bad impression in the mind of new members, and especially those upon whom the Ceremony is being performed.

Further, the interruptions and reports caused by the arrival of late-comers are a great hindrance to the smooth progress of the ceremonies, and a source of delay, and 'late dinner.'

One used to hear *years ago* of members who were seldom in the Lodge 'when the Brethren were at labour,' and seldom absent 'when they were at refreshment,' thereby gaining for themselves the title of 'knife-and-fork Freemasons.' This, however, belongs to an age now happily passed away, and with it the reputation for an inordinate love of feasting, which to some extent our Order once had, as many now living can well remember.

CHAPTER XIX

THE CEREMONIES

In considering the Etiquette of the Ceremonies in detail, it may be necessary to touch upon questions which would appear to belong rather to Ritual than to Etiquette. The truth is, it is extremely difficult to define the limits and boundaries of each; they so intermix and overlap here and there that it is next to impossible to say where the domain of the one ends and that of the other begins. On the one hand, one is bound to point out errors and defects in practice and procedure; and on the other, to point out the correct way; thus words, and forms of words, must be included, as well as gesture, position, and demeanour.

It is true Etiquette to do the right thing in the right way, at the right time, and in the right place, as it is equally Etiquette to say the right thing in the right way, at the right time and place.

This doctrine, as applied to our Ritual and Ceremonies, forbids us even to wish to add or to alter words or actions, to render the meaning, in our opinion, 'more clear,' or the diction 'more harmonious,' 'more dignified,' or 'more worthy' of 'our ancient and honourable Fraternity.'

The temptation to introduce our own individuality is the source of all deviation, and is the origin of all the trouble which has arisen with regard to the Ritual; and accounts for the very regrettable lack of uniformity which unfortunately prevails.

Once admit the right of one person to make one alteration, and how can the right of any person to make any alteration be denied?

The true principle is to conform completely and unflinchingly to the actual ceremonies of the Ritual as settled by the Lodge of Reconciliation, and approved by Grand Lodge in 1816.

This principle has been steadily kept in view in the preceding chapters; it will be the guiding principle in those which are to follow.

*　　*　　*　　*

The 'superstructure' of eventual excellence in working, 'perfect in its parts, and honourable to the builder,' can only be raised upon a sound foundation of knowledge; both theoretical and practical; and details, apparently small and trivial, but nevertheless subserving some useful end, should not be overlooked. These details, small or great, are more readily committed to memory, and are better carried out in practice, if one *knows the reason why*, as regards time, place, and manner of performance. *Experto crede.*

*　　*　　*　　*

Opinions differ as to the number of Candidates upon whom either of the Ceremonies should be performed at one time—that is, supposing there be more than one Candidate, shall they be taken together, or one at a time?

There is no law upon the subject, for or against. Rule 192 in the Book of Constitutions states that 'not more than two persons shall be initiated on the same day'—nothing more. It is therefore perfectly in accordance with the Constitutions to Initiate, Pass, or Raise more than one Candidate at one time.

Two are easily managed, but it is not desirable to go beyond two. In the case of three, four, or five Candidates presenting themselves, it is better to take them two and one, or two and two, up to and including the Obligation, and (in the Initiation) the restoration; and when the other detachment has reached the same stage, to take all together to the end.

Of course, cases frequently do occur in which two or even three Candidates taken at one time are initiated, passed, and raised, as efficiently and with as much impressiveness as could have been the case if they had been taken seriatim; but this method is not to be commended except under pressing circumstances, and is then only permissible when all the Officers concerned are adepts in their several duties.

The advocates of the custom of performing each Ceremony separately, upon each Candidate—e.g., up to and including the Obligation, and (in the Initiation) the restoration to L., and the explanation of the emblematical Ls.—maintain that the Ceremony is more impressive with one only, than with two together; and that with more than one some confusion is certain to occur. There is solid foundation for these objections. So much depends upon the manner in which the Worshipful Master, the Wardens, and more especially the Deacons, are able to perform their several duties; the impressiveness depends in a great measure upon the Master; the orderliness and the avoidance of confusion and muddle depend upon the other officers.

The 'Golden Rule' will apply here as elsewhere. The governing factor should be due consideration for the rights and interests of the Candidate. He is about to pass through one of the most solemn ordeals of his life— one which will leave its impress upon him for the remainder of his career. It can only happen to him once. Is it worth while to risk the possibility of marring a beautiful spiritual exercise for some mundane consideration such as lack of time or spoiling dinner?

It is a crime to ruin a Candidate's first impressions.

*　　　*　　　*　　　*

A preliminary word of caution may be given here. No Officer should 'help' another. Much confusion is created by interference, however well meant.

The Officers should know their work and each should do his own. If a mistake should occur, give the W. Master time to put it right quietly. Confusion is made worse confounded if everyone tries his hand at correction. Of course, no Visitor, however competent or however highly placed, would dream of saying or doing anything to direct the course of the ceremony. Attendance at the Lodge of Instruction will minimize all risk of error.

*　　　*　　　*　　　*

(A.) INITIATION

The preparation of the Candidate for the Ceremony of Initiation is discussed in a later chapter (Chapter XXIII), to which the reader is referred (p. 302), for a full explanation of the origin and the intention of every detail of that preparation. The theory and practice of the various and appropriate Ks. are fully detailed and explained on pp. 305-307.

We will suppose the Candidate to have been properly prepared, the Ks. to have been given, the Report made to the Worshipful Master, and the Candidate ordered to be admitted. The Organist should immediately commence to play impressive and suitable music —*e.g.*, 'Lead, kindly Light'—and should continue until the Candidate reaches the K. S. On his way to the door, the Senior Deacon places K. S.; after which the Inner Guard opens the door, and both the Deacons receive the Candidate at the door; but the Junior Deacon has him in his especial charge, and leads him to K. S. Here an important question is asked, as to the Candidate's eligibility. The Junior Deacon should be from the commencement always on the alert to suggest the proper answers to this and other questions asked by the

Worshipful Master from time to time. The two Deacons cross their wands over the Candidate during the Prayer, during which all stand with Sn. of R. At the words 'S. M. I. B.,' whether said by the Immediate Past Master alone or sung by all the Brethren together, the Sn. of R. is 'dropped,' not 'drawn.' When the Prayer is concluded, amid solemn silence that most important question is asked which, with its affirmative answer, constitutes 'the first and most important of the Antient Landmarks of the Order.' The Candidate's answer should come, unprompted, freely and voluntarily from his own heart; but in case of need the Junior Deacon will assist the Candidate. The response having been given and the Worshipful Master having expressed his satisfaction therewith, the attention of the Brethren is called to the fact that the Candidate is about to pass in view before them. When the Worshipful Master has finished speaking, the Senior Deacon replaces K. S., takes the P. to the Worshipful Master, and resumes his seat, unless there is more than one Candidate; in that case the Senior Deacon, as a matter of course, takes charge of one of them; but the Junior Deacon leads throughout the Ceremony.

The Junior Deacon takes the Candidate's

right hand in his own left and they walk side by side ('squaring' the L.) up the N., across the E., down the S.; the Candidate is halted on the Junior Warden's right and interrogated. He is then conducted to the Senior Warden's right; the questions are asked and answered as before and the Candidate again receives permission to 'Enter free,' etc. He is then presented to the Worshipful Master by the Senior Warden, 'a Candidate properly prepared to be made a Mason.'

During the questions which follow the presentation, the Junior Deacon should be ready to suggest the proper reply to each. It is better to prompt the replies than to leave them to the Candidate, whose form of words in reply may perhaps be not well chosen.

'The method of adv. to the P. in due form' is unfortunately often not well understood by the Junior Deacon himself. In the first place the Candidate should be taken 'diagonally' to the suitable spot. The t. ir. Ss. must not be wrongly dictated. They consist of right lines and angles, and morally teach upright lives and well *squared* actions. The position of the feet should therefore be carefully watched. (The Junior Deacon must remember that it is useless to attempt to use his Wand to point out the method of adv.) This position must be carefully distinguished in the minds of the Junior Deacon and Candidate from a later position, as to which the Candidate is informed, 'That is the first R. S. in Freemasonry,' and in which the feet are placed quite differently, as directed by the W. M. The t. ir. Ss. in advancing from West to East, are, and should always be, separate and distinct from the first 'R. S.' The confusion of these Ss., the one form with the other, is inexcusably frequent; it cannot be too strongly reprobated.

The Senior Deacon arrives at Ped. at the same moment as the Candidate.

The instruction given to the Candidate by the Worshipful Master as to his posture during the Ob. contains these words, '. . . your . . . formed in a S.' If he has been properly adv. to the P. by the Junior Deacon, his . . . will be already in that position.

There will therefore be no need for any pulling or pushing, in order to get the position indicated. The Junior Deacon should see that the Candidate's . . . is *well forward*, do the best he can as to the angle, study the balance of the body in an easy position, and accept that position as a sufficient fulfilment of the requirement of the case. Great discomfort—at times amounting to physical pain—must frequently be the result of the Deacon's ill-directed energy.

Deacons cross Wds. during Ob., and all stand with P. S. of E. A.

When the words 'hereby and hereon' are spoken, the Worshipful Master should place his left hand lightly—for a moment—upon the hand of the Candidate, and then upon the V. S. L. The word 'hele' used in the Ob. is an Old English word which signifies 'to hide, or to cover or conceal'. It is derived from the ancient Saxon word 'hælan,' from which we derive, *inter alia* the word 'hell.' The word 'hele' is still used colloquially in Celtic districts (*e.g.*, Cornwall) and is there pronounced 'heel.' In Masonry it is pronounced 'hail.'

On conclusion of Ob. the P. S. is dis. and the Worshipful Master removes Cs.

Where musical services are in use, the sealing of the Ob. on V. S. L. should be marked by an appropriate instrumental *Kyrie eleison*; this must on no account be sung.

The Rn. to L. requires very great care on the part of the Junior Deacon; he has to be ready to suggest the proper word in reply to the Master's question, and at the same time to have all prepared for the denouement *at the proper moment*. It is well also for all the Brethren to look to the

East, so that the salute may be given by all *as by one man*. A volley, and not a dropping fire, should welcome the Candidate on his Rn. to L. The proper motions are P. L. R. ━┫. The Worshipful Master alone uses the gavel, not the Wardens. The Brethren use their hands, not their Badges. The effect of the whole may be, and often is, marred by want of proper attention to the details here mentioned.

The Junior Deacon restrains the Candidate from movement, and the Worshipful Master then points out to the attention of the Candidate the three great though emblematical Ls., and welcomes the Candidate as a newly obligated Brother among Masons.

After directing the attention of the Candidate to the three L. . . .r Ls. and to other matters, the Worshipful Master communicates the Ss. without leaving his place. He should be careful at the proper moment to take the Sp. and place the f. in the form of the first R. S.

When the Candidate is conducted, still normally 'squaring,' to the Junior Warden, and presented, the examination* should

* The Junior Deacon, after himself saluting the Wardens, does not again give signs or salutes with the Candidate; he merely directs the Candidate to give them.

proceed as far as the W. only, and should not include the derivation and the interpretation, etc. These, however, should always be given to the Senior Warden in full. It should be clearly understood that the import of the W. is *not* S. but *in* S.

The examinations concluded, the Senior Warden presents the Candidate and receives the Worshipful Master's command to invest the new-made Brother with the ancient and honourable distinguishing badge of a Mason —a Lambskin, entirely white: the badge of Innocence and bond of Friendship; a Symbol of a new and spiritual Service; an indication that he is now a Worker and Builder in the service of God and Man; a badge which, if he never disgraces it, will never disgrace him. At this point the Brethren strike their Badges, not their hands.

In adjusting the E. A. badge, the S. W. should see that the 'flap' is up.

After a few observations by the Worshipful Master the Candidate is placed in the N. E. to receive that touching if embarrassing Charge by the Worshipful Master which has thrilled the hearts of thousands on thousands, and to which may be traced the impulse of that Universal Masonic Charity which knows no bounds save those of prudence.

The presentation of the Working Tools,

and the exhibition of the Warrant, follow in due sequence.

Mention is made in Chapter XVI, p. 146, of the custom of actually presenting a copy of the Book of Constitutions, and one of the By-laws, to every Entered Apprentice. Good reasons are there given for this practice, and to these the reader will do well to refer.

The newly initiated Brother is told that on his return a Charge will be delivered. He is then conducted along the N. side (no 'squaring') to the L. of the S. W., where the Deacon instructs* his charge to 'Salute the Worshipful Master as a Mason'; and he should, if necessary, correct any informality or slovenliness in the performance of the salute. The hand should be raised at once to the appointed position; and the sign should be completed without bowing or bending of the body before or after. This position, and the manner of assuming it, should be uniformly practised by every member when entering or leaving the Lodge, or when commanded to stand to order. A Perfunctory or solvenly manner of giving the salute or of standing to order is a breach of Masonic etiquette.

The Junior Deacon accompanies the Candidate to the door and resumes his seat.

* See footnote on p. 205.

After a brief interval the Candidate returns. The Junior Deacon receives him, conducts him to the left of the Senior Warden and directs* him to 'Salute the Worshipful Master as a Mason.' The Charge is given to the Candidate at this stage and while he is in this position.

It is by no means a rare occurrence to hear the Senior or the Junior Warden or some Past Master deliver the Charge in this Degree. This is a relief to the Master, and an advantage to the Wardens, as being good practice in anticipation of their higher duties in the future. (See p. 328.)

The Junior Deacon remains in attendance on the Candidate while the charge is given, and at the conclusion of it he conducts the Candidate to a seat and resumes his own.

* * * *

Brethren generally evince a warmer interest in, and will make more strenuous efforts to be present at, the ceremony of Initiation than at either of the other two. It is naturally to be expected that this would be the case, because it is the formal reception of a new member into our Order, and most of us feel an excusable curiosity to see what manner of man the Candidate is, and how he

* See footnote on p. 205.

will conduct himself under the entirely new circumstances in which he will find himself placed.

Most of us have heard newly-initiated Brethren express themselves to the effect that they understood and appreciated the Ceremony of Initiation in far greater measure after having witnessed and heard it performed with some other Candidate than they did at their own Initiation. Naturally this would be the case; the whole surrounding circumstances, the action, the moral teaching, even the phraseology of the Ceremony, being so far removed from anything within the range of their experience in the outer world, so different from any 'opinion preconceived' of that which actually takes place in the Lodge.

A very curious psychological study would be produced by a transcript of the various impressions made upon the minds of the majority of the newly-elected Members of our Order by the First Ceremony. It may be assumed generally that those impressions —favourable or the reverse—would be just in accordance with the degree of carefulness, accuracy, and impressiveness (or with the absence of those qualities) with which the Ceremony had in each case been performed. Instances of very varied results, consequent upon the Ceremony having been well or ill conducted, are within the experience of perhaps every member of mature years among us.

'A tree is known by its fruits,' and increasingly numerous as our Fraternity is, we may conclude that, as a general rule, the seed sown in our Lodges is good seed, well planted, well nourished, or it would not—as it has done, and is doing—'take root downward, and bear fruit upward, a hundred-fold,' as the number of new Lodges year by year added to the registry of the Grand Lodge abundantly testifies. Nevertheless in very many Lodges complaint is made of the falling away of good men and Brethren from our midst, and of the coldness and apathy of many who retain their membership, but whose visits to the Lodge are few and far between. This is perhaps inevitable. It is not given to everyone to appreciate at its proper value our excellent Institution, or to derive 'profit and pleasure' from its moral teaching.

(AB.) Entrusting the Entered Apprentice

The Junior Deacon with his left hand takes the right hand of the Candidate, and leads him towards the left of the Senior Warden.

The Ceremonies (Entrusting)

The Junior Deacon 'backs,' bringing the Candidate to the proper position, facing the Worshipful Master. There is no 'advance' or 'salute' at this moment. The Worshipful Master examines the Candidate by asking the prescribed questions. If the Candidate should falter it is the duty of the Junior Deacon to correct and prompt him.

At the conclusion of the prescribed questions the Worshipful Master announces that he will put others if any Brother wishes him to do so.

What would happen if any Brother did so 'wish' we will not inquire. At this point some Brethren make a point of ejaculating, 'Very well answered, Worshipful Master!' This is not orthodox, and should be discouraged in all cases; even in those cases where the commendation is earned.

The Junior Deacon (instructing the Candidate, *sotto voce*, about L. F.) then conducts the Candidate, direct (there is no 'squaring' on this occasion), to the N. side of the Worshipful Master's Pedestal, where, after preliminary assurances are given, the P. G. and P. W. are communicated to him.

The Candidate is then taken straight back the way he came (there is no 'squaring' on this occasion) towards the left of the Senior Warden, the Junior Deacon 'backing' as before; and the Candidate is directed* to 'Salute the Worshipful Master as a Mason.' The Junior Deacon conducts him to the door and resumes his seat.

(B.) PASSING

It is stated in Chapter XXIII (p. 296, *q.v.*) that when a Candidate for the Second Degree is conducted by the T. to the outside of the door of the Lodge, the Ks. of the First Degree should be given; and the reasons are there fully explained why those Ks., and no others, should be given.

We will, as in the previous Degree, suppose the Candidate to have been properly prepared, the Ks. of E. A. to have been given, the Report made to the Worshipful Master, and the Candidate ordered to be admitted.

The Organist commences his introductory music (which he continues until the Candidate reaches the K. S.). On his way to the door the Junior Deacon places the K. S.; after which the Inner Guard opens the door and both the Deacons receive the Candidate at the door; but this time the Senior Deacon has him in his especial charge, and leads him to the K. S., where he directs the Candidate to 'Advance as a Mason.' Senior Deacons

* See footnote on p. 205.

should note the employment of this phrase when the Candidate is 'advancing' from one Degree to another. The two Deacons cross their wands over the Candidate during the Prayer, during which all stand with the Sn. of R. At the words 'S. M. I. B.,' whether said by the Immediate Past Master alone or sung by all the Brethren together, the Sn. of R. is 'dropped,' not 'drawn.' When the Prayer is concluded the Junior Deacon replaces the K. S. and resumes his seat; unless there is more than one Candidate; in that case the Junior Deacon, as a matter of course, takes charge of one of them; but the Senior Deacon leads throughout the Ceremony.

As soon as the way is clear, and without any preliminary remarks from the Worshipful Master, the Senior Deacon takes the Candidate's right hand in his own left, and they walk side by side, 'squaring' the L.

During the first perambulation the Candidate has to prove to the Brethren that he has been duly initiated; and for this purpose he is halted at the W. M.'s Pedestal, and directed* by the Senior Deacon to 'Salute the Worshipful Master as a Mason.' This the Candidate should do without turning his head or body towards the W. M. He is then halted at the R. of the Junior Warden and

* See footnote on p. 205.

directed to 'Advance to the Junior Warden as such'; he is subjected to an examination, in which he is called upon to show the Sn. and communicate the T. and W. This having been accomplished, the Senior Deacon directs the Candidate to 'Salute* the Senior Warden as a Mason'; he then passes the Senior Warden's pedestal; and having thus made one circuit, the Senior Deacon pauses; and the Brethren are bidden to observe that 'Bro. —— is about to pass in view before them, to show that he is the Candidate properly prepared,' etc. In the second round he has to 'Salute the Worshipful Master as a Mason,' 'Salute the Junior Warden as a Mason,' 'Advance to the Senior Warden as such, showing the Sn., and communicating the P. G. and P. W.,' leading from the First to the Second Degree.

When the two rounds have been completed nothing more in the way of examination has to be done, and the Candidate is presented to the Worshipful Master by the Senior Warden as a Candidate properly prepared to be passed to the Second Degree.

* The Senior Deacon should in all cases bring the Candidate to a complete standstill before issuing directions; and the Candidate should salute without turning the head or body. The Senior Deacon does not illustrate the Candidate's salutes or signs. He merely superintends them.

The Ceremonies (Passing)

The Candidate should be then placed on the North side of the Lodge, about six feet to the West of the Master's pedestal, and facing full South, and the method of advancing to the East in due form should then be verbally explained and physically described by the Senior Deacon; the Candidate's imitation in 'due form' will bring him to the proper place; at which the Junior Deacon should arrive at the same moment on L. of the Candidate.

Some of the remarks made upon the posture during the Ob. in the First Degree apply with equal force to the one in the Second, and the reader would do well to refer to pp. 202 and 203. If the Candidate has been properly instructed, the . . . will already be formed in a S. without any necessity for further movement. A mistake is often made in placing the L. A. in the proper position; the . . . should rest in the angle of the S. with the . . . elevated, with the t.i.t.f.o.a.S., and pointing over the L. S.

The Deacons cross Wds. during Ob., and all stand with the P. S. of F. C.

When the words 'hereby and hereon' are spoken, the Worshipful Master should place his left hand lightly—for a moment—upon the hand of the Candidate, and then upon the V. S. L.

At the conclusion of the Ob. the P. S. is 'drawn,' and the Junior Deacon removes the S. On sealing the Ob. on V. S. L., the Organist plays the *Kyrie eleison*; after which the Worshipful Master says, 'Rise, newly-obligated Fellow-Craft Freemason.'

The Junior Deacon then resumes his seat. The Senior Deacon places the Candidate at R. of the Worshipful Master for communication of the S. T. and W.

The Worshipful Master should be careful, when he rises, to take the Sp., placing the f. in the form of the Second R. S.

In imparting the Ss., the Worshipful Master should see that the Candidate makes each portion of the three forms accurately, fairly, and squarely; especially in the H. S., in which, not only is the L. A. placed at 'an angle of ninety Degrees,' but the . . . is also, and is clearly pointed over the L. S.; and not, as a visitor to various Lodges in some Northern Provinces too often sees, stretched out across, with the . . . of the hand visible. An opinion upon this point has been obtained from high authority, and the custom here condemned has been pronounced to be entirely wrong.

As to the historical basis of the H. S., a great difference of opinion exists as to the locality in which these words were uttered, as well as in the rendering of the words themselves.

An unprejudiced examination of the facts, which undoubtedly connect the miracle with Joshua, and both with a certain locality (see Josh. x 11-13), must lead to the conclusion that our H. S. is derived from the events recorded in those verses.

The words and signs used in the various portions of the Ritual are 'according to our traditions,' and therefore, not professing that they are the very words of the Bible, the use of them is not open to serious objection.

After the Worshipful Master has finished, the Candidate is conducted to the Junior Warden, and presented by the Senior Deacon for examination. The Senior Deacon, in presenting the Candidate, of course salutes the Junior Warden, but when the Candidate's turn to salute arrives, the Senior Deacon does not duplicate the Sns.; he merely instructs the Candidate what to do. The Junior Warden's examination should proceed, as in the first Degree, as far as the W. only; and should not include the derivation and the interpretation, etc. These, however, should always be given to the S. W. in full.

The examinations concluded, the Senior Warden receives the Worshipful Master's command to invest the Brother with the distinguishing badge of a Fellow-Craft Freemason—a badge which bears two rosettes, and now has the flap down. After a few observations by the Worshipful Master, the Candidate is placed in the S. E. to mark the progress he has made in the Science.

*　　*　　*　　*

The 'Presentation of the Working Tools of the Second Degree' gives occasion to point out one of the greatest anomalies in the Ceremonies of the three Degrees. In the Ritual the explanation of the Square, Level, and Plumb-rule is given with extreme brevity in the Ceremony of Passing to the Second Degree, whereas in the explanation of the Tracing Board of the First Degree they—the Working Tools of the Second Degree—are explained at unusual length.

Very little consideration is needed to show how inconsistent this is. The explanation of the First Tracing Board must of necessity be given when the Lodge is opened in the First, or Entered Apprentice, Degree, and in it the Ritual gives the long Explanation of the Working Tools of the Second, or Fellow-Craft's, Degree; and then in the

Ceremony of Passing, during which alone the Working Tools of the Second Degree can lawfully be explained, they are slurred over with a brevity not to be found in the Explanation of the Working Tools of the First or of the Third Degree.

This *bouleversement* ought to have been reversed; the lengthy explanation of the uses of these Tools in Operative Masonry, and of their moral signification, should have been expunged from the First Tracing Board, and should have been included in the Ceremony of Passing, to which they legitimately belong.

The implements in question, being the 'Movable Jewels' of the Lodge, and being severally the distinctive badges of the Master and the two Wardens, must of necessity be mentioned in the Tracing Board of the First Degree; but not necessarily described and moralized upon. They should be mentioned only in the quality of Movable Jewels, and as designating the three Principal Officers of the Lodge; it is unconstitutional to explain them in the First Degree.

The description of their uses and the excellent moral lessons which they teach (the latter being far too good to be lost) should have been transferred bodily from the Tracing Board to their proper place in the Second Ceremony. Without this longer ex-

position of the Working Tools, the Ceremony
of Passing is poor and meagre as compared
with the Initiation and the Raising; whereas
with the full explanation it will compare not
unfavourably with the First and the Third
Ceremonies.

*   *   *   *

After the presentation of the Working
Tools, the Candidate receives permission to
retire.

Accordingly the Senior Deacon takes him
(no squaring) to the L. of the Senior Warden,
and instructs* him to 'Salute the Worshipful
Master as a Fellow-Craft, first as an Entered
Apprentice.'

The Senior Deacon then accompanies the
Candidate to the door, and resumes his seat.

On the return of the Candidate after a
short interval, the Senior Deacon (only)
meets him, conducts him to the L. of the
Senior Warden, and instructs* him to 'Salute
the Worshipful Master as a Fellow-Craft,
first as an Entered Apprentice.'

The Worshipful Master then proceeds to
the head of the Tracing Board.

The Senior Deacon leads the Candidate to
the foot of the Tracing Board. The Junior
Deacon arrives (L.) at the same moment,

* See footnote on p. 214.

and hands his wand to the Worshipful Master, who gives the Explanation of the Second Tracing Board.

Towards the conclusion of the Explanation, and when the W. M. pronounces the letter 'G,' the I. P. M., S. W., and J. W. successively give ━┫; and *after* the W. M. has said 'denoting God' (not before), the Sn. of R. is placed, and in due course dis.

At the conclusion the Senior Deacon conducts the Candidate to a seat, and then resumes his own.

Sometimes the Worshipful Master delegates the duty of giving this Lecture to some other Brother, thus lightening his own labours and at the same time varying what is apt to become the monotony of the proceedings.

(BC.) ENTRUSTING THE FELLOW-CRAFT

The Senior Deacon, in this ceremony, does exactly as the Junior Deacon does in the ceremony (AB.) Entrusting the E. A. (*q.v.*); except that at the conclusion, on arriving at the left of the Senior Warden, the Candidate is directed to 'Salute the Worshipful Master as a F. C., first as an E. A.' The Deacons ext. Ls. and lay S.

(C.) Raising

When a Candidate for the Third Degree is conducted by the T. to the outside of the door of the Lodge, the Ks. of the Second Degree are given. The reason for this is given on p. 305.

We will, as in the previous Degrees, suppose the Candidate to have been properly prepared, the Ks. of F. C. to have been given the Report made to the Worshipful Master, and the Candidate ordered to be admitted.

The Organist commences solemn and specially selected music, and continues it until the Candidate reaches the K. S.

On his way to the door the Junior Deacon places the K. S.; after which the Inner Guard opens the door; and both the Deacons receive the Candidate at the door, but, as in the Second Degree, the Senior Deacon has him in his especial charge, and leads him to the K. S., where he directs* the Candidate to 'Advance as a Fellow-Craft, first as an Entered Apprentice.' (Senior Deacons should note the employment of this phrase when the Candidate is 'advancing' from one Degree to another.) The two Deacons cross their wands over the Candidate during the Prayer, during which all

* See footnote on p. 214.

222

stand with the Sn. of R. At the words
'S. M. I. B.,' whether said by the Immediate
Past Master alone, or sung by all the
Brethren together, the Sn. of R. is 'dropped,'
not 'drawn.' When the Prayer is concluded
the Junior Deacon removes and subsequently replaces the K. S. and follows the
Senior Deacon closely all the time. In the
case of more than one candidate the Junior
Deacon, as a matter of course, takes charge
of one of them; but the Senior Deacon
leads throughout the Ceremony.

As soon as the way is clear, and without
any preliminary remarks from the Worshipful Master, the Senior Deacon takes the
Candidate's right hand in his own left, and
they walk side by side, squaring the L.,
closely followed by the Junior Deacon. They
have to make three perambulations.

During the first circuit, the Candidate is
directed by the Senior Deacon to 'Salute
the Worshipful Master as a Mason,' and to
'Advance to the Junior Warden as such,
showing the Sn. and communicating the T.
and W.' Thus he has to prove to the
Brethren, through an examination conducted by the Junior Warden, that he has
been regularly initiated into Freemasonry.

During the second round the Candidate
is directed to 'Salute the Worshipful

Master as a Fellow-Craft'; to 'Salute the Junior Warden as a Fellow-Craft'; to 'Advance to the Senior Warden as such, showing the Sn., and communicating the T. and W. of that Degree.' Thus he has to prove to the Senior Warden that he has been duly passed to the Second, or Fellow-Craft's, Degree.

The Deacons and the Candidate then halt on the North side of the Senior Warden's pedestal, and the Brethren are requested to observe that the Candidate 'is about to pass in view before them, to show that he is the Candidate properly prepared,' etc.

During the third round the Candidate is directed* to 'Salute the Worshipful Master as a Fellow-Craft'; to 'Salute the Junior Warden as a Fellow-Craft'; to 'Advance to the Senior Warden as such, showing the Sn., and communicating the P. G. and P. W. he received from the Worshipful Master previously to leaving the Lodge.' Thus he has to prove to the Senior Warden that he is in possession of the P. G. and P. W. leading from the Second to the Third Degree.

Now, inasmuch as it is the invariable rule in each Degree that the Candidate shall undergo *one* examination—no more, and no

* See footnote on p. 214.

less—during *each* of these preliminary perambulations, it is clear that the correct rule
is that there shall be one perambulation for
the First Degree, and no more; two for the
Second Degree, no more and no less; and
three for the Third Degree, no more and no
less.

The Senior Warden then presents the
Candidate to the Worshipful Master, 'a
Candidate properly prepared to be raised to
the Third Degree'; and then, by command
of the Worshipful Master, directs both the
Deacons to instruct the Candidate to 'Advance to the E. by the proper Sps.'

The Senior Deacon (Junior Deacon still
following) takes the Candidate to the N.,
where the Junior Deacon takes temporary
charge of the Candidate.

The Senior Deacon by example instructs
the Candidate; the Sps. should be well
squared with the body erect; concluding
with four distinct Sps. and the completion
of the last one. The Junior Deacon arrives
at the same time on the L. of the Candidate.

The Deacons cross Wds. during the Ob.,
and all stand to order with the P. S. of
M. M. When the words 'hereby and hereon' are spoken, the Worshipful Master
should place his left hand lightly—for a
moment—upon the hand of the Candidate,

and then on the V. S. L. At the conclusion of the Ob. the P. S. is 'drawn' and 'recovered.'

On sealing the Ob. on the V. S. L., the Organ plays the *Kyrie eleison*; after which the Worshipful Master says, 'Rise, newly-obligated Master Mason,' and the Deacons and the Candidate step back a little.

When the Worshipful Master breaks off in the narrative, and says, 'Brother Wardens,' the Wardens should leave their places, bringing the L. and the P. R., and silently take the places of the Deacons; who open out to R. and L., and then resume their seats. The S. W. stands on the left of the Can., the J. W. on his right; and the J. W. directs him to 'c. h. f.'

The Wardens should be especially careful not to perform their respective functions too soon; a good deal has to be said before the proper moment for action arrives, and the appropriate action should come after the corresponding word is spoken, not before. Each Warden should wait for the cue—*e.g.*, 'temple, 'sink,' &c.; and the instant the Worshipful Master utters the word, the Warden should perform his duty.

At the moment of the final action, the Senior Warden may in a whisper caution the Candidate to be perfectly passive. If, as sometimes happens, the Candidate be allowed to move, he cannot be placed where preparation has been made for him. The Junior Warden c. h. f.

At this point the Organist should play some suitably solemn movement or hymn, such as 'Days and moments, quickly flying,' but on no account must any singing take place.

After the ineffectual efforts of the Wardens, the Worshipful Master descends from his Pedestal, and with their assistance . . . . him on the f. ps. o. f.

The Wardens then resume their seats, and the Worshipful Master, facing N., is left in charge of the Candidate, who faces S.

The Candidate should be placed well back on the North side of the Lodge, having the Emblems of M. and the representation of the . . . on his right; so that in the address which follows, the Worshipful Master may direct his attention to the one and the other without a change of position.

After the solemn address the Worshipful Master reverses the respective positions, and the Candidate then faces N.

In making this movement, the W. M. keeps himself between the Candidate and the Ped.

When the Worshipful Master communicates the Ss. of this Degree, the Candidate is instructed to advance to him as a Fellow-

Craft, first as an Entered Apprentice; and then to take another S. P.

After the Worshipful Master has communicated the Ss. he gives the Candidate permission to 'retire in order, etc.,' and the Worshipful Master resumes his seat.

The *newly-made Master Mason* is conducted by the Senior Deacon (no 'squaring') to the L. of the Senior Warden, and instructed* to salute the Worshipful Master in the three Degrees; (P. S. only of Third Degree on leaving), and he is then conducted by the Senior Deacon to the door of the Lodge.

The Senior Deacon puts his wand by his chair; and both Deacons take up the furniture, restore the Ls., and resume their seats.

*   *   *   *

When the newly-raised Brother is brought back to the Lodge, after a short interval, he is met at the door by the Senior Deacon only, who places him at the L. of the S. W., and directs* him to 'Salute the Worshipful Master in the three Degrees. (Full signs.)' The Senior Deacon then hands him to the Senior Warden, by whom he is invested with the distinguishing badge of a Master Mason.

* See footnote on p. 214.

The Ceremonies (Raising)

After a short address by the Worshipful Master concerning the badge, the Senior Deacon places the Candidate before the Worshipful Master, who gives the remaining portion of the Traditional History, which should always be narrated; the Working Tools with which H. Ab. was S. should be mentioned; and attention should be directed to the Emblems of M. After this, the remaining two of the Ss. are communicated, and the Working Tools presented. After which the Senior Deacon conducts the Master Mason to a seat and resumes his own.

*　*　*　*

The Ritual includes among the Emblems of M. the C. These were unknown in the East before and after the date assumed in the Ceremony. The use of the winding-sheet was universal.

As to 'the Ornaments of a Master Masons' Lodge,' there is no foundation in the Bible for the descriptions given of the 'Porch, Dormer, and Square Pavement'; they never had an existence except in the imagination of the old compilers of the Ritual. See Appendix, p. 415, wherein also the question of the 're-interment' is mentioned.

The proper title of H. Ab. would be 'our Grand Master,' he having been one of the three *Grand* Masters (the others being Solomon, King of Israel, and Hiram, King of Tyre) who presided over the Craft during the building of the Temple.

*   *   *   *

In Lodges here and there scattered about the country the latter portion of the Traditional History is seldom or never narrated; in fact, in very many Lodges the Degree is too often given with maimed rites. This should not be. The Candidate is entitled to know all that we in the Ceremonies have to teach, and if he be of an inquiring mind, and if the narrative, etc., be not completed, he will be led to consider that the Ceremony, which began with great solemnity, and with a most interesting historical narrative, had come to an abrupt and a very lame and impotent conclusion. An imperfect or ill-conducted performance of the Ceremonies is an injustice to the Candidate and to Freemasonry itself.

As it is true etiquette to do the right thing in the right way, at the right time, and in the right place, then the details of position and of action here given are not out of place in the Etiquette of Freemasonry which is intended to be carried through upon the lines laid down in the Introduction. These details, perfectly intelligible and easy of accomplishment though they are, still require considerable care; and it is not too much to expect of the Principal Officers of a Lodge that they should exercise the care necessary to prevent a hitch or a fiasco in the performance of the Ceremonies.

(D.) Installation of a Master

This ceremony was specially considered and agreed to by the Board of Installed Masters and sanctioned and approved by the Grand Master in 1827. (See pp. 117-118.)

It is one of the prized privileges of the Worshipful Master to instal his successor, and it is becoming quite the rule for the retiring Worshipful Master to exercise this function. To avoid any confusion, however, in the following description of the ceremony he will be styled Installing Master.

While the Lodge is still in the First Degree the Installing Master should appoint Past Masters to the Wardens' chairs.

There should be no declaration that 'all offices are vacant.' In the first place it is not in accordance with Recognized Ritual, and in the second place no one is empowered to make any such declaration. An officer retains his position until the new Worshipful Master appoints and invests a successor.

The Lodge is then opened in the Second Degree, and a Past Master (either the Immediate Past Master or the Director of Ceremonies) presents the Master Elect for the benefit of Installation. On receiving the Installing Master's reply the Past Master resumes his seat, leaving the Master Elect standing alone.

N.B.—No Warden can be installed as Master of a Lodge (except by Dispensation from the Grand Master) unless he has served the Office as an Invested Warden for a full year—that is to say, from one regular Installation Meeting until the next regular Installation Meeting.

No Installing Master may proceed unless satisfied of such service or Dispensation.

After addressing the Brethren generally and the Master Elect in particular, the Installing Master directs the attention of the Master Elect to the Secretary, who reads the Summary of the Ancient Charges, to all of which the Master Elect signifies his unqualified assent by the Sn. of F. taking the Sp. on the first occasion. The Sn. should be given with the same care as all other Sns. There should be no bowing by the Master Elect.

The Master Elect then turns again to the Installing Master, and gives his promise to support them, and then, on instructions, advances to take the Ob. as regards his duties as Master of the Lodge.

All the Brethren stand to order with the P. S. of F. C.

At the conclusion of the Ob. the P. S. of F. C. is dis. in unison.

The Lodge is then opened in the Third Degree, the Master Elect standing in his place. All under the rank of Installed Master are invited to retire. Officers should leave their collars on their chairs.

The Master Elect remains standing in his place.

*   *   *   *

☞ *(Here follows the Esotery of Installed Masters. Any Installed Master may have this on application and on establishing his right to possess it.)*

On their re-admission the Master Masons are ranged in the N. Preceded by the Installing Master, they pass round and salute the Worshipful Master as M. Ms. (See p. 336.)

The Installing Master in the E. then proclaims the Worshipful Master for the first time, and leads the M. Ms. in greeting the Worshipful Master.

The Installing Master then presents to the Worshipful Master the Working Tools of a M. M. These _must_ be presented _in extenso_; and the Lodge is then closed in the Third Degree. (See p. 337.)

It is, unfortunately, too common to see the Lodge 'resumed' on the plea of 'want of time.' If the Worshipful Master is capable of doing his work he will be well advised to take this opportunity of demonstrating his fitness to rule and direct his Lodge.

The F. Cs. are then admitted, and the same process repeated.

The Working Tools of the F. C. should be presented to the Worshipful Master _in extenso_; and the Lodge closed in the Second Degree.

The E. As. are then admitted, procession and greeting as before, the Working Tools of an E. A. presented, and the Brethren directed to resume their seats.

The Installing Master then delivers the Warrant, presents the Book of Constitutions and the By-laws of the Lodge, each with appropriate advice; and then calls on the Worshipful Master to appoint and invest his officers.

This is done in order of precedence, as set out on p. 91.

All the officers are 'appointed' except the Treasurer and Tyler, who are 'elected.'

If the officer to be invested is already an Installed Master he is conducted to the S. side of the Pedestal; if not, to the N. side.

The Installing Master should, with his left hand, hold the right hand of the officer he is conducting.

When the Installing Master accompanies the newly-invested officer to his place, he should under no circumstances forget to conduct the Past Master, so displaced, to a seat amongst the Past Masters.

On Installation Nights it is customary in some Lodges to salute each officer as he takes his place with a single clap in volley. This is not 'orthodox'; and although it is a kindly and unobjectionable custom, and quite 'Masonic', it were better avoided.

All officers within the Lodge having been invested, the Worshipful Master summons the Tyler or Outer Guard with the proper ⟶.

The Tyler, having saluted on entrance from the L. of the S. W., advances alone to

the Worshipful Master to be invested, and
this having been done, he retires and salutes
alone.

In the event, however, of the Tyler being,
as is often the case, a very old officer and not
quite so active as formerly, the Installing
Master will lose nothing of his dignity if he
fraternally conducts the Tyler also to the
Worshipful Master for investiture.

In either case, if the before-mentioned
unorthodox salute in 'volley' has been given
to the other officers, it should on no account
be omitted on the withdrawal of the Tyler,
who is a Brother; and 'he who is placed on
the lowest spoke of Fortune's wheel is equally
entitled to our regard.'

*   *   *   *

All the officers present having been invested, the Installing Master proceeds to
deliver the three Addresses: the first, to the
Worshipful Master, he delivers from the
left of the Senior Warden; the second, to
the Wardens, from the left of the Worshipful Master. The Wardens should remain
seated during this address. Some make a
point that the Wardens should stand; but
there is not even any logic in it, as they do
not suggest that all the Brethren should
stand during the third and last address,

which is delivered by the Installing Master from the left of the Worshipful Master.

*   *   *   *

At the conclusion of these addresses, it is customary for a Past Master to move that a vote of thanks be accorded to the Installing Master and recorded on the Minutes, expressing the appreciation of the assembled Brethren of the admirable manner in which the Installation Ceremony has been performed. Of course if the Installing Master is also the Immediate Past Master, this occasion is taken to pin on his breast, with appropriate words, the P. M. Jewel, which has been, no doubt, already voted to him.

(E.) CALLING OFF AND CALLING ON

These useful ceremonies will be found in the Ritual *in extenso*, and there is no occasion for any detailed comment thereon, except that there is no legal necessity for the Junior Warden to remain in his seat during the recess as one has sometimes seen.

(F.) CONSECRATION OF A LODGE
ORDER OF CEREMONY*

1. THE Brethren assemble in the Lodge Room.

2. The Consecrating Officer having entered
   in procession with the Grand Officers,
   takes the Chair and appoints his
   Officers.

3. The Lodge is opened in the Three
   Degrees.

4. *Opening Ode*

   Hail Eternal, by Whose aid
   All created things were made,
   Heaven and earth Thy vast design;
   Hear us, Architect Divine.

   May our work begun in Thee
   Ever blest with order be;
   And may we when labours cease
   Part in harmony and peace.

   By Thy glorious Majesty,
   By the trust we place in Thee,
   By the badge and mystic sign,
   Hear us, Architect Divine.

   So mote it be.

5. The Consecrating Officer addressing the
   Brethren on the Motive of the meeting.
   C. O.—'Brethren, we are assembled on
   the present occasion for the purpose
   of Constituting and Consecrating a

---

* This chronological order is official; but to be
consistent, item 3 should come after item 4.

New Lodge, and I am commanded by the M. W. G. M. to act as Deputy *pro tem.*, and perform the requisite Ceremony. I therefore call on our worthy Brother, the Chaplain, to give the

Opening Prayer

Chaplain.—'O Lord, our Heavenly Father, Architect and Ruler of the Universe, Who dost from Thy Throne behold all the dwellers upon earth! Direct us in all our doings with Thy most gracious favour, and further us With Thy continued help, that in all our works begun, continued, and ended in Thee, we may glorify Thy holy Name.'

6. Chant (*Omnes*): 'So mote it be.'
7. The Director of Ceremonies addresses the Consecrating Officer.

'R. W. M., a number of Brethren, duly instructed in the mysteries of the Craft, who are now assembled, have requested me to inform you that the M. W. G. M. has been pleased to grant them a Charter or Warrant of Constitution, bearing date the   day of   , 19 , authorizing them to form and open a Lodge of F. and A. Masons at . . . ., in the county of............, and are desirous that their Lodge should be consecrated, and their Officers installed and invested, according to the ancient usages and established customs of the Order, for which purpose they are now met, and await your pleasure.'

8. The Consecrating Officer replies, and gives directions.

C. O.—'I will thank those Brethren who signed the petition to stand in the body of the Lodge, whilst the D. of C. reads the petition, and also the Warrant or Charter from the M. W. G. M.'

9. The Brethren of the New Lodge are then arranged in order on each side of the Lodge Board.

10. The Director of Ceremonies reads the Petition and Warrant.

11. The Consecrating Officer inquires of the Brethren if they approve of the Officers named in the Warrant.

C. O.—'After due deliberation, the M. W. G. M., by virtue of the authority vested in him by the United G. L. of England, has granted to the Brethren of this new Lodge a Charter, establishing them in all the rights and privileges of our Order, and I now inquire of the petitioners, if they approve of the Officers named in the Warrant to preside over them.'

12. The Brethren signify their approval in Masonic form.

C. O.—'Then we will proceed to constitute these Brethren into a regular Lodge, and to consecrate it according to ancient usage. I therefore call on our worthy Brother, the Chaplain, to deliver an Oration on the Nature and Principles of the Institution.

13. *An Oration*

On the Nature and Principles of the Institution, by the Chaplain.

14. *Anthem*

'Behold how good and joyful a thing it is, brethren, to dwell together in unity!
'It is like the precious ointment upon the head, that ran down unto the beard, even unto Aaron's beard, and went down to the skirts of his clothing.
'It is like the dew of Hermon which fell upon the hill of Zion.
'For there the Lord promised His blessing, and life for evermore.'

So mote it be.

15. *Dedication Prayer (First Portion)*

C. O.—'Almighty Architect of the Universe, Searcher and Ruler of all worlds, deign from Thy Celestial Abode, from realms of light and glory, to bless us in all the purposes of our present assembly. We humbly invoke Thee to give us Wisdom in all our doings; Strength of Mind under all our difficulties; and the Beauty of Love and Harmony in all our communications. Permit us, O Thou Author of Light and Life, great Source of Love and Happiness, to erect this Lodge, and now solemnly to consecrate it to the Honour and Glory of Thy most Holy Name.'

16. Chant (*Omnes*): 'So mote it be.'

17. *Sanctus:* 'Holy, Holy, Holy, Lord God of Hosts; Heaven and earth are full of Thy glory. Glory be to Thee, O God.'

18. The Brethren turn towards the East, and the Consecrating Officer pronounces

The Invocation

C. O.—'O Lord God of Israel, there is no other God like unto Thee, in Heaven above, or in the Earth beneath, Who keepeth covenants and showeth mercy unto Thy servants who walk before Thee with all their hearts.

'Let all the people of the Earth know that the Lord He is God, and that there is none else.

'Let all the people of the Earth know Thy name, and fear Thee.

'Let all the people of the Earth know that I have built this House, and consecrated it to Thy service.

'But wilt Thou, O God, indeed dwell upon the Earth? Behold, the Heavens, and Heaven of Heavens, cannot contain Thee; how much less this House that I have built?

'Yet, have respect unto my prayer, and to my supplication, and hearken unto my cry.

'May Thine eyes be opened towards this House by day and by night; and when Thy servants shall pray towards this House, hearken unto their supplications; hear them in heaven Thy dwelling-place: and when Thou hearest, forgive.'

19. Chant (*Omnes*): 'So mote it be.'
20. The Chaplain reads 2 Chron. ii 1-16.
21. The Consecrating Officer directs Lodge Board to be uncovered.

The Lodge Board is uncovered by the D. of C., who arranged the petitioning Brethren as before on each side of the Board, with a sufficient space between to allow the procession of C. O. and Ws. to pass. The Cornucopia filled with corn, and the vases with wine and oil, are handed by the D. of C. to the C. O. and Ws., and are carried by them round the Lodge, and the elements poured on the floor during their progress. Soft and gentle music.

The Consecration (during which the Elements of Consecration are carried round the Lodge).

22. Before the first circuit the Brethren sing:
'When once of old, in Israel,
Our early Brethren wrought with toil,
Jehovah's blessings on them fell
In showers of Corn, and Wine, and Oil.'

23. The Consecrating Officer scatters Corn—the symbol of Plenty, saying:
'I scatter corn on this L. as a symbol of plenty and abundance. And may the blessing of morality and virtue increase under its auspices, producing fruit an hundredfold.'

24. *Musical Response:* 'Glory be to God on High.'

25. The Chaplain reads Ps. lxxii 16.
26. Before the second circuit the Brethren sing:

'When there a shrine to Him alone
    They built, with worship sin to foil,
On threshold and on Corner Stone
    They poured out Corn, and Wine, and Oil.'

27. The Consecrating Officer pours Wine—the symbol of Joy and Cheerfulness, saying:

'I pour wine on this Lodge as a symbol of joy and cheerfulness.'

28. *Musical Response:* 'Glory be to God on High.'
29. The Chaplain reads Neh. x 39.
30. Before the third circuit the Brethren sing:

'And we have come, fraternal bands,
    With joy and pride, and prosperous spoil,
To honour Him by votive hands,
    With streams of Corn, and Wine, and Oil.'

31. The Consecrating Officer pours Oil—the symbol of Peace and Unanimity, saying:

'I sprinkle this Lodge with oil as a symbol of peace and unanimity.'

32. *Musical Response:* 'Glory be to God on High.'

33. The Chaplain reads Exod. xxx 25, 26.

34. Before the fourth circuit the Brethren sing:

'Now o'er our work this salt we shower,
Emblem of Thy conservant power;
And may Thy presence, Lord, we pray,
Keep this our temple from decay.'

35. The Consecrating Officer sprinkles Salt —the symbol of Fidelity and Friendship, saying:

'I scatter salt on this Lodge, the emblem of hospitality and friendship; and may prosperity and happiness attend this Lodge until time shall be no more.'

36. *Musical Response:* 'Glory be to God on High.'

37. The Chaplain reads Lev. ii 13.

38. *The Consecrating Officer dedicates the Lodge saying:*

'To God and His Service we dedicate this Lodge! and in memory of the three original G. Ms., under whose auspices many of our Masonic mysteries had their origin.'

39.   *Anthem.*

'O how amiable are Thy dwellings, Thou Lord of Hosts! My soul hath a desire and longing to enter the courts of the Lord; my heart and my flesh rejoice in the living God. Blessed are they that dwell in Thy house: they shall be always praising Thee. Hallelujah!'

40. The Chaplain takes the Censer round the Lodge three times, saying:

'And Aaron shall burn thereon sweet incense every morning; when he dresseth the lamps, he shall burn incense upon it, and when Aaron lighteth the lamps at even, he shall burn incense upon it, a perpetual incense before the Lord throughout your generations.'

41. *Dedication Prayer (Second Portion)*

C. O.—'Grant, O Lord, that those who are now about to be invested with the government of this Lodge may be endued with wisdom to instruct their Brethren in all their duties: may brotherly Love, Relief, and Truth ever prevail amongst its members; and may this bond of union increase and strengthen the several Lodges throughout the world. Bless all our Brethren wherever dispersed over the face of the earth and water, and grant a speedy relief to all who are oppressed or distressed. We especially and affectionately commend to Thy especial care and attention all the members of the Fraternity; may they increase in knowledge of Thee, and love of each other. And, finally, may we finish all our work here below with Thy approbation; and then leave this earthly abode for Thy Heavenly Temple above, there to enjoy Light, Bliss, and Joy evermore.'

42. Chant (*Omnes*): 'So mote it be.'
The D. of C. then arranges the petitioning Brethren as before, on each side of the Lodge Board, when—

43. *The Consecrating Officer constitutes the Lodge, thus:*

'I now constitute this Lodge, denominated the..........Lodge, numbered ...... in the Register of the G. L. of England, through the blessing of Divine Providence, to the purposes of Freemasonry, and, in the name of the M. W. G. M., I constitute and form you, my good Brethren, into a Lodge of F. and A. Masons; henceforth I empower you to Initiate, Pass, or Raise Candidates for Freemasonry, and to perform all the Rites and Ceremonies conformably with the ancient Charges,

and the Constitutions of the Order.
And may the G. A. O. T. U. prosper,
direct, and counsel you in all your
proceedings.'

44. Chant (*Omnes*): 'So mote it be.'

45.   *Hymn*

'Glory to God on high!
Let heaven and earth reply,
    Praise ye His name.

Masons His love adore,
Arched in their mystic lore,
And cry out evermore,
    Glory to God!'

46.   *Patriarchal Benediction*

'The Lord bless and preserve thee;
The Lord make His face to shine upon
        thee,
    And be gracious unto thee;
The Lord lift up His countenance upon
        thee,
    And grant thee peace.'

47. Chant (*Omnes*): 'So mote it be.'

———

(*End of Consecration Ceremony.*)

*   *   *   *

48. The Lodge is resumed in the Second
    Degree.

C. O. to D. of C.—Have you examined the M. nominated in the Warrant, and found him well skilled in the noble science, and duly instructed in our mysteries?

D. of C. to C. O.—I have.

C. O. to D. of C.—Then let him be presented in due form.

D. of C. to C. O.—R. W. M., I present to you Bro. A. B., to be installed Master of this Lodge, whom I believe to be of good morals and great skill, true and trusty, and a lover of the whole fraternity, and who, I feel assured, will discharge his duty with zeal and fidelity.

49. Installation of Worshipful Master.

* * * *

50. Election of Treasurer.
51. Election of Tyler.
52. Appointment and investiture of Officers.
53. Election of Committee to frame By-laws.
54. The W. M. rises for the first time.
Votes of thanks to Consecrating Officers —Offers of Hon. Membership—Gift of Souvenirs, etc.
Propositions for Initiation and Joining Members.

55. The W. M. rises for the second time.
56. The W. M. rises for the third time.
57. The Lodge is closed.

58.   *Closing Ode*

'Now the evening shadows closing
    Warn from toil to peaceful rest,
Mystic arts and rites reposing
    Sacred in each faithful breast.
God of light! whose love unceasing
    Doth to all Thy works extend,
Crown our order with Thy blessing,
    Build, sustain us to the end.
Humbly now we bow before Thee,
    Grateful for Thine aid Divine.
Everlasting power and glory,
    Mighty Architect, be Thine.'

                      So mote it be.

59. Procession out of the Lodge as directed
    by the Director of Ceremonies.

(G.) LAYING A FOUNDATION STONE, OR CHIEF CORNER STONE

As a rule some high dignitary of the Craft lays the stone. In this copy of the Ceremony the title of Provincial Grand Master will be used.

A Craft Lodge is opened in a convenient room, and there the procession is formed;

the Provincial Grand Director of Ceremonies, assisted by the local D. C., arranging the Brethren in the proper order.

The Provincial Grand Master having arrived at his station on a platform, a flourish of trumpets is given, or a hymn or an ode is sung, or music is played, as may have been arranged.

The Provincial Grand Master delivers an address, either composed to suit the occasion, or in general terms, as follows:

PROVINCIAL GRAND MASTER'S ADDRESS

Men and Brethren, here assembled to behold this Ceremony! Be it known unto you, that we be true and lawful Freemasons, the successors of those ancient Brethren of our Craft, who from time immemorial have been engaged throughout the civilized world in 'the erection of stately and superb edifices,' to the glory of God, and for the service of mankind! From those ancient Brethren have been handed down from generation to generation certain secrets 'by which Freemasons are known to each other, and distinguished from the rest of the world.' These secrets are lawful and honourable, and 'are in no way incompatible with our civil, moral, or religious duties'; and as we have received them from our predecessors in the Order, so we hand them down pure and unimpaired to those who are to succeed us.

Our Order has always been distinguished for loyalty to the Throne, for obedience to the laws and institutions of the country in which we reside, for good citizenship, for goodwill to all mankind, and especially for 'that most excellent gift—Charity!' By the exercise of these qualities we have in all ages enjoyed such distinction, that princes and nobles of high degree have been Members of our Order, 'have patronized our mysteries, and joined in our assemblies.' Under such powerful protection, and by the fidelity and zeal of its Members, Freemasonry has endured through the ages, and has been enabled 'to survive the wreck of mighty empires, and to resist the destroying hand of time.'

We have met here to-day, in the presence of this great assembly, to lay the [Chief Corner] Stone of this building, which is about to be erected to the honour and glory of the Most High, and in humble dependence upon His blessing.

As Freemasons, our first and paramount duty in all our undertakings is, to invoke the blessing from T. G. A. O. T. U. upon that which we are about to do; I therefore call upon you to give attention to the Provincial Grand Chaplain, and to unite in prayer to Him from Whom alone cometh every good and every perfect gift.

(*The stone will now be raised.*)

(*Prayer by the Provincial Grand Chaplain.*)

Chant (*Omnes*).—So mote it be.

P. G. M.—I now declare it to be my will and pleasure that the Chief Corner Stone of this building be laid. Bro. Provincial Grand Secretary, you will read the inscription on the plate. (*Which is done.*)

(*The stone will be lowered about nine inches: during the process of lowering the Choir will sing the first verse of 'Prosper the Art.'*)

SOLO

When the Temple's first stone was slowly
    descending,
  A stillness like death the scene reigned
    around;
There thousands of gazers in silence were
    bending,
  Till rested the ponderous mass on the
    ground.

CHORUS

Then shouts filled the air and the joy was
    like madness,
  The Founder alone, standing meekly
    apart;

Until from his lips burst—flowing with
　　gladness,
　The wish that for ever might prosper the
　　Art.

P. G. M. — Bro. Provincial Grand
Treasurer, you will deposit the vessel containing the coins and other articles in the
cavity.

*(The Bottle containing the Parchment, with
an account of the undertaking, and the names
of the principal personages taking part in the
Ceremony, various current coins of the Realm,
and copies of local papers, will be placed in
the cavity. The cavity should now be filled
with powdered charcoal. The plate will then
be cemented in its place over all.)*

*(The Stone is again lowered nine inches,
during which the Choir will sing the second
verse of 'Prosper the Art.')*

SOLO

When the Temple had reared its magnificent
　　crest,
　And the wealth of the world had em-
　　bellished its walls,
The nations drew near from the East and
　　the West,
　Their homage to pay in its beautiful
　　halls.

CHORUS

Then they paused at the entrance, with
feelings delighted,
Bestowing fond looks ere they turned to
depart;
And as homeward they journeyed with
voices united,
They joined in full chorus, with 'Prosper
the Art.'

*(The Provincial Grand Master descends
from the platform, the trowel is presented to
him, with some appropriate remarks, and the
Provincial Grand Master spreads the cement.)*
*(Solemn music may be played, or the
'Gloria' may be sung, while the Stone is
lowered into its place.)*

P. G. M.—Bro. Junior Warden, what is
the Emblem of your Office?
J. W.—The Plumb-rule, Right Worshipful Provincial Grand Master.
P. G. M.—How do you apply the Plumb-rule?
J. W.—To try and adjust uprights, while
fixing them on their proper bases.
P. G. M.—Bro. Junior Warden, you will
apply the Plumb-rule to the sides of the
Stone. *(This is done.)*
J. W.—Right Worshipful Provincial Grand

Master, I find the Stone to be perfect and trustworthy.

P. G. M.—Bro. Senior Warden, what is the Emblem of your Office?

S. W.—The Level, Right Worshipful Provincial Grand Master.

P. G. M.—How do you apply the Level?

S. W.—To lay levels and prove horizontals.

P. G. M.—Bro. Senior Warden, you will prove the Stone. (*Done.*)

S. W.—Right Worshipful Provincial Grand Master, I find the Stone to be level and well founded.

P. G. M.—Worshipful Master, what is the Emblem of your Office?

W. M.—The Square, Right Worshipful Provincial Grand Master.

P. G. M.—How do you apply the Square?

W. M.—To try and adjust rectangular corners of buildings, and assist in bringing rude matter into due form.

P. G. M.—You will apply the Square. (*This is done.*)

W. M.—Right Worshipful Provincial Grand Master, I have applied the Square, and I find the Stone to be well wrought and true.

(*The Provincial Grand Master himself applies the Plumb-rule, the Level, and the Square.*)

P. G. M.—I find the Stone to be plumb, level, and square, and that the Craftsmen have laboured skilfully.

(*The mallet is presented to the Prov. G. M. with some appropriate remarks.*)

(*The Prov. G. M. gives three knocks on the Stone with the mallet.*)

P. G. M.—May T. G. A. O. T. U. look down with favour upon this undertaking, and may He crown the edifice of which we have laid the foundation with abundant success.

(*Flourish of Trumpets, or Music, or the Choir and the Assembly may sing the following Chant:*)

CHAPLAIN.—'Except the Lord build the house: their labour is but lost that build it.

'Except the Lord keep the city: the watchman waketh but in vain.

'It is in vain that ye rise up early, and late take rest: for so He giveth His beloved sleep.

'If the foundations be destroyed: what can the righteous do?

'Her foundations are upon the holy hills: the Lord loveth the gates of Zion more than all the dwellings of Jacob.

'That our sons may grow up as the young plants: and that our daughters may be as the polished corners of the temple.

The Ceremonies (Laying Stone)

'Happy is the people that is in such a case: yea, happy is that people whose God is the Lord.'

(The Provincial Grand Superintendent of Works, or the Architect, presents the plans.)

P. G. S. of W.—Right Worshipful Provincial Grand Master, it is my duty to present these Plans of the intended building, which have been duly approved.

(The Provincial Grand Master inspects the Plans and returns them to the Architect.)

P. G. M.—I place in your hands the Plans of the intended building, having full confidence in your skill as a Craftsman; and I desire that you will proceed without loss of time to the completion of the work, in conformity with the plans and designs now entrusted to you.

BEARER OF THE CORN.—Right Worshipful Provincial Grand Master, I present to you Corn, the sacred emblem of Plenty.

(The P. G. M. strews Corn upon the Stone.)

CHAPLAIN.—'There shall be a handful of corn in the earth upon the top of the mountains: the fruit thereof shall shake like Lebanon: and they of the city shall flourish like grass of the earth.' *(Psalm lxxii 16.)*

BEARER OF THE WINE.—Right Worshipful Provincial Grand Master, I present to you Wine, the sacred emblem of Truth.

(The P. G. M. pours Wine on the Stone.)

CHAPLAIN.—'And for a drink-offering thou shalt offer the third part of a hin of wine, for a sweet savour unto the Lord.' (*Numbers* xxviii 14.)

BEARER OF THE OIL.—Right Worshipful Provincial Grand Master, I present to you Oil, the sacred emblem of Charity.

(The P. G. M. pours Oil upon the Stone.)

CHAPLAIN.—'And thou shalt make it an oil of holy ointment, an ointment compound after the art of the apothecary: it shall be a holy anointing oil.

'And thou shalt anoint the tabernacle of the congregation therewith, and the ark of the testimony.' (*Exodus* xxx 25, 26.)

P. G. M. (*or Chaplain*).—May the All-bounteous Creator of the Universe shower down His choicest blessing upon this (*names the building*), and grant a full supply of the Corn of nourishment, the Wine of refreshment, and the Oil of Joy.

Chant (*Omnes*).—So mote it be.

(The Provincial Grand Master reascends the platform. Some money for the workmen is placed on the Stone by the Provincial Grand Treasurer. If the building be for a charitable institution, a voluntary subscription is made in aid of its funds during the singing of the Anthem or Te Deum.)

The Ceremonies (Laying Stone)

After which the Chaplain pronounces the

Benediction

CHAPLAIN.—May the Glorious Majesty of the Lord our God be upon us; prosper Thou the work of our hands upon us, yea, the work of our hands establish Thou it.

Chant (*Omnes*).—So mote it be.

(The following Masonic Version of the National Anthem may be sung:)

God save our gracious Queen,
Long live our noble Queen,
   God save the Queen.
Grant her victorious,
Happy and glorious,
Long to reign over us,
   God save the Queen.

Hail! mystic light Divine,
Long may thy radiance shine
   O'er sea and land.
Wisdom in thee we find,
Beauty and strength combined;
May we be ever joined
   In heart and hand.

Sing, then, ye Sons of Light,
In joyous strains unite,
   God save the Queen.

The Ceremonies

Long may Queen Elizabeth reign
Lord of the azure main.
Freemasons! swell the strain,
God save the Queen.

*   *   *   *

(End of the Ceremony.)
(Procession, formed as before, returns to the place from which it started, and the Lodge is closed.)

(H.) FUNERAL CEREMONY

(To follow the usual funeral service of the religious denomination to which the deceased Brother belonged.)

The Worshipful Master reads as follows:

Brethren.—The melancholy event which has caused us to assemble on the present occasion cannot have failed to impress itself on the mind of everyone present. The loss of a friend and Brother—especially of one whose loss we now deplore—conveys a powerful appeal to our hearts, reminding us as it does of the uncertainty of life, and of the vanity of earthly hopes and designs.

Amid the pleasures, the cares, and the various avocations of life we are too apt to forget that upon *us* also the common lot of all mankind must one day fall, and that Death's dread summons may surprise us even in the meridian of our lives, and in the full spring-tide of enjoyment and success.

The ceremonial observances which we practise during the obsequies of a departed Brother, are intended to remind us of our own 'inevitable destiny,' and to warn us that we also should be likewise ready, for we know not the day nor the hour when in the case of each of us 'the dust shall return to the earth as it was, and the spirit shall return unto God who gave it.'

Then, Brethren, let us lay these things seriously to heart; let us strive in all things to act up to our Masonic profession, to live in accordance with the high moral precepts inculcated in our Ceremonies, and to practically illustrate in our lives and our actions the ancient tenets and established customs of the Order. Thus, in humble dependence upon the mercy of the Most High, we may hope, when this transitory life, with all its cares and sorrows, shall have passed away, to rejoin this our departed friend and Brother in the Grand Lodge above, where the world's Great Architect lives and reigns for ever.

Chant (*Omnes*).—So mote it be.

(The following supplications are then offered by the Master:)

MASTER.—May we be true and faithful, and may we live in fraternal affection one towards another, and die in peace with all mankind.

RESPONSE (*to be sung*).—So mote it be.

MASTER.—May we practise that which is wise and good, and always act in accordance with our Masonic profession.

RESPONSE (*to be sung*).—So mote it be.

MASTER.—May the Great Architect of the Universe bless us, and direct us in all that we undertake and do in His Holy Name.

RESPONSE (*to be sung*).—So mote it be.

(*The Secretary then advances and throws his roll into the grave, while the Master repeats, in an audible voice.*)

MASTER.—Glory be to God on high! on earth peace! goodwill towards men!

RESPONSE (*to be sung*).—So mote it be, now, henceforth, and for evermore!

There is a calm for those who weep,
    A rest for weary pilgrims found;
They softly lie and sweetly sleep,
    Low in the ground! low in the ground!

The storm that wracks the winter sky
    No more disturbs their deep repose
Than summer evening's latest sigh,
    That shuts the rose! that shuts the rose!

The Ceremonies (Funerals)

Ah, mourner! long of storms the sport,
   Condemn'd in wretchedness to roam,
Hope thou shalt reach a sheltering port,
   A quiet home! a quiet home!

The sun is like a spark of fire,
   A transient meteor in the sky;
The soul, immortal as its sire,
   Shall never die! shall never die!

(*The Master then concludes the ceremony at the grave in the following words:*)

MASTER.—From time immemorial it has been the custom among the Fraternity of Free and Accepted Masons, at the request of a Brother on his death-bed, to accompany his corpse to the place of interment; and there to deposit his remains with the usual formalities of the Order. In conformity with this usage, and at the special request of our deceased Brother, whose loss we deeply deplore, we are here assembled as Freemasons, to consign his body to the earth, and, openly before the world, to offer up in his memory the last tribute of our fraternal affection, thereby demonstrating the sincerity of our esteem for our deceased Brother, and our inviolable attachment to the principles of the Order.

* [With all proper respect to the established customs of the country in which we live, with due deference to all in authority in Church and State, and with unlimited goodwill to all mankind, we here appear as Freemasons, clothed with the insignia of the Order, and publicly express our submission to order and good government, and our wish to promote the general interests of mankind. Invested with 'the badge of innocence, and the bond of friendship,' we humbly bow to the Universal Parent; we implore His blessing on our zealous endeavours to promote peace and goodwill; and we earnestly pray for His grace, to enable us to persevere in the *practice* of piety and virtue.]

The Great Creator having been pleased, in His infinite wisdom, to remove our worthy Brother from the cares and troubles of this transitory life, and thereby to weaken the ties by which we are united to the world, may *we* who survive him, anticipating *our* own approaching end, be more strongly cemented in the bonds of union and friendship, and, during the short space which is allotted to us in our present existence, may we wisely and usefully employ our time in

* The paragraph between the brackets [ ] may be omitted.

the interchange of kind and fraternal acts, and may we strive earnestly to promote the welfare and happiness of our fellow-men.

Unto the grave we have consigned the body of our deceased friend and Brother, there to remain until the general resurrection, in the fullest confidence that both body and soul will then arise to partake of the joys which have been prepared for the righteous from the beginning of the world. And may Almighty God of His infinite goodness, at the last grand tribunal, extend His mercy towards him, and all of *us*, and crown our hope with everlasting bliss, in the realms of a boundless eternity! This we beg, for the honour of His Name, to Whom be glory, now and for ever.

Chant (*Omnes*).—So mote it be.

It is decreed in heaven above,
That we, from those whom best we love,
    Must sever.
But hard the word would be to tell,
If to our friends we said farewell,
    For ever.

And thus the meaning we explain—
We hope, and be our hope not vain,
That, though we part, we meet again.
A brief farewell; then meet again
    For ever.

(Then the Brethren, led by the Worshipful Master, pass round the grave, and each Brother casts a sprig of acacia on the coffin.)

(End of Funeral Ceremony.)

Masonic Mourning

In the event of the death of any high dignitary in the Craft, an order is sent by the Grand Secretary to each Lodge that mourning shall be worn by every Brother for a certain period of time. In the case of a similar loss in a Province or District, the Provincial or District Grand Secretary would send a like order to every Lodge in his Province or District.

The regulation form of mourning dictated on these occasions is as follows: For Officers present and past of Grand Lodge, or of Provincial or District Grand Lodges, and for Officers of private Lodges, a black crape Rosette near the point of the collar above the jewel; and for all Master Masons, Officers included, a similar crape Rosette to cover the three blue Rosettes, one just above the point of the flap of the Apron, and one on each of the lower corners.

For Fellow-Crafts and Entered Apprentices, two black crape Rosettes, to cover the blue Rosettes on each corner of the bottom of the Apron.

Black or white ties, and white, or, *preferably*, grey gloves, with black stitchings, should be worn. In either case uniformity is much to be desired; on this point an expression of the wish of the Worshipful Master may be added to each circular.

If it be thought necessary or desirable that the Lodge-room should be put into mourning, the following plan or any portion thereof may be adopted:

Each of the three pedestals may have a black cloth cover to fit the top, with a fall round the front and the two sides eight inches deep, with a black bullion fringe of five inches round the lower edge.

The Master's and the two Wardens' chairs may have a cap of black cloth fitted to the shape of the top of the back of each chair, about twelve inches deep, fringed on the lower edge the same as the covers on the pedestals. The three candlesticks and the columns should each have a trimming of crape; so also should the Deacon's wands.

If the Banner of the Lodge be displayed, it should have a large black crape Rosette on or near the top of the staff, and one of the same size (or nearly) on each of the four corners. If there be cords and tassels, they may be trimmed with crape.

If the occasion justify any further demonstration of mourning, advantage may be taken of any salient portion of the room and the furniture, such as the tops of windows and doors, and the Secretary's table, the organ or harmonium, upon which crape or cloth may be placed. Much may depend upon the occasion of the mourning, whether it be for a high dignitary in the Craft (as previously mentioned), or for one of the then Principal Officers, or a Past Master of the Lodge.

In the case of the death of an ordinary member, it is unusual for the Lodge room to be put into mourning; the Brethren wear their crape Rosettes at the next meeting; and a letter of condolence to the family of the deceased, signed by the Master and the Wardens, is generally considered to be proper and sufficient. This mark of respect should not by any means be omitted.

(I) THE CEREMONY OF OPENING A PROVINCIAL OR DISTRICT GRAND LODGE

The Craft Lodge having been opened in the three Degrees, the Provincial or District Grand Master and the Provincial Grand

Officers, present and past, make their formal entry (see p. 70).

(We will use the initials of a Provincial Grand Master with the prefix of R. W. for Right Worshipful. A District Grand Master is also Right Worshipful. If a Deputy Provincial or Deputy District Grand Master should preside, he would be addressed as Very Worshipful, etc.)

R. W. P. G. M. (—▮ *followed by Provincial Grand Wardens*).—Brethren, assist me to open this Provincial Grand Lodge.

(All rise.)

R. W. P. G. M.—Bro. Provincial Grand Pursuivant, where is your situation in Provincial Grand Lodge?

P. G. P.—Within the Inner Porch of Provincial Grand Lodge Right Worshipful Provincial Grand Master.

R. W. P. G. M.—What is your duty?

P. G. P.—To give a proper report of all approaching Brethren, and to see that they are properly clothed and ranged under their respective banners.

R. W. P. G. M.—Do you find them so placed?

P. G. P.—To the best of my knowledge, Right Worshipful Provincial Grand Master.

R. W. P. G. M.—Where is the situation of the Provincial Junior Grand Warden?

P. G. P.—In the South, Right Worshipful Provincial Grand Master.

R. W. P. G. M.—Bro. Provincial Junior Grand Warden, whom do you represent?

P. J. G. W.—...., the Prince of the People on Mount Tabor.

R. W. P. G. M.—Bro. Provincial Junior Grand Warden, where is the situation of the Provincial Senior Grand Warden?

P. J. G. W.—In the West, Right Worshipful Provincial Grand Master.

R. W. P. G. M.—Bro. Provincial Senior Grand Warden, whom do you represent?

P. S. G. W.—...., the Assistant High Priest on Mount Sinai.

R. W. P. G. M.—Bro. Provincial Senior Grand Warden, where is the situation of the Deptuy Provincial Grand Master?

P. S. G. W.—At the right of the Right Worshipful Provincial Grand Master.

R. W. P. G. M.—Bro. Deputy Provincial Grand Master, whom do you represent?

D. P. G. M.—H. A. B., the Prince of Architects.

R. W. P. G. M.—What is your duty?

D. P. G. M.—To lay lines, draw designs, and assist the Right Worshipful Provincial Grand Master in the execution of the work.

R. W. P. G. M.—Very Worshipful Deputy

Provincial Grand Master, where is the situation of the Provincial Grand Master?

D. P. G. M.—In the East.

R. W. P. G. M.—Whom does he represent?

D. P. G. M.—The Royal Solomon, on his throne.

R. W. P. G. M.—Then, Brethren, after the Worshipful Bro. Chaplain has invoked the blessing of T. G. A. O. T. U., I shall, in the name of the Royal Solomon, declare this Provincial Grand Lodge open. (*All adopt the sign of R.*)

[*The Prayer by the Chaplain.*]

(*At the conclusion of the Prayer the Sn. of R. is 'dropped,' not 'drawn.'*)

R. W. P. G. M.—Brethren, in the name of the Royal Solomon, I declare this Provincial Grand Lodge opened in due* form. (⚊⚌ *followed by the Provincial Grand Wardens; the Provincial Grand Pursuivant gives ks., and the Tyler replies.*)

* * * *

P. G. D. of C.—Brethren, I call upon you to salute the Right Worshipful Provincial Grand Master with seven, taking the time from me. To order, Brethren!

(*All present, including Provincial Grand Officers, give the Gr. or R. Sn. seven times.*)

* See No. 79, 'Book of Constitutions.'

P. G. D. of C.—Brethren, I call upon you to salute the Very Worshipful Deputy Provincial Grand Master with five, taking the time from me. To order, Brethren!

(All present give the Gr. or R. Sn. five times· Then the Provincial Grand Officers sit down.)

P. G. D. of C.—Brethren, I call upon you to salute the Provincial Grand Officers past and present, with three, taking the time from me. To order, Brethren!

(This is done by those who have remained standing.)

P. G. D. of C.—Brethren, be seated.

CEREMONY OF CLOSING PROVINCIAL OR DISTRICT GRAND LODGE

R. W. P. G. M. (—❚ *followed by Provincial Grand Wardens).*—Brethren, assist me to close this Provincial Grand Lodge.

(All rise)

R. W. P. G. M.—Bro. Provincial Grand Pursuivant, prove the Provincial Grand Lodge close tyled. *(This is done.)*

P. G. P. (with Sn.).—Right Worshipful Provincial Grand Master, the Provincial Grand Lodge is close tyled.

(The Ceremony proceeds exactly as in the opening.)

(At the proper moment all adopt the Sn. of R.)

[*Prayer and Praise by the Chaplain.*]
(*At the conclusion of Prayer and Praise the Sn. of R. is 'dropped,' not 'drawn.'*)

R. W. P. G. M.—Brethren, in the name of the Royal Solomon, I declare this Provincial Grand Lodge closed in due* form. (*Gives the ▬Ӏ, followed by the Prov. Grand Wardens.*) (*The Provincial Grand Master, followed by his Officers present and past, leaves the Lodge, the Brethren all standing, and the Organist performing his duty.*)

(*End of Ceremony of Closing Provincial or District Grand Lodge.*)

* * * *

(*The Worshipful Master, and the Officers, resume their several places, and the Craft Lodge is closed in three Degrees.*)

(J) CEREMONIES OF OPENING AND CLOSING GRAND LODGE

The Ceremonies of Opening† and Closing Grand Lodge are precisely the same as detailed on pp. 270-274, except that—

1. The Pro-Grand Master is styled *Most Worshipful.*
2. The words 'Provincial' are omitted.
3. Grand Lodge is not 'proved close tyled.'

* See No. 79, 'Book of Constitutions.'
† See No. 51, 'Book of Constitutions.'

CHAPTER XX

THE CHAPLAIN AND HIS DUTIES

THE Constitutions provide that the Master 'may' also appoint a Chaplain; and in any Lodge which has among its members a duly qualified Brother, it is desirable that a Chaplain should be appointed; and, as a matter of course, all the devotional portions of the opening and the closing in each Degree and in each of the three Ceremonies would then be performed by him. The impressiveness and the solemnity of the whole proceedings may be enhanced by having a Chaplain to perform those important duties.

The following optional address may be delivered to the Chaplain on his investiture:

(W. M.) 'W. Bro......., I appoint you Chaplain of the Lodge, and now invest you with the Jewel of your Office, the Open Book. This represents the Volume of the Sacred Law, which is always open upon the Master's Pedestal when the Brethren are at labour in the Lodge. The V. of the S. L. is the greatest of the three great, though emblematical, lights in Freemasonry. The Sacred

Writings are given as the rule and guide of our Faith. The Sacred Volume will guide us to all Truth, direct our steps in the paths of Happiness, and point out to us the whole Duty of man. Without it the Lodge is not "just"; and without an openly avowed belief in its Divine Author, no Candidate can be lawfully initiated into our Order. Your place in the Lodge is near the Worshipful Master, and as, both in the opening and the closing of the Lodge in each Degree, as well as in each of the three Ceremonies, the blessing of the Almighty is invoked on our proceedings, it will be your duty, as far as may be possible, to attend all the meetings of the Lodge, in order that you may exercise your sacred office in the devotional portions of our Ceremonies.'

*   *   *   *

If the Chaplain recites the Prayers, he must follow the Worshipful Master in this manner:

OPENINGS

First Degree

W. M.—The Lodge being duly formed before I declare it open. . . .

CHAPLAIN.—. . . . let us invoke, etc. . . . . harmony.

I. P. M.—So mote it be.

Second Degree

W. M.—Before we open the Lodge in the Second Degree. . . .

CHAPLAIN.—. . . .let us supplicate, etc. . . . science.

I. P. M.—So mote it be.

Third Degree

W. M.—We will assist you to repair that loss. . . .

CHAPLAIN.—. . . .and may Heaven aid our united endeavours!

I. P. M.—So mote it be.

CLOSING

First Degree

W. M.—Brethren, before we close the Lodge. . . .

CHAPLAIN.—. . . .let us, with all reverence, etc. . . . . virtue.

I. P. M.—So mote it be.

CHAPTER XXI

THE DIRECTOR OF CEREMONIES AND HIS DUTIES

THE Director of Ceremonies is not a 'regular' Officer of a Lodge, and no place is assigned to him in the Recognized Ritual of the Regular Ceremonies of Initiation, Passing, Raising, and Installation.

Nevertheless, a capable Director of Ceremonies is of great advantage to any Lodge which appoints him. His duties are multifarious and onerous, and his influence for good can be made to extend to every department of Lodge working.

It is very desirable that he should be a Past Master, not only by reason of the experience he has gained in serving the various offices, but because a continuity of service in that capacity is important.

He should, of course, be well versed in the Ritual and in the requirements of the various degrees, so as to guard against all imperfection in the ceremonies.

It is he who organizes the processions in and out of the Lodge, receives the visitors and assigns to them their correct precedence in the Lodge, and at table; settles all questions of etiquette among the Brethren; and contributes to the dissipation of difficulties when they arise.

He will probably be consulted by the Worshipful Master on points of procedure; and on the order of business; and if any Officer should be prevented, by the pressing emergencies of his avocation, from fulfilling his duties, he will most probably be asked to advise as to a substitute.

In the Ceremony of Consecration important duties are assigned to him, and in public ceremonial he is, of course, an indispensable factor.

One important duty attached to the Office of Director of Ceremonies is 'to marshal all processions and demonstrations of the Brethren.' We may remark in connection with this subject that a rule exists which gives to the Rulers of the Order the power to put a check upon too frequent public demonstrations of the Brethren. Rule No. 178 of the Book of Constitutions expressly states that no Brother shall appear in Masonic clothing in public without a dispensation from the Grand Master or the Provincial or District Grand Master.

As a matter of course, the petition for a

The Director of Ceremonies and his Duties

Dispensation would set forth fully and clearly the object of the demonstration. The petition would necessarily be sent to the Grand Secretary, or in the Provinces or Districts to the Provincial or District Grand Secretary, as indeed etiquette demands that all written communications to the high dignitaries mentioned should invariably be so sent.

One general rule would appear to apply to the marshalling of all processions of our Order, some details being occasionally superadded to suit the varying purposes of the demonstration. The Tyler, with a drawn sword, heads the procession; next follow Entered Apprentices two and two; then Fellow-Crafts, followed by the Master Masons, juniors leading; next the Assistant Officers of the Lodge, the lowest first; then Past Masters, juniors first; next the Immediate Past Master; the Banner of the Lodge; the Worshipful Master, supported on the right by the Senior Warden, and on the left by the Junior Warden, each of the Wardens carrying his Column. After these come Provincial or District Grand Officers, the lower in rank going first, Grand Officers bringing up the rear; among the Provincial, or District, or Grand Officers, being probably the one appointed to perform the Ceremony, if any. He would be in the last rank, supported on each side by Brethren of distinction and of high rank in the Craft.

It is necessary that all (except those mentioned as being supported right and left) should form *two deep*, as will be seen in the next sentence. On arriving at the appointed place, the Tyler halts, and the whole of the Brethren, down to, but not including, the rear rank, separate and form two lines. Those in the rear rank walk forward between the lines, and each two of the Brethren as they are reached fall in behind, and so on until the whole order of the procession is inverted, and those—the juniors—who were first, become the last.

* * * *

If the occasion be the laying of a foundation, or Chief Corner Stone, the requisite number of distinguished Brethren are appointed to bear the Square, the Level, and the Plumb-rule, the Heavy Mall, and the Trowel, the Corn, the Wine, and the Oil. Others carry the bottle containing the coins, etc., the brass plate with the inscription, and whatever else it may be thought necessary to carry in the procession. The Architect carries the plans of the building.

If the edifice to be erected be a Church or

Church Schools, the open Bible with the Square and Compasses is carried frequently by the Tyler. A board of the necessary size, covered probably with crimson velvet or cloth, with a cushion upon it, would be provided. Two broad straps or ribbons passed over the Tyler's shoulders would enable him to carry the whole with perfect ease, and he would have his right hand free to carry the sword.

On one occasion the open Bible was carried upon a board made for the purpose, having four handles extending horizontally, two in front and two at the back. The bearers were four little boys, *each boy a Lewis.* Nothing in the whole procession attracted so much interest as those four little bearers of the Bible, all apparently under ten years of age. The Deputy Provincial Grand Master who laid the Chief Corner Stone, afterwards sent an enduring memento of the occasion to each of the boys. It would be interesting to know if they—or any of them—eventually became Freemasons.

Once the members of a Lodge in the far West of England erected a Masonic Hall. The Chief Corner Stone was laid by the Deputy Provincial Grand Master, assisted by a number of Provincial Grand Officers. One of these of high rank regulated the

whole proceedings. On that occasion the
Tracing Board of the First Degree, on a
light frame with four handles—an enlarged
edition of that mentioned in the preceding
paragraph—ornamented white and gold,
was carried by four Past Masters of the
Lodge. This Tracing Board was supposed
to represent the Lodge in a symbolic sense.

It would probably have been more correct to have had the three Tracing Boards.
At the Consecration of a Lodge in a large
public building—not the Lodge-room—the
three Tracing Boards, piled (horizontally)
one upon another, were placed upon a stand
in the centre of the hall, presumably representing the Lodge. A Very Worshipful
Brother, high in Office in Grand Lodge, was
the Presiding Officer; the Wardens were
also Very Worshipful Members of Grand
Lodge, and the then Grand Director of
Ceremonies assisted, so no doubt can be
entertained of the strictly correct manner
in which everything was carried out.

Customs, however, vary in different Provinces, and a practice which is held to be
strictly correct in one Province would be
utterly condemned in another. In all cases
of Public Ceremonial, if any doubt or difficulty should arise, application should be
made to the Grand or Provincial, or District

Grand Secretary, according to locality, for counsel and guidance.

When the chief Functionary is the Provincial, or District Grand Master, or his Deputy, or any of his past or present Officers specially appointed to officiate in his stead, the Provincial, or District Grand Secretary, would, as a rule, take the control of the proceedings, assisted, of course, by the Officers of the Lodge, or Lodges, chiefly interested in the Ceremony to be performed. In the case of the Grand Master himself, or the Pro-Grand Master, or the Deputy Grand Master, or other high Officer of Grand Lodge officiating, the Grand Secretary would dictate the course of the proceedings, and would give his instructions to the Brethren who, under him, would have the charge of the preparations.

The Ceremony of laying a Foundation, or Chief Corner, Stone will be found on pp. 251 to 264.

*　　*　　*　　*

One other occasion for a 'public procession of Freemasons clothed with the Badges of the Order' is a Masonic funeral. Widely divergent opinions will be found to exist in different Provinces, and even in different portions of the same Province, as to the desirability, or otherwise, of continuing the practice of this undoubtedly ancient custom in the Craft. In some Provinces it may be considered obsolete, or is possibly almost, or altogether unknown.

In one Province, where the custom of burying with Masonic Ceremonial was rather frequently practised, a feeling adverse to the custom was known to exist on the part of some two or three Provincial Grand Officers (not the highest in authority), and an attempt was made to pass a resolution in Provincial Grand Lodge interdicting the practice in that Province; the motion, however, was negatived by a substantial majority, chiefly representative of Lodges favourable to its continuance.

Very much may be said upon both sides of the question. Of its lawfulness there is no doubt whatever; it is upon its expediency that the doubt may arise. As supplementary to the comprehensive and beautiful Burial Service of the Church of England, the tacking on of our Masonic Service at the end appears to many to be a supererogatory proceeding; to some an anti-climax. Many, on the other hand, especially older members of the Craft, regard it with an extreme reverence, and believe in its impressiveness and solemnity, and in its possibly lasting good effect upon the hearers.

The Director of Ceremonies and his Duties

Three cases may here be cited. A Nonconformist Brother, a zealous Freemason, and an old Past Master, had—on his deathbed (a necessary condition)—expressed the desire to be buried with Masonic Ceremonial. A programme of the full Ceremony was furnished, a few days previously to the funeral, to the minister who was to officiate on the occasion. He, the minister, being bound by no rule or Ritual, so composed and arranged his portion of the service as to lead up to and to fit in with the Masonic Ceremony. The result was that all went admirably and harmoniously as two component parts of one perfect whole. There was no incongruity, no superfluity.

The second case was that of the oldest Past Master in the district in which he had spent a long and active life; he had been highly distinguished in Freemasonry for many years, and had borne high office in Provincial Grand Lodge. He had a long, lingering illness, the fatal result of which he never doubted. He repeated his wish again and again, that his obsequies should be performed with Masonic Rites.

The interment took place in a country churchyard, near to the birthplace of the deceased. The Vicar (who had been made fully aware that some Masonic Ceremonial

would be performed), immediately upon the
conclusion of the Burial Service of the
Church, took his departure, without a word,
and remained in the vestry until those concerned went in to pay the fees, after the conclusion of the Masonic Ceremony. Very
many present, including a number of non-
Freemasons, considered that the Vicar had
showed a bigoted and intolerant spirit. It
is possible, however, that he acted in accordance with his conscientious convictions; he
probably felt that a service, not sanctioned
by the Church, should not be performed
upon ground consecrated by the Church.
Such a view may be narrow; but if it be
conscientiously held, it is entitled to respect.

The third instance was the interment of
the remains of a Provincial Grand Master—
a man of mark in his county, a territorial
magnate, and a zealous Freemason. A very
large gathering of the Brethren of the deceased's own and of the neighbouring
Province assembled, including the majority
of the then present and past Provincial
Grand Officers. A choir—Freemasons, with
some female voices—had been provided.
Two at least of the sons of the deceased, who
were Freemasons, were 'clothed with the
Badges of the Order.' The aged widow sat
by the grave-side. The Burial Services of

the Church and that of our Order were admirably rendered—there appeared no want of harmony between them; the effect of the whole was solemn and impressive in a high degree. The clergy remained throughout, up to the end. The eldest son became Grand Master of his Province, and a Warden in Grand Lodge.

The foregoing have been given here in order to show that the advocates for the retention of the custom in question are not without precedents, supplying good arguments in favour of their views: that the practice—if it be at all an anachronism—is not obsolete; that men of high degree, as well as those of a lower grade, continue to express the wish that the Brethren with whom they have been associated in life should join with their immediate connections in 'paying this last sad tribute of respect to departed merit.'

The fact, also (previously mentioned), should not be lost sight of, that no such Ceremony, nor, indeed, any demonstration of Freemasons (in clothing), can take place without the permission of the Grand Master, or of those to whom he may delegate the authority to grant dispensations for such public occasions. The power of veto therefore always rests with the authorities, and we may presume that in every case good cause must be shown for the application or it would not be granted.

(See Masonic Mourning, p. 268.)

CHAPTER XXII

THE ORGANIST AND HIS DUTIES

THE adoption of instrumental music is on the increase; hence the office of Organist has become much less of a sinecure than it used to be. It is not a regular office; the Organist being one of those whom the Worshipful Master 'may' appoint. His duties are set forth in the following optional address, which may be delivered to him when he is invested with the jewel of his Office, as follows:

'Bro....., I appoint you Organist of the Lodge, and I now invest you with the Jewel of your Office. The Lyre is the emblem of Music; one of the seven liberal Arts and Sciences, the study of which is inculcated in the Fellow-Crafts' Degree. The records of Ancient History, both sacred and secular, testify that from the earliest times Music has borne a more or less important part in the celebration of religious rites and ceremonies; that Pagans and Monotheists, the Ancient Hebrews, and the more comparatively modern Christians, have in all Ages made full and free use of music, as an aid to devotion, and in the expression of praise and thanksgiving in the services of their several systems of religion. In like manner Freemasonry, from the earliest period of its history, has availed itself of the aid of music in the performance of its rites and ceremonies; and we must all feel how much of impressiveness and solemnity is derived from the judicious introduction of instrumental music into those ceremonies. Music has been defined as "the concord of sweet sounds." In this aspect it typifies the concord and harmony which have always been among the foremost characteristics of our Order. Your Jewel, therefore, the emblem of Concord, should stimulate us to promote and to maintain concord, goodwill, and affection, not only among the members of our own Lodge, but with all Brethren of the Craft.'

* * * *

A few words must, however, be added upon the subject of the musical services in the three degrees.

Any Brother who visits other Lodges is able to mark the contrast between a Ceremony performed with accompanying instrumental music, and one without that accompaniment, and in which the voice of the Worshipful Master alone is heard from the beginning to the end, with only the slight break here and there of the little which the Wardens have to say. The impression made upon the mind of the Candidate by the musical addition to the Ceremony is far deeper, and consequently is calculated to be far more enduring than that formed by a Ceremony unrelieved by the effect of the Divine Art of Music.

Great care must be taken to exercise this art within the boundaries of the Constitutions.

At one time there was a tendency to introduce the singing of hymns and anthems during the ceremonies, the perambulations, and at certain noticeable points.

This was dangerous. Masonry is universal, and finds adherents among the followers of many creeds, demanding from them only the common acknowledgment of a supreme Governor of the Universe.

Hymns and anthems, therefore, which would seem innocuous to some might contain words and references which, if vocalized, would offend others; and thus friction might arise.

It was in these circumstances that on April 20, 1875, the Board of General Purposes passed a resolution that: 'Hymns form no part of the Masonic Ritual; and the singing of hymns in a Lodge is an innovation to which the Board of General Purposes strongly objects.'

On June 17, 1902, there was a Resolution of the Board of General Purposes reaffirming above; and on September 3, 1902, a similar Resolution was reported by the Board of General Purposes to Grand Lodge, and adopted.

There is no objection to singing the Masonic Opening Ode before the Lodge is opened; and none to singing the Masonic Closing Ode after the Lodge is closed.

There is no objection to chanting 'So mote it be' at the conclusion of the Prayers because that is part of the Ritual.

What is objected to is the interpolation of words not found in the Ritual. Thus, while there is no objection to the Organist playing a kyrie eleison at the conclusion of the Obn., there is objection to the Brethren singing the words, although free from dogma.

The plain rule to be deduced is therefore that no words other than those used in the Ritual may be sung in any part of the ceremonies.

There are many points in the ceremony when the introduction of suitable instrumental music is very useful; but it should always be unobtrusive, furnishing a gentle accompaniment to a solemn occasion; in fact, when it becomes noticeable it is a nuisance.

* * * *

Besides the musical portions of the ceremonies within the Lodge, it often becomes the pleasurable duty of the Organist to arrange and supervise the musical entertainment during and following the Banquet.

On important occasions, such as Installation, professional artistes are usually engaged by the W. M.; but on ordinary occasions it is possible to construct an enjoyable programme by the aid of the talent of the members. (See p. 355.)

This scheme of pleasure is not restricted to musical performance. Many greatly varying items may be included—*e.g.*, Anecdotes, Glees, Part Songs, Recitations, Sleight-of-hand, Records of Travel, Masonic Facts, and even Masonic Fictions.

It is respectfully submitted that so-called 'comic songs' should be rigidly avoided, and that no 'smoking-room stories' of questionable colour should be permitted.

CHAPTER XXIII

THE TYLER AND HIS DUTIES

IT will be convenient at this stage of our work to consider in some detail the multifarious duties of that very useful Officer the Tyler, some of whose duties will be found to have a distinct bearing upon our subject.

We will first, however, discuss briefly the Tyler himself, and consider what manner of man he should be. Experience gained in a number of different Lodges enables one to divide them into at least three classes.

The first of these would consist of old Past Masters. These are now comparatively few in number, and are gradually becoming more and more rarely to be found. These may be subdivided into two classes, one class consisting of those who continue to subscribe to the Lodge, and are unwilling to be out of Office, and who perform the duties of Tyler with perfect efficiency without fee or reward. The other subdivision will include those 'who perhaps from circumstances of unavoidable calamity,' etc., are glad to retain their connection with

Freemasonry by serving the Office of Tyler, the fees of membership being remitted, and the small emoluments of the Office being of value to them in their low estate.

The second main division would comprise members of certain Lodges in which it is the custom to have no permanent Tyler, paid or otherwise, that Office being year by year filled by a junior member, and constituting the first step upon the Official ladder, and without which no one can attain to any higher Office.

This custom has certain advantages. It goes to the very root of the matter, and if the aspirant should go on step by step through all the gradations of Office, until he attains to the chair of Worshipful Master, his experience will be unquestionable, and he will have the satisfaction of feeling that, having begun at the very beginning, he has literally worked his way upward to the Chair. Against this custom may be set the disadvantages of the want of age and of experience in the work of the Lodge. Zeal and ability, care and attention, will, however, soon enable even the youngest in experience to perform his duty with a fair degree of efficiency and success.

The third, and by far the most numerous division, will comprise those who are paid for their services (excluding the second subdivision of the Past Masters mentioned in the first division). Some of these are Initiated with this express intention. They are called 'serving brethren,' and in many Lodges they act as waiters at Banquets, etc. Where Lodges are held in Hotels, it is not unfrequently thought desirable to initiate one of the waiters (preferably the head of his department), but in this case he does not always undertake the duties of Tyler.

Other paid Tylers are older Freemasons (who have not passed the Chair) who have fallen upon evil days, and who are glad to serve the Lodge in a humble capacity, and to receive the small emoluments of the Office, and who rank as ordinary members of the Lodge, but without paying any subscriptions. These are as a rule faithful and efficient Officers, zealous and energetic in the performance of their duties.

Some mention should be made of those who have formerly been members of Military Lodges—generally pensioners—and, foremost among these, retired non-commissioned officers are especially to be commended. If they possess medals and a goodly number of clasps, and have testimonials of good conduct, as most of them have, so much the better. Old soldiers, if they have encouraged habits of sobriety, may be depended upon to keep sober under all circumstances. They have in addition learned the lesson of perfect obedience. They have been accustomed to rigid discipline, and have become strict disciplinarians themselves, and when— in the event of any public procession of the Order—they march at the head of their Lodge, they handle the sword and set and maintain the pace as few civilians are able to do.

* * * *

The duties defined in the address to the Tyler at his Investiture, and partially repeated by the Junior Warden in the opening of the Lodge in the First Degree, are these: 'To see that the Candidates are properly prepared; to give the proper reports on the door of the Lodge, when candidates, members, or visitors require admission; to keep off all intruders and cowans to masonry, and suffer none to pass but such as are duly qualified.'

In addition to the before-named duties of a Tyler, others of equal importance and indispensably necessary to the working of the Lodge, and to the convenience of the Officers and Brethren, come within the scope of his supervision. The furniture and implements, the collars and jewels, and, in short, all the belongings of the Lodge, are under his care, and he is responsible for their being kept always in good condition. He has to prepare the Lodge for all its meetings, and to see that everything that can be required in each Degree shall be in its proper place ready for use.

The Tyler's multifarious duties have much to do with 'Freemasonry and its Etiquette,' which may be freely rendered, as 'the right way in which to do the right thing, at the right time, and in the right place.' This, applied to the work of the Lodge through the several Degrees, will show that the Tyler, in the preparation of the Lodge, and in providing that everything that can possibly be wanted shall be in its proper place, has a very close connection with the subject of this treatise.

Foremost among all the duties previously detailed, must be mentioned the duty of the preparation of the Candidates in each of the Degrees, and of a thorough comprehension of the theory and practice of the Ks. or proper reports on the door of the Lodge. The word 'theory' may well be applied to both these subjects, for one can seldom go wrong in the practice of either of them if one knows the reason why a certain form is practised at one time and not at another. These subjects will be discussed in the following pages.

*   *   *   *

PREPARATION OF CANDIDATES

Attention may here be called to the desirability of the Director of Ceremonies (or some Past Master) leaving the Lodge and superintending the preparation of the Candidates in each Degree, or, at least, inspecting them before they claim admission. The Tyler is liable to have his attention distracted by members or visitors coming or going, by having to answer the Ks. upon the door when the Lodge is being opened in the higher Degrees; and in many ways his thoughts may be diverted from the work in hand; and a mistake may be made in the preparation of the Candidate, however efficient generally the Tyler may be.

Another equally cogent reason may be given for the Tyler having the assistance of some Past Master. In the preparation of a Candidate for the Ceremony of Initiation, there are certain processes which may well cause some surprise in the mind of a stranger. In such a case—perhaps it would be well to say in all cases—it is desirable that a Past Master should assure the Candidate that nothing is being done without a meaning; that there is a good historical or traditional reason for every detail; and that in due time the whole will be explained, and will be made perfectly clear to him.

Probably some few of the Officers and Brethren who witness or assist at this preparation of a Candidate for Initiation are themselves partially, or even totally, unaware of these reasons. In order that such of those as may read these pages may be instructed upon this subject, and that when in office they may be enabled to give the assurance contained in the previous paragraph with perfect truthfulness, a full explanation, of the origin of and the reasons for the several processes of the preparation, is here given.

Preparation in the First Degree

The following explanation consists chiefly of excerpts from the second section of the First Lecture.

The Candidate is divested of m....l and h. w. d., his r. a. l. b. and k. m. b., his r. h. s. s. and a c. t. placed about his n.

He is divested of all m....l, firstly, that he may bring nothing offensive or defensive into the Lodge to disturb its harmony; secondly, having been received into Freemasonry in a state of p....y, he should always thereafter be mindful of his duty to relieve indigent Brethren, as far as may be consistent with his own circumstances in life, and with the needs, and more especially with the merits, of the applicant; and thirdly, because at the erection of King Solomon's Temple 'there was not heard the sound of metallic tool.' Following the pious example of King Solomon at the building of the Temple, we do not permit the Candidate to enter the Lodge with any metallic substance about him, except such as may necessarily belong to the articles of clothing which he may have upon him.

In 1872 the then Grand Secretary, Bro. Hervey, wrote a letter, *with the personal approval of the Grand Master*, stating 'that in the present day the rule was to be taken to represent metals of value, money, or weapons.'

The Candidate is h. w., firstly, that in the event of his refusal to go through any of the Ceremonies which are usual in the Initiation of a Freemason, he may be led out of the Lodge without discovering its form; secondly, as he is admitted into Freemasonry in a s. of d., it should remind him to keep all the world so with respect to our Masonic mysteries, unless they come legally by them, as he is then about to do; and, thirdly, that his heart may conceive before his eyes are permitted to discover.

The r. a. of the Candidate is m. b., to show that he is able and ready to labour; his l. b. is made b., so that nothing may be interposed between it and the p. of the P. extended thereto by the Inner Guard at the door of the Lodge; and further, in order to distinguish beyond a doubt the sex of the Candidate. The l. k. is m. b., in accordance with the immemorial custom of the Order, which prescribes that the Obn. of an Entered Apprentice shall always be taken upon the l. k. b. and b.

The r. h. is s. s., in allusion to a certain passage of Scripture, where the Lord spake thus to Moses from the Burning Bush: 'Put off thy shoes from thy feet, for the place whereon thou standest is holy ground.'

The Candidate has a c. t., with a r. n. about his n., to render any attempt at retreat equally fatal.

This completes the preparation in the First Degree, and, being thus properly prepared, he is conducted to the door of the L., where, after having sought in his mind, asked of his friends, and knocked, the door of Freemasonry is opened to him, and after strict examination he is admitted.

The Tyler and his Duties

Then, after solemn prayer, being neither naked nor clothed, barefoot nor shod, but in an humble, halting, moving posture, the Candidate is led round the Lodge, figuratively to represent his seeming state of poverty and distress.

PREPARATION IN THE SECOND DEGREE

The Candidate's preparation in the Second Degree is in a manner somewhat similar to the former, save that in this degree he is not h. w. His l. a. b. and r. k. are m. b. and his l. h. s. s. He is admitted by the Ks. of an E. A. on the S.

PREPARATION IN THE THIRD DEGREE

The Candidates b. as b. bs. and b. ks. are m. b. and b. hs. s.s. He is admitted by the Ks. of a F. C. on b. ps. of the Cs. presented to b. bs.

*　　*　　*　　*

REPORTS

The next subject in connection with the duties of the Tyler which demands our attention is the series of Ks. or reports on the door of the Lodge. Either from carelessness or from an innate maladroitness, the Ks. are too often jumbled, or so imperfectly sounded as to necessitate correction, which to a great extent interferes with the smooth and correct working of the Lodge. The Ks. severally of the three Degrees are simple in the extreme, and when the theory of their arrangement is once understood, a mistake need never be made in giving them.

When a Candidate for Initiation is conducted to the door, the Ks. of the Can. must be given by the Tyler, in allusion to an ancient and venerable exhortation: seek and ye shall find; ask, and ye shall have; knock, and it shall be opened unto you.'

(See remarks on p. 161.)

When a Candidate for Passing is brought to the door (the Lodge being at that time open in the Second Degree), the Ks. of the First Degree should be given, in order that the Brethren within the Lodge may be warned that one who is not a Fellow-Craft is seeking admission.

The same reason exactly applies to the Third Degree. When the Candidate for Raising is brought to the door the Ks. of the Second Degree should be given, and the Brethren within the Lodge are thereby informed that the Candidate (necessarily a Fellow-Craft) seeks admission.

The Tyler and his Duties

In brief; for a Candidate in the First Degree the Ks. of the Can.; for a Candidate in the Second Degree, the Ks. of an Entered Apprentice; and for a Candidate in the Third Degree, the Ks. of a Fellow-Craft.

When the Lodge is open in the First Degree, for a member or a well-known Visitor seeking admission, the Ks. of the E.A. Degree are given by the Tyler. In the Second Degree, for a member or a visitor who is known to have taken that Degree, the Ks. of the F.C. Degree are given. In the Third Degree for a member or visitor those of the M.M. are given. In each and in all of these cases the Ks. so given are respectively the Ks. of the Degree in which the Lodge is opened at that particular time.

In the case of late comers, the Tyler should be particularly careful not to disturb the Lodge by making his announcement on the door of the Lodge at an inconvenient moment. If, for example, a ceremony is in progress, it must not be interrupted except at recognized points; and, however important the late arrival may be, the Tyler must remember that the interests of the Candidate are even more important.

* * * *

ADMISSION OF VISITORS

Pleased as we are to receive Visitors, their admission into our Lodges should be the subject of careful attention.

The W. M. promises that no Visitor shall be received into his Lodge without due examination and producing proper vouchers of his having been initiated in a Regular Lodge.

Most of our Visitors are naturally our own friends who are members of English Lodges, and about them there is no need to say anything. The fact that they are introduced by members of the Lodge is ample warranty, and quite sufficient authority to the Tyler to announce them. But occasionally come Visitors from other Constitutions, and then arises the necessity for caution. In the event of a stranger professing to be a Freemason seeking admission, the Tyler should immediately summon the Junior Warden to his aid, so that the responsibility of either granting or refusing admission to the Lodge may not rest upon himself alone. Etiquette, even ordinary politeness, requires that a probably well-qualified Brother shall not be turned back simply upon the *ipse dixit* of the Tyler, but that one of the Principal Officers of the Lodge—that is, the Junior Warden—shall be the arbiter in such a case.

The Tyler and his Duties

It is not sufficient that the Brother himself should express his belief in the G. A. O. T. U. He must have been initiated on the V. S. L. in a Lodge acknowledging the same supremacy. There is no compromise possible, and no exception may be made. All strangers must be proved with Masonic rigidity, and the Tyler must suffer none to pass but such as are duly qualified.

* * * *

A custom appears to prevail in the United States of admitting strangers who profess to be Freemasons, but who have no friend or acquaintance to vouch for them, who have with them no certificate, and who apparently are subjected to little or no examination, but who nevertheless are received into the Lodge upon taking that which they call the Tyler's obligation. This is, in plain English, the meaning of the words in italics in the following extract from Bro. Dr. Mackey's Masonic Law. The words mentioned are capable of being thus paraphrased: '. . . they may still be admitted by the production of their certificate, or by an examination as to their knowledge of Freemasonry; or, dispensing with both these safeguards, they may be admitted by the Tyler's obligation.' A very loose and reprehensible custom, which we devoutly hope may never be imported into this country. The extract runs thus:

'But many brethren who are desirous of visiting are strangers and sojourners, without either friends or acquaintance amongst the members to become their vouchers, in which case they may still be admitted *by certificate, examination, or the aid of the sacred volume*—commonly called the Tyler's obligation, which in the United States runs in the following form: "I, A. B., do hereby and hereon solemnly and sincerely swear that I have been regularly initiated, passed, and raised to the sublime degree of a Master Mason in a just and legally constituted Lodge; that I do not stand suspended or expelled, and know of no reason why I should not hold Masonic communication with my Brethren."' The doctor concludes with the dictum: 'And this is all that Freemasonry needs to provide'! We in England think this is not *all* by a very long way.

CHAPTER XXIV

MISCELLANEOUS MATTERS

LODGES usually have two classes of Members. those who pay a full rate of subscription, which is fixed to cover Banquets, etc.; and those who pay a lower rate, which does not include, or which does only partially include, refreshments, as may be fixed by the By-laws.

The former are usually termed Full Members or Dining Members (happy phrase!). The latter are usually styled Country Members or Non-Dining Members.

No such distinction is recognized so far as Grand Lodge is concerned.

The same Quarterage is payable to Grand Lodge, and they are all equally Members of the Lodge, and have the same right of voting.

In some Lodges Country Membership is considered a disqualification for Office, and common sense and convenience generally would seem to support that view; but apart from any By-law bearing on the subject, there does not seem to be any constitutional disability which would preclude a Non-Dining Member from accepting Office if able to discharge its duties satisfactorily.

* * * *

In some Lodges, where the rate of subscription is insufficient to cover all the outgoings, especially where some of those outgoings are of a personal nature (such as a Past Master's Jewel), there may be found a more or less surreptitious form of income under the denomination of Fees of Honour.

This impost is usually levied in a graduated scale upon all the Officers of the year. Commencing at, say, 10s. from the Inner Guard, 20s. from the Junior Deacon, 30s. from the Senior Deacon, 40s. from the Junior Warden, 50s. from the Senior Warden, 60s. from the Worshipful Master, it amounts to the respectable sum of £10 10s.

This is the amount which many Lodges vote to the Master's List if he goes up, as he ought during his year of Office, as a Steward for one of the Great Masonic Charities.

* * * *

The subject of Honorary Membership is hedged with difficulties. The status of an Honorary Member must be strictly confined to the Lodge which so elects him, and can in no way give him any position in the Craft outside the door of that Lodge.

He cannot therefore hold any Office in the Lodge, or vote on any subject which might even remotely affect the Craft at large.

In short, his status and privileges as an Honorary Member entitle him to attend the meetings, and partake of its refreshments, without the necessity of being introduced by a subscribing member. Honorary Members have no other right or privilege whatever.

Until recently there was an additional pitfall. Constitution No. 127 says: 'No Brother who has ceased to be a subscribing member of a Lodge shall be permitted to visit any one Lodge more than once until he again become a subscribing member of some Lodge,' and this Law was invoked against an Honorary Member who had been unfortunate enough to bring himself within its provisions (by a Secretary who must have desired to exemplify that 'the letter killeth, but the Spirit giveth Life'). Accordingly, March 4, 1914, Grand Lodge added: 'But this Rule shall not apply to the visits of a Brother to any Lodge of which he has been elected a non-subscribing or Honorary Member.'

This is the first recognition by the Book of Constitutions of an Honorary Member.

An Honorary Member must not be included in the Returns to Grand Lodge. Even his refreshment is a matter of doubt in the minds of the meticulous. It is suggested that the above phraseology merely entitles the Honorary Member to dispense with an introduction to the table; but that he must pay for his own meal!

It is apprehended, however, that if the Lodge Subscription covers, as is usual, the subsequent refreshment, the Honorary Membership of that Lodge would do so likewise.

A Brother is even ineligible for Honorary Membership while he is an ordinary member of the Lodge in which it is proposed to 'honour' him.

It will be seen therefore that current and generally accepted ideas as to Honorary Membership, and the dignity thereby conferred, are not applicable in Freemasonry.

An Honorary Membership of a Lodge would appear to be a negligible quantity (such as when conferred on Consecrating Officers, who are never likely to see the inside of that Lodge again), and not by any means to be classed as a reward (*e.g.*) for meritorious service to a Lodge rendered by one who has perhaps been a member of it for many years, and who, with increasing age and diminishing resources, might have gladly accepted such honorary membership as a token of appreciation.

Grand Lodge recognizes, as Members of Lodges, only those whose dues to Grand Lodge are duly paid, and whose subscriptions to the Lodge are not further in arrear than the By-laws of the Lodge, and ultimately the Constitutions (B. of C., 148), permit. The dues to Grand Lodge must be paid in respect of Secretaries (and others) whose services are considered equivalent to their subscription (B. of C., 104).

A Lodge has no power to elect a Life Member, and Grand Lodge does not permit the commutation of future dues by a single payment or otherwise.

It would seem, therefore, that an Honorary Member is not a Member of the Lodge at all.

He possesses:—

(a) The ordinary unrestricted right common to all Masons of visiting the Lodge, without invitation, so long as he is a Subscribing Member of some other Lodge (Const. 167).

(b) The recently conferred right of visiting unrestrictedly the Lodge (in which he has the title of

Honorary Member), even though he is not a Subscribing Member of some other Lodge (Const. 127, as amended).

(c) The right to sit at the table of the Lodge without invitation (the question of payment for his refreshment being determined by the custom of the Lodge).

(d) The right to employ his Honorary Membership as a cloak to conceal the fact that he is really a Visitor, though signing the Attendance Book as a Member.

*   *   *   *

It sometimes happens that a Warden of a Lodge is unable or unwilling to accept election as Master, and therefore he stands aside.

This is unfortunate, as when he ceases to be a Warden he ceases to have the right to attend Grand Lodge.

*   *   *   *

If, however, he has completed his full year of service as Invested Warden (see p. 92), he will always be eligible, *cæteris paribus*, in any Lodge, as its Worshipful Master, without any further qualifying period of service as Warden.

It occasionally happens that from circumstances quite beyond control the investiture of a Warden does not take place on the regular date of Installation, and the full qualifying period cannot be legally satisfied. In such a case—but only on good cause shown—a remedy may be provided by Dispensation (Const. 109).

It has also been known that a Warden served part of a year as Junior Warden and part of a year as Senior Warden, and under the special circumstances of his case the broken periods (amounting to sixteen months) were allowed to be equivalent to the regulation year from Installation to Installation.

*　　*　　*　　*

When a Brother, usually the Senior Warden, has been elected to fill the Worshipful Master's Chair for the ensuing year, he receives the title of Master-Elect. It is quite wrong to style him 'Worshipful-Master-Elect,' as he does not become entitled to the prefix 'Worshipful' until he has been 'placed in the Chair of K.S. according to ancient Custom.'

It often happens, however, that a Brother who is already a Past Master in another Lodge is elected to the Master's Chair.

That Brother, being already entitled to the prefix 'Worshipful,' is, in fact, a Worshipful Master-Elect (not a Worshipful-Master Elect); but in view of the confusion likely to arise in the minds of junior Members, it is most advisable to adhere in all cases to the term 'Master-Elect.'

*   *   *   *

As regards the necessity of confirming the [Minutes of] the Election of Master before the Installation Ceremony can proceed (p. 156), the employment of the word 'Minutes' in Law 105 is perhaps a little misleading in this connection. It is the election itself which must be confirmed, and until the election is so confirmed the Master is not 'deemed to be elected.' The interval is evidently intended as an opportunity for reflection on so important a subject. Minutes as such can only be confirmed or rejected on the score of their accuracy or inaccuracy of record. Strictly speaking, therefore, if the Minutes of a Lodge accurately record *inter alia* the fact of the election of a Master, the Minutes ought to be confirmed even though the election itself be not confirmed.

The motion for the non-confirmation of the election might properly be based on the substantial ground of a change of opinion; or on the more formal ground that the Master-Elect was not eligible, and that consequently his election was invalid; or on the technical ground that the election itself was improperly conducted, and was, therefore, void.

Neither of these reasons would form a proper basis for refusing to confirm the Minutes.

The principle, therefore, cannot be too clearly urged upon the attention of Masters and Secretaries that the mere formal confirmation of the Minutes does not *ipso facto* include, however much it may imply, the confirmation of those matters mentioned in the Minutes which may in themselves require confirmation.

Those matters 'arise out of the Minutes,' and should be so dealt with.

* * * *

A reigning Worshipful Master is not only paramount in his own Lodge, but he is entitled to precedence over all Past Masters during his year of Office.

* * * *

The status of a Past Master of a Lodge is not achieved solely through having been elected and installed as Worshipful Master of that Lodge.

A Worshipful Master must have filled that office in that Lodge for one year (see Const., No. 9) (and that year is usually, though not invariably, counted from the regular date of Installation 'until the next regular period of election within this Lodge and [not or] until a successor shall have been duly elected and installed in his stead') before he becomes entitled to rank as a Past Master of that particular Lodge; so that if for any cause a Worshipful Master is displaced before the completion of his period or 'year of Office,' he thereby, and to that extent, fails to become entitled to the position and status of a Past Master of that Lodge. It is conceivable that he might be already, or might subsequently become, otherwise qualified for that position.

Having regard to the obligation taken by a Master-Elect, the voluntary resignation of his Office by a Worshipful Master is not contemplated by the Constitutions; indeed, it would be quite unmasonic, and in a strict sense illegal.

Constitution 119 provides that 'if the Master shall die, be removed, or be rendered incapable of discharging the duties of his office . . .' (see p. 94).

Now, it is not at all clear by whom the Master could 'be removed.' Certainly his own Lodge has no power to remove him. And if the conduct of the Master were such as to justify his impeachment before Grand Lodge, his rights and privileges as Master and Past Master would be determined by, or deducible from, the judgment of that august Tribunal.

If the Master were 'rendered incapable'— *e.g.*, by accident or illness of body or mind, no doubt his year of office would run its normal course, the Lodge being ruled in his absence in accordance with the provisions of Constitution 119.

Therefore the mere absence, from whatever cause, of an Installed Master during the greater part of his year of office is not necessarily or *ipso facto* a disqualification for his Past-Mastership of that particular Lodge.

Occasionally, however, a vacancy occurs by the death of the Worshipful Master, and consequently a broken period has to be filled. In such a case it is advisable to elect a Past Master of the Lodge to fill the vacancy, as the broken period would not qualify a new occupant of the Chair for a Past Mastership, and to complete the full year would necessitate breaking in upon another regular year, and so on.

On the other hand, an Installed Master of an English Lodge becomes thereby entitled to certain privileges as such. For example, he becomes entitled to attend any Board of Installed Masters under English, Irish, or Scotch Constitutions, and to count as one of necessary quorum. If invited to do so, but not unless, he may preside, and may instal a Master under the English Constitution; and he may do the like under Irish or Scotch Constitutions in the remote contingency that no Master or Past Master of that Lodge's own Constitution is present.

Of course, a Past Master of any Lodge retains the privileges of Grand Lodge to which he has become entitled so long as he continues a subscribing member of any Lodge (see p. 60).

When a Past Master of a Lodge visits another Lodge, he is not legally entitled to sit with the Past Masters of that Lodge on the left of the Worshipful Master. To do so would be to displace some Past Master of that Lodge, and would therefore be a breach of etiquette.

When a Past Master joins another Lodge (see p. 164), he is entitled to sit with the Past Masters of that Lodge according to the rule of precedence there mentioned.

A Brother who becomes a Past Master of one Lodge while remaining an ordinary member of another or others, becomes, under the same rule, entitled to rank and precedence in all Lodges of which he is a member, without altering his number on the Lodge List.

* * * *

On vacating the Master's Chair, the Immediate Past Master finds himself on a pedestal entirely his own. His title is recognized in the Constitutions, and in the Ritual; his place in the Lodge is settled by established custom; and on certain occasions, notably in the absence of the Master, he has the first right to the Master's Chair; but his rank and precedence are nowhere defined. He is not mentioned in the Table of Precedence of Regular Officers. His status is, apparently, the growth of immemorial usage.

In the Lodge he sits on the immediate left of the Master.

Most Lodges assign to him during the year of his Immediate Past Mastership a precedence ranking immediately after the Worshipful Master and before the Wardens, though how far this can be theoretically justified is open to doubt, as the Government of the Lodge is vested in the Master and his two Wardens, *tria juncta in uno* (see 'Landmarks,' p. 65).

Nevertheless, he is a very useful sort of

person, and no one grudges him the consolations which accompany and, let us hope, soften his journey from his high estate of Worshipful Master through the paths of his Immediate Past Mastership, to the abysmal depths of his position as Junior Past Master, from which only the lucky incident of a Past Master joining can save him.

* * * *

Should a member be three years in arrear he thereupon ceases to be a member of the Lodge, and can only become a member again by regular proposition and ballot. Secretaries and others whose services to the Lodge are deemed equivalent to the payment of their subscriptions should see that due provision concerning them is made in the By-laws of the Lodge, otherwise trouble may arise.

* * * *

The length of the Cable Tow is the distance within which attendance at the Lodge is deemed obligatory upon a Master Mason. In the old charges it varies from five to fifty miles. Nowadays it seems to be made of elastic. The collars worn by the Officers are said to be survivals of the Cable Tow.

* * * *

Miscellaneous Matters

In these days of feminine association with some masonic and semi-masonic functions, such as Ladies' Festivals, Lodge Dances, etc., and the consequent admission of non-Masons of both sexes to Banquets, etc., it may not be amiss to recall what the Antient Charges enjoin with respect to 'Behaviour in presence of strangers not masons:—

'You shall be cautious in your words and carriage that the most penetrating stranger shall not be able to discover or find out what is not proper to be intimated.'

And with respect to 'Behaviour at home and in your neighbourhood':—

'You are to act as becomes a moral and wise man; particularly not to let your family, friends, and neighbours, know the concerns of the Lodge, etc.'

* * * *

Dispensations are permission granted (on due cause shown) by the M.W.G.M. for a temporary or occasional infraction of the General Law.

Dispensations are frequently required in the administration of a Lodge—*e.g.*, to hold a Lodge on an irregular date or at an unusual place; to wear Masonic clothing in Public—*i.e.*, outside the Lodge; to be Worshipful Master of more than one Lodge at the same time; to continue as Worshipful Master of a Lodge for more than two years; to initiate more than five Candidates on the same occasion; to initiate any person under the age of twenty-one. All these and other occasional circumstances require a Dispensation and, needless to add, a fee—10s. 6d. for London, 5s. for a Province.

Apart from the benefit thus created for the Fund of General Purposes, these Dispensations are of value as manifestations of loyalty to the Constitutions and as indications of good Masonic discipline.

* * * *

One of the proudest moments of a Freemason's early career is that when he receives his Certificate from Grand Lodge. It is of course signed by him at the Secretary's table in open Lodge, and the Worshipful Master should then present it to the newly-fledged Master Mason with appropriate words, which will ring in his ears and be remembered by him in years to come, even as the Senior Warden's address when investing him with the badge can never be effaced from his memory.

* * * *

'The Charges of a Freemason extracted from the Antient Records of Lodges beyond Sea, and of those in England, Scotland, and

Ireland, for the Use of Lodges, to be read at the making of new Brethren, or when the Master shall order it,' will be found *in extenso* in the Book of Constitutions.

These Ancient Charges are, unfortunately, greatly neglected in the majority of Lodges, and it is suggested that the Worshipful Master of every Lodge should find or create opportunity for their being read at least once during his year of Office.

When there is 'no work to do,' the time could not be better occupied than in reminding ourselves of what our Ancient Brethren considered the Code of Good and True Men.

The announcement of such intention on the Summons convening the meeting would add importance to the occasion.

William Preston, in his 'Illustrations of Masonry' (twelfth edition), writes:—

'A rehearſal of the Ancient Charges properly ſucceeds the opening and precedes the cloſing of the Lodge. This was the conſtant practice of our ancient brethren, and ought never to be neglected in our regular aſſemblies. A recapitulation of our duty cannot be diſagreeable to thoſe who are acquainted with it; and to thoſe to whom it is not known, ſhould any ſuch be, it muſt be highly proper to recommend it.'

*　　*　　*　　*

Strictly speaking, the Charge after Initiation ought to be delivered by the Master himself, and, of course, from the Master's Chair.

If a Past Master delivers it, he should temporarily occupy the Master's Chair for that purpose.

If the Master is unwilling to vacate his position, although delegating some of his duties, the next best thing is for the Past Master to deliver the Charge from the left of the Worshipful Master; and if a Warden or a brother of lesser degree be invited to deliver it, it should be recited from the left of the Worshipful Master. The Warden should not deliver it from his Pedestal, and the position of the Candidate at the left of the Senior Warden's Pedestal should not be varied.

* * * *

Any procedure by which the secrecy of the Ballot is or may be infringed is entirely irregular. Consequently a proposal—usually made on the score of 'saving time'—that the 'Ballot shall vest in the Worshipful Master' is quite out of order.

Any public announcement by a Brother of how he intends to vote, or how he has voted, is an infringement of the secrecy of the ballot, and may entail the annulment of the proceedings.

If the Master, on inspecting the Ballot Box, has reason to believe that by some accident or carelessness the result of the ballot is not what was intended, he may, in his absolute discretion, order a Second Ballot to be taken then and there, warning the Brethren of the fatal consequences of a second mistake.

* * * *

A few words may not be out of place as to the Ethics of Balloting. Although the use of the black ball is provided for in the Constitutions, and although the power of employing it is one which it is essential to possess, and to keep in reserve, it is a power which should only be employed in extreme cases. There are other means of effecting the same object more masonically.

If there are serious reasons for objecting to the admission of a new Member, representation may be made, confidentially if need be (but, better, quite openly), to the Standing Committee, or, if that does not exist, to the Worshipful Master or Secretary. In this way opportunity may be given to the Proposer to withdraw the name without the infliction of any indignity upon the Candidate.

Hundreds of reasons may be considered sufficient reasons for refusal of admission, without implying any reflection on the Candidate. Even personal dislike or political differences—though not very noble—can be understood and accepted as amply sufficient, as it is inadvisable to introduce into a Lodge any element likely to cause resignations or destroy the Love and Harmony which should characterize all Freemasons.

The Golden Rule is the unfailing Guide, and happy the Lodge whose Minutes record the passing of its Resolutions 'unanimously'!

* * * *

There are various Rules and Regulations as to voting in Lodge, according to the subject-matter of discussion.

Rule 105, Book of Constitutions, provides on the occasion of the ballot for the election of a Master for a bare majority of those present who vote—that is to say, if there are any present who do not vote, their abstention from voting does not count against the Candidate for the Chair.

The same principle applies in the case of the ballot for a Candidate for Initiation (see p. 165), the ballot for a Joining Member

(p. 164), the ballot for the Treasurer (p. 93), and the show of hands for the Tyler (p. 93).

All the general questions which come before the Lodge are determined by show of hands and a bare majority (see p. 338). But for the removal of a Lodge a majority is required of two-thirds of those present who vote at a special meeting convened for the purpose (Const. 141*b*).

In the case of a formal complaint by the Master against any of the Officers, Const. 120 provides that the matter shall be dealt with at a Regular Meeting, with seven days' notice in writing to the Brother complained of (see p. 94).

Nothing is said about the matter appearing in the Agenda of the Summons convening the meeting.

In this case a majority of the Brethren present is required, and it is apprehended that if there were any present who did not vote, their abstention from voting would be counted against the complaint.

In the case of a proposal to exclude a Member, Const. 181 provides that the power of exclusion can only be exercised by a majority of not less than two-thirds of the Members present at a meeting appointed for the consideration of the complaint of which the said Member shall have had due notice.

Nothing is said about giving notice to the other Members in the Summons convening the meeting, but it is assumed that such notice would be given.

In these circumstances, if there were any Brethren present who did not vote, their abstention from voting would count against the motion for exclusion.

Assuming, therefore, an attendance of, say, thirty-five, twenty-four would have to vote for the motion to entitle the Master to declare it carried.

The Second or Casting Vote of the Master in the Chair (p. 99) should (if necessitated) be judiciously exercised, and, generally speaking, should be used to negative the proposal, and to preserve the *status quo ante*.

It is a counsel of perfection to suggest that motions should as far as possible be carried unanimously.

In every case, however, a ready acquiescence in all votes and resolutions duly passed by a majority of the Brethren is expected from all good Masons.

*   *   *   *

A Resignation of Membership is effectual and irrevocable as soon as it is communicated to the Lodge; it may be withdrawn by the writer at any time before being so communicated. If a Brother intimates his resignation, and if it is desired to ask him to reconsider his intention, care should be taken not to read his letter to the Lodge until after his final decision has been ascertained.

On the other hand, the resignation, when so communicated to the Lodge, is effective from the date on which it is written, and not from the date on which it is communicated to the Lodge. It does not require 'acceptance'; being complete without it.

On the Minutes it may be 'recorded' with regret.

Resignation takes effect, as above stated, whether dues are in arrear or not; but if any Member resigns without having complied with the By-laws of his Lodge, or with the general regulations of the Craft, he is not eligible to join another Lodge unless and until that Lodge has been made acquainted with his former neglect.

Any Lodge failing to make proper inquiry is liable to pay the arrears due to the other Lodge.

When a Member resigns, he may require a certificate stating the circumstances under which he left, and this must be produced to any Lodge he proposes to join.

In the case of a joining Member who has not resigned, a similar inquiry as to dues must be made, and a certificate procured from the other Lodge or Lodges that he is 'in good standing.'

This certificate is commonly called a Certificate of Clearance.

*　　*　　*　　*

Occasionally it happens that a man wishes to become a Mason in circumstances which necessitate haste, and constitute what is known Masonically as an emergency.

If in the opinion of the Master the emergency be real, he may direct the Secretary to include the necessary particulars of the proposed Candidate in the Summons; and if the ballot be in his favour, he may be Initiated.

This procedure is known as the FIAT of the Worshipful Master. But in no case can a Candidate be initiated unless full particulars appear on the Summons, and at least seven days' notice given.

*　　*　　*　　*

Although a brother has, so long as he continues to be a subscribing member of a Lodge, an inalienable right to visit (if duly vouched) any Regular and Recognized Masonic Lodge without any invitation, and to remain during the whole time of the transaction of its masonic business (see 'Landmarks,' p. 65), there are occasions when it would be good taste to retire voluntarily.

He has, for example, a complete right to hear the reading of the Minutes; and if the conduct of a member were under consideration with a view to his exclusion from the Lodge, the Visitor would have an undoubted right to remain and to hear the discussion, as the decision of such a matter would affect the interests of the whole Craft. He is entitled also to remain during the performance of any ceremony which his masonic rank may entitle him to witness.

On the other hand, discussions as to a Lodge's finances (in which even Grand Lodge has no *locus standi*) are matters in which the presence of a visitor might be irksome, both to himself and the Lodge, and his temporary retirement would be a testimony to his Masonic good feeling.

This right to visit is, however, subject to the power of the Master to refuse admission to any visitor whose presence may disturb the harmony of the Lodge; or to any visitor of known bad character (Const. 126).

* * * *

An Inventory of the Furniture and other possessions of the Lodge should form an

integral part of the annual Audit of the
Accounts of the Lodge; and this opportunity
should be taken to consider the question of
repairs and renewals, thus keeping the Furniture and appointments of the Lodge in a
state of efficiency.

Many — perhaps most — Lodges content
themselves at their Audit with a Statement
of Receipts and Expenditure for the year;
but it is submitted that a Balance Sheet is a
desirable form in which to exhibit the result
of the year's working and the present financial position.

*　　*　　*　　*

When the Board of Installed Masters is
closed, the Master Masons, on re-entering
the Lodge, do not salute until directed to do
so by the Installing Master; but all Master
Masons, Visitors as well as Members, should
pass round and salute. If there are too
many for comfort, perhaps Visitors might
be seated after saluting as M.M.s.

On this subject Brother Henry Sadler, in
his 'Notes on the Ceremony of Installation,'
says: 'I will merely direct attention to
another innovation, which, although of less
moment, is, in my opinion, almost as objectionable. I allude to the practice now in
vogue of visitors below the chair resuming

their seats on their return to the Lodge after the Installation, and not performing the usual perambulations, etc. Certainly no such privilege was allowed in my early days, and I must confess that I fail to see any reason why visitors in particular should be exempt from the customary act of homage and respect paid to the new Presiding Officer. I can only account for the omission by the knowledge that at recent large gatherings of the fraternity, such as Consecration Meetings, the Director of Ceremonies has permitted the visitors to resume their seats—(I presume more as a matter of convenience than for any other reason)—and hence the idea has got abroad that it is the right thing to do at all Installations. I know many old Masons who feel rather strongly on this point, and the sooner we revert to the ancient custom the better it will be for those who, like myself, occasionally perform the ceremony of Installation, and do not believe in innovations, however trivial they may appear, and are sometimes under the necessity of insisting upon visitors taking their places in the ranks instead of acting the part of mere spectators of the proceedings.'

* * * *

Although, for the convenience of working the Programme of Business in the Lodges, it is permissible, after opening in the three Degrees, to 'resume' up and down (see p. 172), the Lodge should, at the conclusion of ceremonial work, always be resumed in the third Degree, and formally closed in each degree. Any other procedure is not only technically incorrect, but implies inability on the part of the Master and his Officers. The excuse of 'want of time' is too thin.

* * * *

The Deacons' Jewel is now, and has been since the Union, officially 'a dove bearing an olive branch'; but 'in the olden time before then' the 'Athol' or 'Antient' Lodges used to employ a figure of Mercury. In some of the older Lodges this emblem is still retained upon the Deacons' collars, presumably through a disinclination to discard such interesting evidences of antiquity.

* * * *

In certain circumstances, and on good cause shown, a Lodge may (with the approval of the M.W. Grand Master) change its name (Const. 98), but not its number.

No provision is made in the Constitutions as to the voting necessary to achieve this result; but official requirements, in certain instances, have been—

(*a*) Notice of Motion, in open Lodge, at a Regular Meeting.

(*b*) Printed Notice, on Summons of such Regular Meeting.

(*c*) Bare majority of those present and voting.

(*d*) Printed Notice of Confirmation on Summons of next Regular Meeting.

(*e*) Bare majority at such meeting.

(*f*) Extracts of Minutes transmitted to Grand Secretary.

(*g*) Endorsement of Warrant, with subsequent publication in the Transactions of Grand Lodge.

* * * *

When the accuracy of the Minutes has been confirmed, either in their original form or as amended, the Minute Book should be taken, by the Senior Deacon, to the Worshipful Master in order that it may be signed by him as a correct record.

In adjusting the Minute Book for signature, the Senior Deacon should take care not to place it on the V.S.L.

In some Lodges the minutes are signed by the Wardens also.

* * * *

No excuse, except sickness or the pressing emergencies of public or private avocations, is available as a justification for failure to attend the duties of the Lodge (see p. 88).

Of course, if an Officer is unavoidably prevented from attending in his place, timely notice to the Worshipful Master, enabling the provision of a substitute, is the least which may be expected; and no doubt this intimation should be accompanied or followed by suitable explanation and apology for absence.

Ordinary members might very well accept it as incumbent on them also (though not perhaps so obligatory) to render similar courtesy to the Worshipful Master in the event of inability to obey the summons.

Such thoughtful manifestations of respect to the Chair are greatly appreciated and reciprocally bring their own reward.

*   *   *   *

Brethren should not be too ready to believe the mere verbal assertion that Grand Lodge wills this, or disapproves of that, as such observations are often made in good faith, but with very imperfect knowledge. The truth or otherwise of such statements is to be discovered without much difficulty through the proper official channels, and in cases of grave doubt or difficulty no Brother need hesitate to make inquiry; he may be sure of a courteous reply, always presuming that the case is of importance. Perhaps we may say that the Secretary of a Lodge would in most cases be the best channel of communication for obtaining information as to all matters affecting the interests of a particular Lodge.

*   *   *   *

We may here mention briefly the mode of addressing any written communication to those in authority over us. No one would be so presumptuous as to address H.R.H. the Grand Master, except in the form of a petition, which would be forwarded to the Grand Secretary. The heading of such a petition will be found in Article 94 of the Book of Constitutions. The Pro. Grand Master is entitled to the prefix Most Worshipful, in virtue of his Office as the immediate representative of the Grand Master. The Deputy-Grand Master, and all Provincial and District Grand Masters, are entitled Right Worshipful. Deputy-Provincial Grand Masters, and the higher Officers of Grand Lodge, including the Grand Secretary and the Grand Registrar, are Very Worshipful. The Master of a Lodge, as every Freemason knows, is entitled Worshipful. Whether it be in oral or written addresses, the several titles should always be strictly observed. We venture, however, again to caution Brethren that all written communications to the higher authorities should always pass through the hands of the Grand, or Provincial, or District Grand Secretary; and, even then, that Brethren should not address those high Officers without good and sufficient reason.

* * * *

The following are the nineteen Lodges now entitled to recommend Grand Stewards:

1.	Grand Master's	(c.), †1759
2.	Antiquity	Time Imm.
4.	Royal Somerset House and Inverness	(c.), Time Imm.
5.	St. George's and Corner Stone,	†1756
6.	Friendship	1721
8.	British	(c.), 1722
14.	Tuscan	(c.), 1722
21.	Emulation	(c.), 1723
23.	Globe	(c.), 1723
26.	Castle Lodge of Harmony	(c.), 1725
28.	Old King's Arms	(c.), 1725
29.	St. Alban's	(c.), 1728
46.	Old Union	(c.), 1735
58.	Felicity	(c.), 1737

c. = Centenary warrant.
† 'Athol' or 'Ancient' Lodge.

60. Peace and Harmony	..	1738
91. Regularity	.. ..	(c.), 1755
99. Shakespeare	.. ..	(c.), 1757
197. Jerusalem	.. ..	(c.), 1771
259. Prince of Wales	.. ..	(c.), 1787

These Lodges are colloquially termed 'Red Apron Lodges,' from the red edging worn on the aprons by their members.

CHAPTER XXV

'THE FESTIVE BOARD'

THE etiquette of the table, or in old Masonic parlance 'the festive board'—Brethren are besought not to call it 'the Fourth Degree'—differs in no material degree from the order and rules observed when a number of men meet and dine or sup together upon any occasion.

It is not generally remembered that theoretically all 'refreshment' is under the immediate supervision of the Junior Warden 'as the ostensible Steward of the Lodge.'

The Worshipful Master will already have announced in Lodge whether the brethren are to dine 'in full Masonic clothing' or only 'officers in collars.'

The duty rests upon the Director of Ceremonies to see that the places at the table for visitors and for members are assigned in accordance with their rank in the Craft; allowing, of course, a certain degree of freedom of choice; that is to say, if a distinguished visitor be assigned a place at, or near the top of the table, and if he prefers a lower seat beside the Brother who introduces him, or with whom he may be more or less intimate, his wish would, of course, be complied with. On the other hand, it would be bad taste for a Brother who bears no rank of any importance to aspire, on the plea of sitting next to a friend, to occupy one of 'the chief seats at feasts, lest haply a more honourable man than he come in,' etc.

Visitors should be ranged in the order of their rank and precedence on the right of the Worshipful Master. The only exception is the Initiate, who, on the night of his Initiation, takes precedence of visitors, Grand Officers included, and sits on the immediate right of the Worshipful Master.

Past Masters of and in the Lodge should be ranged, in the order of their Masonic rank and of their seniority in the Lodge, on the left of the Worshipful Master; the Immediate Past Master being, of course, on his immediate left (pp. 164, 322-323).

There is as a rule more freedom from form and ceremony at the table after the ordinary meetings of the Lodge; still, order and regularity should not be neglected; rules should be observed as far is as compatible with freedom from unnecessary restraint, but they should not by any means be ignored. At Festivals (annual or other) a certain degree of state and ceremony should be observed, and the ordinary rules regulating the proceedings on such occasions should be even more strictly enforced; and precedence should be given to rank and station in the Craft.

* * * *

When Grace is said (that is, when it is not sung), if the Chaplain be present he should say it.

We have a good old Masonic form of 'Grace before meat,' and of 'Grace after meat,' which should not be allowed to fall into disuse. They run thus: 'May T. G. A. O. T. U. bless that which His bounty has provided for us. So mote it be'; and 'May T. G. A. O. T. U. give us grateful hearts, and supply the needs of others. So mote it be.'

* * * *

During the meal the Worshipful Master 'takes wine with the Brethren.' This operation is sometimes performed in sections; and sometimes the ingenuity of the Immediate Past Master or of the Director of Ceremonies is responsible for a great variety of excuses for the 'taking of wine.'

It is usually: 'Brethren, the Worshipful Master will take wine with the Brethren on his left'; then with those 'on the right.'

'The Festive Board'

On these occasions the Worshipful Master should always stand. He is in the capacity of a host welcoming his friends to his table, and courtesy demands that he should rise. It is perhaps for this reason that he makes these occasions collective rather than individual.

The Brethren, on their part, have an inveterate habit of 'challenging' each other in the course of the meal; but even in this free and easy habit etiquette prevails.

No one may challenge the Worshipful Master at all. No one may challenge a Grand Officer or superior officer or senior member. He should wait until the superior or senior challenges him.

Of course in the case of a little forgetfulness or too great absorption of—mind—on the part of the 'high and mighty,' there is nothing to prevent a succession of 'nods, becks, and wreathed smiles' to indicate that the junior is anxious and willing to be challenged.

In this connection it may be remarked that Officers of the Lodge should be spoken to and spoken of by the name of their Office —*e.g.*, 'Worshipful Brother Immediate Past Master,' 'Brother Senior Warden,' 'Worshipful Brother Treasurer,' 'Brother Inner Guard.'

*   *   *   *

347

During refreshment the Stewards should be quietly and unostentatiously active in looking after the comfort and satisfaction of all the Brethren, but especially of the Visitors, that they may be encouraged to wish to come again.

* * * *

The custom of proposing certain regular toasts, and occasionally of drinking to the health of any particular Brother or Brethren who may be present, if not universal, is still general as of old. Numbers of men advocate the entire abandonment of the practice; and suggest that, as at military mess dinners, one toast only—'The Queen'—should be given.

It may well be doubted if the abolition, or even the partial abandonment of the custom, or the serious curtailment of the lists of toasts which we have been accustomed to find upon the programmes of our Festivals, would be acceptable to any but a very small minority of the Members of the Craft. The custom of giving toasts and of drinking healths at social gatherings, dinners, etc., in our own houses, is happily a thing of the past; but with Masons the case is different. We profess to be, and we are, very properly tenacious of 'The ancient Landmarks of the Order.' The custom of toasts at our festive meetings is so old as to have become a social landmark—it should not be lightly abandoned, or tampered with to any serious extent.

Some of the peculiar Masonic toasts are said to have been 'revived' in 1719 by Dr. Desaguliers, who was then Grand Master.

The forms will necessarily vary to some extent in different Provinces or Districts, or even in neighbouring Lodges; but in their main features and in their order of sequence there is no great variation.

Even in the same Lodge some difference is generally made between the number of toasts given at an ordinary meeting and those included in the list intended for an Installation dinner, or an Anniversary, or any other special occasion.

At the ordinary meetings of the Lodge, it is not expected that the full complement of toasts shall be given, although, even then, a certain routine should be observed, such as: 'The King and the Craft'; 'The high dignitaries and the Rulers of the Order, supreme and subordinate'; 'The Worshipful Master,' and some others at discretion, and in accordance with the probable duration of the sitting.

The list of toasts, however, should not be cut down to poor dimensions upon extraordinary occasions, such as Festivals, Installations, and so on, when large numbers—members and visitors—are expected to be present.

Where so great a variation of practice is certain to exist in different Lodges and different Provinces, one feels some degree of hesitation in even suggesting, and much more in dictating for general adoption, any programme of toasts.

The following is culled from programmes recently used at Installation and Anniversary banquets:

1. The Queen and the Craft.

2. The Most Worshipful Grand Master, His Royal Highness the Duke of Connaught and Strathearn, K.G., K.T., K.P., etc., etc., etc.

[See note on p. 357 as to smoking.]

3. The Most Worshipful Pro Grand Master, the Lord Ampthill, G.C.S.I., G.C.I.E., the Right Worshipful Deputy Grand Master, the Right Honourable Thomas Frederick Halsey, and the rest of the Grand Officers, Present and Past.

4. Brother (name, and titles, if any), Right Worshipful Provincial (or District) Grand Master of (insert the Province or District).

5. Brother (name and rank), Very Wor-

shipful Deputy Provincial (or District) Grand Master, and the Provincial (or District) Grand Officers present and past.

6. The Worshipful Brethren of London Rank (instead of 4 and 5; see p. 380).

7. The Worshipful Master.

7a. The Initiate.

8. The Visiting Brethren.

8a. The Joining Member.

9. The Immediate Past Master, the Installing Master, and the other Past Masters of and in the Lodge.

10. The......Chapter, No.....

11. The Masonic Charities.

12. The Treasurer and Secretary.

13. The Senior and the Junior Warden, and the other Officers of the Lodge.

14. Prosperity to the Lodge (name), Number......

15. All Poor and Distressed Masons (wherever dispersed over the face of Earth and Water, etc., etc.). (See Charge after third section of first Lecture.)

*   *   *   *

It is, perhaps, unnecessary to remind the responsible reader, that no Masonic toast should be proposed, honoured, or acknowledged unless the Banqueting Room be 'close tyled.'

When about to propose the Toasts, the Worshipful Master, or the Brother whom he has deputed, or whose duty it is to propose the Toast, after satisfying himself that the Lodge is 'close tyled,' usually inquires (seated) of the Wardens: 'Brother Senior and Junior Wardens, how do you report the glasses under your respective Columns?' and, having been assured by them that they are 'all charged in the West, Worshipful [Master],' and 'all charged in the South, Worshipful [Master],' he calls upon them to rise, saying, 'Principal Officers upstanding!' so that, in effect, the Toast is proposed by the three Principal Officers, 'the Worshipful Master, and the Senior and Junior Wardens.'

These formulæ are not employed for the Toast of 'The Officers,' or for the 'Tyler's Toast.'

It is a custom in certain Lodges for all the members of the Lodge to stand while the Toast of the Visitors is being proposed.

*　　*　　*　　*

It is no uncommon thing to find on programmes of Festivals and other occasions 'The Queen' as the first toast, without any reference to 'The Craft'; this is wrong.

In the united toast, we express at once

our loyalty to the Throne, and our reverence for 'our ancient and honourable Fraternity.' 'The Queen and the Craft' is the
original and very ancient form among Freemasons; whereas 'The Queen' alone is the
form used at ordinary meetings in the outer
world. We should retain the combined
form by all means; and we should do so
whether the reigning Monarch is or is not a
Freemason.

Similarly, full Masonic Honours should be
given to the combined toast. A circular
issued in 1911 to Masters of Lodges on this
subject concludes with the expression of the
Pro Grand Master's hope 'that the ancient
form of toast "The King and the Craft"
will be generally retained.'

*   *   *   *

Visitors may be present whose rank socially
or Masonically may entitle them to special
mention and a separate toast. No hard-
and-fast line can be or should be attempted
to be drawn upon the subject. All that has
been aimed at above has been to give a
good, useful, practical programme, fairly
comprehensive, and not wearisome.

With regard to 'the honours' after the
Toasts in Provincial Lodges, the following
have been obtained from a very efficient

Provincial Grand Director of Ceremonies, and are those which generally obtain in the Provinces—

The Queen and the Craft	3 times	9
The W.M. Grand Master	3 „	9
The W.M. Pro. G. Master	3 „	9
The R.W. Dep. G. Master	3 „	7
The Grand Wardens	3 „	5
The Rest of Grand Officers	3 „	3
The R.W. Dist. or Prov. G. Master ..	3 „	7
The R.W. Dep. Prov. G. Master (in chair)	3 „	5
The W. Dep. Prov. G. Master (not in chair)	3 times	3
The Prov. G. Wardens	3 „	3
The Rest of Prov. G. Officers	3 „	3

N.B.—When any of the foregoing are grouped, the Honours given are those to which the highest Officer of the Group is entitled.

The W.M.	3 „	5
The P.M.s	3 „	5

N.B.—Occasionally the W.M. and P.M.'s toast is honoured with twenty and one—or Running Fire.

Visitors and Brethren generally ..	3 „	3

They appear to have been well arranged, and are fairly proportioned to the individual rank of the several subjects of the various toasts. There is no authoritative rule and no universal custom. The Worshipful Master and the Director of Ceremonies must always arrange the programme either in accordance with precedent in their Lodge or at their own discretion.

The 'Fire,' after the Toasts in London Lodges, is usually restricted to the P. L. R.

This is often imperfectly given, owing to want of observant attention on the part of those who copy it from those who know; or, still worse, to the misfortune of copying it from those who do not know the absolutely correct method; which is—

P. L. R. P. L. R. P. L. R. one. two. three. (Sn. of E. A.) 1 2 3 (Sn. of E. A.) 1 2 3 (Sn. of E. A.) 1 2 3.

The 'Fire' after the Tyler's Toast is sometimes given with what is called 'silent fire.' This is utterly wrong in principle. It is not a funeral. It is a toast to poor and distressed Freemasons, who may yet, and we all hope they may, find a relief from all their sufferings. So they are entitled to the same joyous 'open fire' as the rest of us.

* * * *

On Anniversaries or Installation banquets as a rule each toast is followed by a song or glee, or some musical performance. These are within the province of the Organist, and whatever may be arranged is set forth— each piece in its proper place—in the Programme. If the songs, glees, etc., be well selected, with some care as to their appropriateness to the toasts which they respectively follow, and if they be fairly well rendered, the entertainment as a whole will be successful and enjoyable, at least, let us hope, to the majority—to those who desire to be happy themselves, and, if it be in their power, to communicate happiness to their Brethren.

In some Lodges a custom exists for the Worshipful Master to propose the first toasts. He then calls upon some Past Master or Senior Warden or the Junior Warden to propose the next. After these have been duly honoured, various Brethren selected by the Worshipful Master (assisted perhaps by the Director of Ceremonies) are requested to propose certain of the remaining toasts; these being allotted to the several speakers according to their special fitness for the duty; derived, it may be, from an intimate knowledge of the subject of the toast with which each speaker is entrusted; or for other good and sufficient reasons.

It is important, however, to be noted that the Brother whom the Worshipful Master deputes to be the proposer of any Toast is entrusted for the time being with the Worshipful Master's gavel. This symbol indicates that the Toast is being proposed by and

with the authority of the Worshipful Master,
and it is intended to be as great a compliment as if proposed by the Worshipful
Master himself.

*　　*　　*　　*

Immediately after the toast of the Grand
Master permission is given to the Brethren
to smoke; then, and not till then, cigars and
other means and appliances for the enjoyment of the nicotian weed are brought into
requisition.

No apology can be needed for the mention
of tobacco in connection with the symposia
of our Order, the habit is so generally,
indeed universally, practised at our meetings.
Still less need we hesitate to allude to the
subject in these days, when, from the lordly
club or social gathering in which princes
occasionally disport themselves, down
through all grades—to the working men's
political or social club—'smoking concerts'
are, as our American cousins would aptly
say, in *full blast.*

*　　*　　*　　*

Some mention must be made of the
speeches of the Brethren in proposing the
various toasts; and of the replies (returning
thanks) of those whose healths—either singly

or in connection with others—have formed the subjects of the personal toasts.

A considerable amount of ridicule is cast upon the quality of post-prandial oratory.

The kind, the manner, and the quality of the speeches one hears at the table at Masonic meetings differ, perhaps, quite as much as the speakers themselves differ the one from the other, and as the toasts vary in importance, and in general or individual interest. It is, therefore, clearly impossible to lay down rules for general adoption.

One hesitates to go so far even as to hint at, or to make the slightest suggestion upon, a subject so varying in all its surrounding circumstances as a list of toasts must necessarily be, comprising, as it does, subjects of the highest dignity and of world-wide interest down to subjects of local interest, and so on. Who shall prescribe—with any hope of even partial success—rules or suggestions for their several introduction in speech?

A Demosthenes is not born every day. Nevertheless, among the members of our Order we may occasionally meet men capable of investing common subjects with the charm of their own fancy, affording an intellectual feast to their hearers. From such men we do not expect brief utterances—we should be disappointed with a short address—we expect something above the average in quantity as well as in quality, and generally we are not disappointed.

Except from men of superior attainments, and of unusual facility and happiness of expression, long speeches upon well-worn topics, such as the routine toasts given at our meetings, are a weariness of the flesh; they should be studiously avoided. There are, however, certain toasts, such as the health of the Worshipful Master, particularly if by the performance of the duties of the lower Offices, and during his Mastership, he have shown exceptional zeal and ability; in such a case a moderately lengthy address is not only permissible, but is eminently desirable.

Again, the toast wishing 'Success to the Masonic Charities' is one that demands much more than a brief introduction. It is very desirable that at least 'once in every year' the members of the Lodge should learn, from some well-informed Brother, the excellent, the beneficent work, which year after year our various Charities are engaged in performing. Some well-selected, and not too minutely-detailed statistics, may well be given upon such occasions. The facts and figures thus produced tend to foster the virtue of Charity in the best possible way—namely, by convincing the Brethren that the various Institutions are conducted with care and efficiency, that the large revenues are carefully administered, and that the results bear in all cases a full proportion to the means employed.

In many Provinces, every Lodge elects yearly a member, whose duty it is to attend to all matters connected with the Charities, both Metropolitan and Provincial, so far as the interests of his own Lodge are concerned. In the Provinces alluded to, there are Charities, educational and otherwise, the benefits of which are restricted to the Provinces in which they exist; and the Brother mentioned is the representative of his Lodge upon the Central Committee of the Province, which conducts the affairs of the Institution. In the case also of an application to the Board of Benevolence in London, the same Brother goes to the meeting of the Board, to support the application, and to answer the searching questions which are always, and very properly, asked before the application is decided upon.

In many Lodges the same Brother is re-elected year after year, with the good result that he becomes as a rule thoroughly well versed in the working of the Charities, and so is able to render eminent service to the Lodge. Who, then, can be a more 'fit and proper person' to propose the toast of 'The Masonic Charities,' or perhaps, better still, to respond to the toast? In the latter case some Brother, selected for his fitness for the duty, might dilate at reasonable length upon 'the distinguishing characteristic of a Freemason's heart—namely, Charity,' in the abstract; and the Charity Representative would follow with such moderate detail of the results of the beneficence of the Craft as will interest and not weary his hearers.

This subject has been here somewhat fully discussed, because Charity being, as it were, the watchword of our Order, the younger Brethren should learn that it is no unmeaning cry, no 'sounding brass or tinkling cymbal,' but a substantial reality among us; that we do minister to the relief of 'our poor and distressed Brethren, and their widows, and their helpless orphan children'; that all is done without degrading the recipients, and without wounding their self-respect; that, judged by results, our Charities are the best managed and the most successful organizations in existence; that, with scarcely an exception, the scholars who have passed through the Boys' and the Girls' Schools respectively have done credit to the Institutions, and in some instances have achieved eminent success in their after-life; and that the closing years of life are rendered comfortable and happy for many an aged Brother, and many an otherwise unprovided for and hopeless widow. Having the knowledge of these good works of our Order imparted by 'one who knows,' 'the best feelings of the heart may be awakened to acts of Beneficence and Charity,' to the lasting advantage of our Charitable Institutions, and to the realization on the part of the givers of the fact that in very deed 'it is more blessed to give than to receive.'

There may be other occasions, such as the presence of a visitor of distinction, or the presentation of an address, or a testimonial (a jewel, or something of the kind), as an acknowledgment of eminent services rendered to the Lodge, when something more than a hasty and perhaps ill-considered address is required of the speaker. A very nice discrimination is necessary in treating these subjects; the speaker is required to avoid, on the one hand, excessive laudation, manifestly beyond the merits of the recipient, and, on the other hand, the equally manifest falling short in the expression of appreciation of those merits, and in giving utterances to the sentiments of those of whom he is the mouthpiece.

A difficult task, generally, is that of replying to the toast of one's own health, or of expressing one's grateful feelings as the recipient of the testimonial mentioned, whatever form it may take. There is always the initial difficulty of having one's self as the topic upon which to dilate.

We should never cease to be natural in our utterances; 'the tongue, being an index of the mind, should utter nothing but what the heart truly dictates,' and if our utterances bear the stamp of truthfulness, if they have the ring of the true metal, be they the utterances of a novice or the well-rounded periods of a practised speaker, they will not fail of their full effect upon the hearers.

A good old custom, in general use some years ago, is now perhaps less observed than it formerly was; but on every occasion when there is an Initiation, immediately after the newly initiated Brother's health has been duly proposed, the Loving Cup should be circulated, and the Entered Apprentice's Song should be sung as a matter of course; indeed, the Brethren should as soon think of omitting the Charge as of foregoing the

E. A.'s Song, with its chorus and the cordial
hand-grasps all round during the singing of
the last verse. All the older Brethren, and
certainly the majority of the younger generation, would consider the ceremony incom-
plete without the good old song.

(Full notes on the Entered Apprentice's
Song will be found in the Appendix, p. 423.)

The Secretary's Toast

One interesting toast which is of remote
origin and rarely heard, is one proposed
occasionally by the Secretary.

To enable it to be proposed properly the
Brethren must arrange themselves all seated,
if not in a circle, in a conveniently continuous chain, which may for this purpose be
deemed to be an irregular circle, as it is
requisite that each Brother should be in
immediate whispering contact with a left-
hand neighbour.

The Secretary commences by whispering
to his left-hand neighbour the words, 'The
Secretary's toast'; and each Brother in
turn whispers the same words to his left-
hand neighbour, until in due course the
Secretary is reached. He then starts the
whisper similarly, 'What is it?' and that
question is passed round the table. In

exactly the same whispered way the following phrases are circulated.

'There's no harm in it!'

'The Mother of Masons.'

'Who is she?'

'No. . . .' (the No. of the Lodge).

Then, in an audible voice, this message is sent round:

'Glass lip high.'

Then the order is similarly circulated:

'Drink.' [And, as each Brother passes on the command, he drinks.]

Then the Secretary, in a loud tone, says:

'Drink all, and all drink.' [And simultaneously all the Brethren drink, and (theoretically) drink all—*i.e.*, to the last drop.]

The 'fire' is correspondingly unique. The Secretary commences with a single knock, and that single knock is passed round the table one after the other until it has made three complete circuits.

Then, led by the Secretary, all the Brethren 'fire' three times rapidly, and raising the firing glass high in the air, finish with one tremendous volley.

CHAPTER XXVI

THE ROYAL MASONIC INSTITUTIONS

1. The Royal Masonic Benevolent Institution

THIS Institution was founded as the result of efforts initiated by Dr. Crucefix about 1834-35 to found a home for aged Freemasons. An annuity fund was formed in 1842 (during the Grand Mastership of the Duke of Sussex), and Grand Lodge voted the sum of £400 a year towards the granting of Annuities to Aged and Distressed Freemasons. As the Institution steadily progressed, it enlarged its sphere of usefulness by establishing, in 1849, a Fund for the Widows of Freemasons. The two funds were later amalgamated, and in recent years help has also been given to the aged and needy Spinster Daughters and Sisters of Freemasons. In 1849 also an amalgamation of this Institution was effected with the Asylum for Aged Freemasons at Croydon—where there was a home for thirty-two residents.

The majority of the Annuitants to-day live in their own homes, but about one hundred of them can live in the self-contained flats which are being built at Harewood Court, Hove. Here they live rent free and are allowed heating and light in addition to their annuities. Medical attendance and nursing are also provided free.

In 1867, the earlier system of classifying the Annuitants according to age was abolished. The maximum payment to a married Brother is now £156 per annum, and to other classes of Annuitants, £104 per annum.

Apart from the Annuitants who are now living, about 550 widows and 200 Brethren have received over £1,000 each from the funds. Nineteen Brethren and sixty-one Widows have been paid over £1,500 each.

There are now about 2,300 Annuitants on the Funds of the Institution, who are paid in the aggregate no less a sum than £183,000 per annum.

2. THE ROYAL MASONIC INSTITUTION FOR GIRLS

(Incorporated by Royal Charter.)

This Institution was founded in 1788 by the Chevalier Ruspini, P.G.Sd.B., a 'Modern.'

Since the foundation nearly nine thousand Girls have been trained or assisted in their education.

One Hundred and Seventy Five Girls were admitted to the benefits of the Institution *without ballot* during the year 1953.

Four hundred special Naval, Military and Air Force Nominations have been reserved for the benefit of the Daughters of Brethren killed or incapacitated during the War.

The *Senior School* (400 Girls) is situated at Rickmansworth, Hertfordshire. The *Junior School* (120 Girls) is situated at Weybridge, Surrey.

Girls are admitted to the Junior School at the age of eight, and proceed to the Senior School at about the age of ten. They remain normally until the age of sixteen, but many are retained until seventeen and even later should circumstances justify that course.

The Royal Masonic Institutions

At present 1,038 girls are receiving the benefits, 520 of whom are in the schools, the remaining 518 being in receipt of Out-Education Grants varying according to age and circumstances from £50 to £75 per annum. In cases of exceptional necessity these grants may be increased up to £150 per annum. Where a Boarding School is necessary an amount up to £200 per annum may be paid and in cases of exceptional necessity may be increased by a further £100.

The school has been very successful in the results attained in the General Certificate of Education Examinations. During the year 1953 14 girls passed at advanced level and 50 at ordinary level.

During the same year 169 girls received grants for further education after their school career was over, 53 of whom studied at University or other Training Colleges.

The income from investments last year was £39,368.

The annual expenses of the Institution approximate to £238,000 per annum, and are likely to increase in future.

3. THE ROYAL MASONIC INSTITUTION FOR
BOYS

(*Incorporated by Royal Charter.*)

The Royal Masonic Institution for Boys
was founded in 1798, mainly by Brother
Burwood, an 'Athol' or 'Ancient' Mason,
since which time 9,826 sons of Freemasons
have been elected to receive benefits of
education, clothing and maintenance.

The object of the Institution is to receive
under its protection, to maintain, clothe and
educate the sons of Freemasons under the
English Constitution of every religious denomination who from circumstances arising
from the death, illness or misfortune of
either or both parents are reduced to and
continue to be in a position requiring the
benefits of the Institution.

This object is achieved within the Schools
of the Institution at Bushey, Hertfordshire,
and also by assistance to boys educated at
schools near their homes or in boarding
schools. For boys out-educated adequate
grants are made for school fees (if any) and
maintenance, while for ex-pupils substantial
scholarships are available for post school

education at Universities, Medical Schools, etc. Extensive provision is also made for ex-pupils to assist them during their early years of employment by paying apprenticeship premiums and supplementing wages until they are able to be self supporting.

1,029 boys are now actually receiving benefits, 691 being at Bushey, 265 being out-educated and 73 being ex-pupils aided from the funds of the Institution.

Boys are admitted by election to the Institution's benefits at five, and are educated at schools near the residences of their parents or guardians until eight years of age, when, according to seniority of age, they may be drafted in the Bushey Schools.

In the Great War 1914-1919, 750 old boys served their King and country; 106 laid down their lives, and many others were wounded. Many distinctions were gained including a C.M.G., O.B.E., D.S.O., forty-nine Military Crosses and Medals, etc.

In the World War 1939-1945, about 1,398 Old Boys were serving in the Services and Merchant Navy. Of this number 533 held Commissioned Rank. 128 laid down their lives or were 'missing.' The many distinctions gained included O.B.E., M.B.E., D.S.O., M.C., D.F.C., D.C.M., D.S.M., D.F.M., A.F.M., B.E.M., etc.

There are four elections in each year, and 144 boys were admitted to benefits in the year 1953. Since 1910, 5,758 candidates have been admitted without a ballot, thus relieving their friends from much anxiety and expense. In addition, 666 duly qualified boys, whose fathers were killed or became incapacitated on or through active service in time of war, have been similarly admitted without a ballot to the benefits of the Institution.

A Royal Charter of Incoporation was granted to the Institution by Letters Patent dated June 15, 1926, and the Institution now enjoys the Royal Patronage of her Majesty the Queen.

CHAPTER XXVII

THE MASONIC LECTURES

THE Masonic Lectures are an elaborate explanation and commentary, not only of the ceremonies of the three Degrees and of the Tracing Boards appertaining to them, but of many important subjects connected with the higher phases of Masonry and Masonic thought. As at present constituted, they are divided as to seven sections in the First Lecture, five sections in the Second Lecture, and three sections in the Third Lecture, making fifteen sections in all. They are catechetical in form, and at some Masonic festivals all the fifteen sections are worked on the same evening!

The system of Lodge Lectures is, as compared with Masonry itself, of modern growth.

Some of the questions would seem to be intended merely to test the *bona fides* of the person examined, as both question and answer are distinctly arbitrary.

It may be accepted as historical fact that previous to 1717 the fraternity was without any such system.

Prior to that time the Charges and Covenants explanatory of the duties of Masons to each other seem to have been read 'at the making of a Freemason,' but these charges contained no instruction as to the symbolism of the Order. (See p. 326.)

The earliest authorized Lectures were apparently arranged by Drs. Anderson and Desaguliers, but they were imperfect and unsatisfactory, and in 1732 Bro. Martin Clare, M.A. (afterwards Deputy Grand Master), was commissioned by Grand Lodge to prepare a system of Lectures 'which should be adapted to the existing state of the Order without infringing on the Ancient Landmarks.'

Oliver says that Clare's version of the Lectures was so judiciously drawn up that its practice was enjoined on all the Lodges.

But Clare's Lectures did not long occupy their authoritative position in the Order. About 1766 Thomas Dunckerley — 'that truly Masonic luminary'—was authorized by Grand Lodge of 'Moderns' to prepare a new course of Lectures.

Dunckerley's Lectures were a considerable amplification of those of Clare, but a considerable modification also, as in them he dissevered the Master's Word from the Third Degree, and postponed it into the Royal Arch Ceremony.

Even Dunckerley's had to give way to the Lectures of William Hutchinson, of the North of England; and while Hutchinson was labouring in the North, another light, of almost equal splendour, appeared in the South, and a system of Lectures was prepared by William Preston, which soon superseded all those that had previously been in use. It is supposed that Hutchinson and Preston united in this undertaking, and that the Prestonian Lectures which were afterwards universally adopted were the result of the combined labours of the two.

In 1787 William Preston organized the Grand Chapter of Harodim in order to thoroughly teach the Lectures he had prepared. Some of the most distinguished Masons of the day became members of the Order.

The Prestonian Lectures continued to be used authoritatively until the Union in 1813, when it was determined to 'revise' the system of Lectures. This duty was entrusted to the Rev. Dr. Hemming. Many alterations of the Prestonian system were made by Dr. Hemming, principally, it is said, in consequence of their Christian references.

It appears from a letter from Bro. Philip Broadfoot (who was one of the members of the Lodge of Reconciliation and founder of the Stability Lodge of Instruction), that Bro. Hemming, after arranging the First Lecture, could not be induced to go on with the Second and Third, and that Bro. Philip Broadfoot was obliged to arrange them himself!

As may well be imagined, this was the subject of debate and controversy, as in 1819 complaint was made 'against Philip Broadfoot and others for working unauthorized Lectures.' Into this we need not enter very deeply. The Board of General Purposes recommended that the Lecture complained of should not be further promulgated, but Grand Lodge thought it unnecessary to adopt the recommendation, and, indeed, the M. W. Grand Master, the Duke of Sussex, stated that it was his opinion that so long as the Master of any Lodge observed exactly the Landmarks of the Craft he was at liberty to give the Lectures in the language best suited to the character of the Lodge over which he presided. This will explain why the Lectures practised by the Stability Lodge of Instruction have since claimed to be considered as legally 'orthodox' as those of the Emulation Lodge of Improvement; but the same considerations apply, though not in the same degree, to the Lectures as to the Ritual, as to the desirability of adhering to a precise and uniform method of working.

In 1819 the Perseverance Lodge of Instruction unanimously passed a resolution 'that the Lectures as heretofore worked in this Lodge be continued.' This was seconded by Bro. J. H. Wilson, subsequently a founder of the Emulation Lodge of Improvement.

In 1821 a similar resolution was carried unanimously.

In 1823 the Emulation Lodge of Improvement was founded by 'several Brethren who considered that the Masonic Lectures were not worked in Lodges upon a sufficiently regulated system, and that if those whose attainments as working Masons placed them as a prominent authority were to meet together and to work efficiently, they might be the means of effecting much improvement.' The work of this Lodge of Improvement was at first confined to the Lectures, but afterwards the Ceremonies were introduced. The Grand Stewards Lodge was, until that time, the only recognized authority for a recognized system of Lectures. The

Lectures then worked at the Grand Stewards Lodge were probably the 'Prestonian' Lectures formerly worked in the Lodge of Antiquity No. 2, William Preston's favourite Lodge. Accordingly, some members of the Grand Stewards Lodge conceived it to be their duty to watch the proceedings; and some Grand Officers, with Bro. Harper, the Grand Secretary, attended, and were greatly pleased with all they saw.

'For how long a period the Lectures as now worked at Emulation were previously in vogue it is impossible to state definitely, but we have every reason for believing that they are almost identical with the Lectures worked in the Perseverance Lodge of Instruction, which were described as "Ancient" in 1821, and they certainly bear a striking resemblance to Lectures known to have been in use about 1798.'

Bro. Thomas Fenn in 1893 stated that Bro. Stephen Barton Wilson admitted having made a few additions to the Lectures. No alteration has been made since, and in their present form they are regularly practised by the Emulation Lodge of Improvement.

William Preston died in 1818, and was buried in St. Paul's Cathedral. He bequeathed, among other Masonic gifts, £500 Consols to the Board of Benevolence, and

£300 Consols as an endowment for the annual delivery of the Prestonian Lecture. This was delivered somewhat intermittently until 1862, since which date it appears to have been forgotten.

CHAPTER XXVIII

LONDON RANK

LONDON RANK was instituted in December, 1907, as a consequence of a widespread feeling that Past Masters of London Lodges should have an opportunity, until then denied them, of attaining a dignity analogous to, and equivalent to, that of Provincial or District Grand Rank.

The honour is the direct gift of the M. W. Grand Master, and exists only during his pleasure, but the recipient is nominated by the Master of the Lodge to which he belongs, and this nomination is usually the result of consultation between the Master, Past Masters, and Wardens, in response to an invitation to that effect from the M. W. Grand Master.

The honour is therefore very highly esteemed as being the result of an expression of confidence by the Lodge itself.

London Rank entitles the holder to precedence in any London Lodge, next to

Grand Officers; beyond the London area, or, in other words, outside the 'Province' of London, that precedence ceases.

The holder is of course entitled during the Grand Master's pleasure to wear the London Rank clothing, consisting of a distinctive Jewel Collar and apron, at all Masonic Meetings, whether in London or elsewhere; with a modification, however, with respect to meetings of Grand Lodge.

On the occasions of his visits to Grand Lodge every holder of London Grand Rank (like his brother holding Provincial or District Grand Rank) attends Grand Lodge in virtue only of his Past Mastership.

The honour is now conferred on about 263 Past Masters every year, representing about one-third of the London Lodges.

There are at present about 1,500 Worshipful Brethren of London Rank, of whom about 450 are members of a voluntary association called London Rank Association.

Proposals have been submitted to Grand Lodge and rejected to divide London into ten Metropolitan Districts and establish ten Metropolitan Grand Lodges. Under that Scheme no further appointments would have been made to London Rank, but the holder of London Rank would have retained his right to wear his London Rank Jewel and

Clothing, and he would have had the same rank and precedence as a Past Metropolitan Grand Senior Deacon; but he would have had this rank and predecence only in the Metropolitan Grand Lodge containing the Lodge originally nominating him for London Rank.

CHAPTER XXIX

MARK MASTERS, AND ROYAL ARK MARINERS

THE Degree of Mark Master is recognized by the Grand Lodge of Scotland and Ireland. It is regrettable, however, that the Degree of Mark Master was not recognized by the United Grand Lodge of England in 1813 as coming within the definition of 'pure and ancient Masonry.'

As part of Speculative Masonry it existed before 1813; indeed, there are authentic records dating September, 1769. It is a complement of the Fellow-Crafts degree of a particularly interesting character. It is, however, conferred only on Master Masons.

In former times it was the custom, in all Fellow-Craft Lodges, for each Fellow-Craft to choose a mark by which his work might be known to his Overseer, the mark selected being one not previously chosen by a Brother of the same Lodge. This mark he presented at the Senior Warden's wicket to receive his wages as a Mark Man.

In due course, when he became a Master

Mason, he had the degree of Mark Master conferred upon him.

It is at this stage that the Legend of the Mark Master who prepared a curious stone commences. He has the mortification of having rejected in the first instance, and subsequently has the ecstatic joy of seeing it placed in one of the most important positions in the Building.

In 1855 a Committee appointed by Grand Lodge reported that, whilst not positively essential, it was a graceful appendage to the degree of a Fellow-Craft.

In March, 1856, it was resolved by Grand Lodge 'that the degree of Mark Mason or Mark Master is not at variance with the Ancient Landmarks of the Order, and that the degree be an addition to, and form part of, Craft Masonry'; but at the subsequent meeting in June this was not confirmed.

Three months afterwards the Grand Lodge of Mark Master Masons was formed, and has proved very successful, controlling 654 Lodges, and has recorded 66,616 advancements of Candidates.

*　　*　　*　　*

The degree of a Royal Ark Mariner is conferred only on Mark Master Masons. It has

been worked from 'time immemorial' (!).
The earliest records are of a date *circa* 1790.

In 1870 the Royal Ark Mariners came under the jurisdiction of the Grand Lodge of Mark Master Masons, and since then these Arks have been 'moored' to Mark Master Masons' Lodges.

The ritual goes back to the time of Noah, and refers to the despatch of the dove which returns with the olive branch. It is distinctly a side degree, and bears no apparent relation to Craft Masonry or its Etiquette.

It is not recognized by the United Grand Lodge of England, but is recognized by the Supreme Grand Chapter of Scotland.

It is only mentioned here on account of its relationship with the Mark Masters.

CHAPTER XXX

THE SUPREME ORDER OF THE HOLY ROYAL ARCH

THE Supreme Order of the Holy Royal Arch is not a degree; it is the completion of the Master Mason's degree, which is interrupted in such an untimely fashion; and without it no Master Mason can consider himself 'fully fledged.'

In early times it was, no doubt, incorporated in the Third Degree; and the true word which constitutes the Royal Arch was found by Dr. Oliver in a Master Mason's Tracing Board, *circa* 1725. The earliest mention of it as a separated ceremony is about 1740, just two years after the separation of the 'Ancients' and the 'Moderns.' Its creation is attributed to the 'Ancients.'

As late as 1758 the 'Moderns' had no Royal Arch, and in the Lecture of the Third Degree the true Master Mason's word was revealed to the Master Mason by the 'Moderns' in the latter ceremonies of the Third Degree, thus precluding the necessity for the Royal Arch.

About 1766 Dunckerley was commissioned by the 'Modern' Grand Lodge to revise the Lectures, and he did so by, *inter alia*, dissevering the true word from the Third Degree, and transplanting it into the Royal Arch ceremony, and to that extent assimilating the Ancient and Modern systems. This radical move owed its success to Dunckerley's popularity and the influence of the Grand Master. It was no doubt a great factor in preparing the ground for the reunion in 1813, when the Royal Arch was declared a part of 'pure and ancient Masonry'; and so it has ever since remained.

The Royal Arch is not recognized by the Grand Lodge of Scotland.

In 1817 the two Grand Chapters of the Royal Arch were amalgamated.

In 1834 the ceremony of exaltation was considerably altered by the Rev. G. A. Browne, at the request of M. W. G. M. the Duke of Sussex; but the general outline of the system was preserved.

In 1853 a Chapter of Promulgation was authorized for the purpose of disseminating the revised Ritual with a view 'to establish a uniformity of Practice and Working throughout the Order.'

The Supreme Grand Chapter governs the Order, and its Ruler is denominated the

Most Excellent First Grand Principal. The most important Grand Officers of Grand Lodge are entitled *ex officio* to similar offices in Grand Chapter (if they are R. A. Masons), so that the government is in practically the same hands.

In former times the ceremony was restricted to those who had passed the Chair. In 1843 the Regulations required only twelve months' service as a Master Mason; while since 1893 any Master Mason who has exercised himself in that capacity for four weeks and upwards is eligible for 'exaltation' in the Order; and there can be no impropriety in urging a brother to complete his Third Degree.

From a practical point of view, it is also very desirable, if otherwise convenient, that a young Mason should join the Royal Arch as soon as possible. While in the first place it gives him a greater comprehension of his 'blue' Masonry and assists him to take an intelligent interest in that, the practical advantage is that of saving time, by enabling him to take office in the Royal Arch as soon as his progress in the Craft warrants it.

No Mason can occupy a Principal's Chair in the Royal Arch until he is an Installed Master in the Craft, but conversely, if he can mount in rotation in the Royal Arch at the same time as he is nearing the Chair in the Craft, there need not be such a long interval as there would be if he were not a member of the two organizations concurrently.

At the present time there are 250 London Chapters and 612 Provincial Chapters.

* * * *

On May 7, 1902, a Resolution 'that it is expedient that all Royal Arch Masons be permitted to be present at the Opening of Private Chapters' was proposed in Grand Chapter and carried 'almost unanimously.'

Prior efforts to achieve the same object in 1880, 1893, and 1896, had been defeated by large majorities.

CHAPTER XXXI

LODGES OF RESEARCH

It is natural that so vast a subject as Freemasonry should induce a spirit of inquiry in those whose thoughts are not circumscribed by the physical aspects of their Lodges.

Our Masonry is to us what we make it. If we confine it to social enjoyment and mundane ambitions, it will yield these things abundantly, and give us the sweets and bitters associated with such matters. If, on the other hand, we enlarge the outlook, then the possibilities are infinitely greater, and we reap a correspondingly greater result.

Simple investigations into the origin of the Fraternity from the historical point of view are interesting if illusory. Speculation as to the more recondite spiritual meaning of our mysteries, and their association with the same mysteries of preceding ages, is an absorbing study; for we must surely realize that our researches are prompted by the same desires as prompted the researches of the ancient seekers after TRUTH.

The labours of our investigators have been limited by the paucity of record, and yet their industry has produced so much that a lifetime would be insufficient to read it all.

And if we could read it and retain it, what more should we know of the Infinite and Eternal than our ancestors knew? Who can say?

But it is a most satisfactory feature that the desire to know more is perennial, and this very proper inquisitiveness has gathered together some of our Brethren, who have encouraged themselves and others to form Lodges of Research, charged with the pleasurable duty of acquiring and disseminating useful knowledge in all branches of Masonry.

Prominent among these is the Quatuor Coronati Lodge, No. 2076, which was established in 1884, to provide a centre and bond of union for Masonic students, and to imbue them with a love for Masonic research. Its membership is limited to forty, but it has an unlimited Correspondence Circle extending to all parts of the world. It meets as a Regular Lodge at Freemasons' Hall six times in the year. At every meeting an original paper is read, which is followed by discussion. Once a year an excursion is arranged.

The fee for the Correspondence Circle is

10s. 6d., and that entitles the subscriber to the Transactions 'Ars Quatuor Coronatorum,' published three times per annum.

The Lodge of Research, Leicester, was founded in 1892.

The Humber Lodge of Installed Masters was consecrated 1894.

There are many other Lodges, Clubs, and Associations having objects similar to these, among which may be mentioned, Manchester Association for Masonic Research, Leeds Installed Masters' Association, Masonic Veterans' Association.

It is to be hoped that every Brother who reads these pages will become a member of at least one of them.

CHAPTER XXXII

OPERATIVE MASONRY

WE have seen in Chapter I (p. 11) that Speculative Masonry is derived from the various systems of Operative Freemasonry which have existed since the earliest periods; and that it is, more immediately, based upon the secret organizations of the Operative Masons of the Middle Ages; but it is insufficiently known and realized by present-day members of our Speculative Lodges that the Craft to which they profess their devotion was, originally, wholly operative; and that the members of it were real Free Masons, engaged in actual construction of buildings; dependent, for their subsistence, upon the excellence of their work; that the Lodge was the place in which the work was carried on; and that the ceremony of Initiation was an actual ordeal through which the candidate had to pass before he could be permitted to learn the practical secrets of the Craft by which he expected to earn his daily bread.

It was only as a concession, and as a compliment to sympathizers of the types mentioned in Chapter I, that the Craft from time to time admitted or 'accepted' a sprinkling of non-working or Speculative Masons, who were not actually Free Masons, but were known as 'Accepted' Masons.

Thus the membership of the Operative Lodges, while almost entirely composed of Operative Masons, consisted, in many instances, of Free Masons on the one hand, and of 'Accepted' Masons on the other.

This was the state of affairs down to 1717 when the Grand Lodge of that date was formed, and Anthony Sayer, himself an Operative, was elected Grand Master.

In this connection attention may be called to the Entered Apprentice's Song, as printed in 1722 (see p. 423), in which the toast is to a Free OR Accepted Mason.

Under the Speculative Grand Lodge the non-working element gradually increased, and indeed soon predominated, to the utter exclusion of the working element, until nowadays the very existence of an Operative is lost sight of in a Speculative Lodge.

We are often reminded in the Ritual that we are not all Operative Masons; but, for the above reason, the phrase is meaningless to most. It is unquestionably a survival of the times when Operatives and Speculatives sat side by side in the same Lodge.

It must not, however, be supposed that Operative Masonry died in giving birth to Speculative Masonry.

The Operative parent system, now enfeebled by various causes, especially by Trade Unionism, continued its existence, notwithstanding the birth, separate life, and extraordinary growth of the Speculative offspring.

Bro. R. B. Grant writes: 'The existing Operative Lodges in England, which are under the Worshipful Society of Free Masons, Operative, have never come under the control of the Grand Lodge of England; and they continue to work their old Ritual, as revised in 1663 and 1686, and as it was before the Speculative Grand Lodge was formed in 1717.'

To Masonic Speculative students the present-day existence of these Operative Lodges must be a matter of intellectual interest, since the ancestry is common to both.

It will be readily conceded that a right understanding of the practical trade of Masonry, the methods employed in delineating the building in a draft or plan for the instruction and guidance of the work-

men, and the working tools and implements
used by them in executing the work, cannot
but be helpful to a clearer appreciation of
the meaning—often the hidden meaning—
of the corresponding speculative aspect of
Masonry, " . . . for many parts are quite
incomprehensible even to learned Free
Masons, without the technical part which
only the Guilds of the Free Masons can
supply." Hence, any research which will
bring us into closer contact with the actual
Operative Lodges of ancient times is likely
to give us clearer insight, and to widen our
range of Masonic vision and comprehension.
On the other hand, it must be admitted that
the endeavour to distinguish and appreciate
the connection of our whole system and the
relative dependency of its several parts will
lead us into a very wide field of research—
one in which, regrettably, there is more opportunity for developing imagination than
for discovering incontrovertible facts.

There are many worthy Speculative
Masons who, feeling mentally unsatisfied
with the meagre and imperfect explanations
provided for their acceptance from speculative sources, and feeling that there must be
a rich harvest of additional knowledge to be
reaped in the field indicated, are devoting
their attention to the Operative aspects of

Masonry; and are attending Operative Lodges; as a result of which Speculative Masonry is, to them, illuminated from the Operative point of view.

These Operative Lodges work their own Operative Ritual, and purport to carry on the work as practised in the ancient Operative Lodges from which they claim to trace their descent both immediate and remote— that is to say, their remote origin is claimed to date from the beginning of building, while their more immediate History, although we read in our Masonic Year Book that St. Alban formed the first Lodge in Britain, A.D. 287, may be said to date from Athelstan, A.D. 926, and the granting of the Charter at York in that year.

Dr. Charles Hope Merz, President of the Masonic Library of Sandusky, Ohio, writes: 'By the Athelstan Charter, granted A.D. 926, the Operative Society had the inherent right to form a kind of private law court in order to preserve its rights. The Masters and Passed Masters held an Assembly regularly, and at this meeting a Charge was read to them. Edward died A.D. 924, and was succeeded by his son Athelstan, who appointed his brother Edwin patron of the Masons. This prince procured a charter from Athelstan, empowering them to meet annually in communication at York, where the first Grand Lodge of England was formed in 926, at which Edwin presided as Grand Master. Here many old writings were produced (in Greek, Latin, and other languages), from which the Constitutions of the English Lodges were originally derived. From this era we date the establishment of Freemasonry in England. There is to-day in the city of York a Grand Lodge of Masons, who trace their existence from this period (Masonic Minstrel, 1818).

'Athelstan (926) gave the Operatives power to correct within themselves faults . . . done within the Craft. This, with the system of fines, is in operation to-day.'

Between A.D. 926 and A.D. 1717 the records are very meagre and tantalizingly insufficient.

The following dates and facts are interesting and indicative, although not in all cases free from doubt:

1349. Ordinance of Labourers (23 Ed. III) respecting Operative Masons (cementarii).

1350. Statute of Labourers (25 Ed. III) respecting Operative Masons, "Master Mason of Free Stone," and "other Masons."

1356. Regulations by the Mayor, Aldermen, and Sheriffs of the City of London concerning Operative Masons.

1358.* Edward III revised the Constitions.

1360. Statute of Labourers (34 Ed. III) "Masons . . . Congregations, Chapters, Ordinances, and Oaths . . . wholly annulled."

13—. Probable date of Halliwell MS.

1376. Two Operative Societies in London (Herbert's Livery Companies). "The Worshipful Society of Freemasons in the City of London," and "The Free Masons Company of London."

1377. Will Humbervyle, styled "Magister Operis," and a "Free Master Mason," was employed as a teacher at Oxford.

1380-1400. Approximate date assigned to document from which the Regius MS. appears to have been copied.

1390-1410. Approximate date assigned to document from which the (Matthew) Cooke MS. appears to have been copied.

1425.* Masons yearly General Chapters prohibited (3 Henry VI). This

* See *Masonic Year-Book.*

Act was virtually repealed in 1562 by (5 Eliz., Cap. 4), and was formally repealed in 1825 bv (6 Geo. IV).

1445. Statute of (28 Henry VI) refers to Frank Mason. This would appear to be the earliest expression in the Statutes which could bear the rendering of Free Mason.

1450.* Henry VI (said to have been) initiated (at the age of twenty-nine).

1481. The City of London made further regulations *re* Operative Masons.

1495. Statute of (11 Henry VII). The words Free Mason appear for the first time in the actual Statutes (see A.D. 1445). Repealed 1497.

1515. 7 Henry VIII. "On the humble petycyon of the Free Masons, rough Masons . . . wythin the Cytie of London."

1550-1575. Probable date of Lansdowne MS.

1562. 5 Eliz., Cap. 4, giving Masons and others the right to take Apprentices.

1583. "Grand Lodge" version of the Operative Constitutions.

1598. Schaw Statutes (No. 1) written in the

*See *Masonic Year-Book*.

Minute Book of the Lodge of Edinburgh.

1600. John Boswell, Laird of Auchenleck, a non-Operative Mason, attended Lodge of Edinburgh and attested the Minutes with his mark like his 'Operative Brethren.'

1607.* Inigo Jones constituted several Lodges.

1637.* Earl of St. Albans "regulated" the Lodges.

1646.* Elias Ashmore (Windsor Herald) initiated October 16 at Warrington.

1655. The Free Masons Company discontinued the use of the word 'Free,' and elected members who had not served seven years at the Trade.

1663. Robert Padgett rewrote the Operative Ritual.

1675. Foundation Stone of St. Paul's Cathedral laid June 21 by Operative Free Masons.

1677. King Charles II granted to the Operative Masons Company another Charter.

1685.* Sir Christopher Wren was Grand Master of Operative Free Masons.

1686. Robert Padgett further revised part of Operative Ritual.

* See *Masonic Year-Book*.

1690.* King William III was initiated.

1691. Sir Christopher Wren (said to have been) 'adopted' a Free Mason.

1708. Last stone laid on dome of St. Paul's, October 25.

1710. Dr. Anderson appointed Chaplain to St. Paul's Operative Lodge.

1715. Dr. Anderson's connection with Operative Masonry severed.

1717. Constitution of Speculative Masonry by the formation of the Grand Lodge of England. (See p. 20.)

It must be remembered that many of the statements made in this chapter emanate from Operative writers, and from Operative sources only, and upon them the responsibility for their accuracy rests, and must, of course, rest, until the production of independent corroborative testimony permits, or, indeed, compels, their unreserved acceptance by Masons generally.

It is stated that Robert Padgett, who was 'the Clearke' of the Operative Society, rewrote their Ritual in 1663; and it is also stated that at Wakefield in 1663 the General Assembly sanctioned the ancient prayer which is still in use by the Operatives.

This Revised Operative Ritual is appar-

* See *Masonic Year-Book*.

ently the Ritual which was taken in hand before 1717 by the Rev. Dr. James Anderson.

Dr. Merz writes: 'In order to show the close relation existing between them, it is only necessary to place the two rituals side by side, and all the remarkable points of similarity will at once become apparent; and the "digestions" of Dr. Anderson may be readily detected.'

Dr. Anderson is said to have been appointed Chaplain to St. Paul's Operative Lodge in London in January, 1710; but it appears that he never became a Master Mason in the seventh degree. It is even alleged that he was expelled from the Operatives in September, 1715, and that he then conceived a system of Speculative Masonry for 'gentlemen who did not work at the trade.'

Dr. Anderson was, of course, an important factor in the organisation of the Grand Lodge of England in 1717, and he was its first Grand Secretary. This Grand Lodge was composed of both Operatives and Speculatives, and the first Grand Master, Anthony Sayer, was an Operative; and, of his Wardens, one was an Operative, the other a Speculative.

The establishment of this Grand Lodge was, therefore, no 'revival' of Freemasonry as some write of it. It was rather a 're-visal' of it.

It was apparently intended to be an alliance between the Free and the Accepted; more or less on the same lines as before, but with their status equal; but events falsified prognostications, and the remarkable growth of the Speculative side of its membership completely overshadowed and eventually crowded out the Operatives.

In September, 1721, Dr. Anderson was commissioned by the Grand Lodge of England, under John, Duke of Montagu, to write a Digest collated from the existing Gothic (*i.e.*, manuscript) documents. In 1722 this Digest was approved, and ordered to be printed under the style of the 'Ancient Constitutions of Freemasonry.' On January 17, 1723, 'G. Warden, Anderson, produced the New Book of Constitutions now in print which was again approved.'

A second edition was published in 1738, in which Dr. Anderson made important alterations, which were unauthorized by Grand Lodge, and gave offence.

One of the most striking of these important alterations is that two degrees—the Apprentice Part and the Fellow-Crafts' or Masters' Part—are officially recognized in the constitutions of 1723, and three—En-

tered Apprentice, Fellow-Craft, _and_ Master
—by the Constitutions of 1738.

Dr. Anderson's characteristics would have
delighted some of the Ritual Reformers of
the present day, as he appears to have
altered the Operative Ritual radically and
ruthlessly, and often 'without rhyme or
reason.'

For instance, in Operative Masonry the
three Masters sit in the West, to see the sun
rise in the East. The Senior Warden sits
in the East 'to mark the setting sun.' The
Junior Warden sits in the North to 'mark
the Sun at its [high] meridian.' The thoughtful Speculative Mason will perceive many
reasons why this arrangement is more suitable.

Operatives open the Lodge in the seventh
degree, and work downwards.

The Degrees are:

VII. Three Ruling Masters.
VI. Certified Master.
V. Intendent and Super-Intendent.
IV. Super-Fellow Erector.
III. Super-Fellow.
II. Fellow.
I. Apprentice.

Operatives explain that, as Dr. Anderson
did not know the seventh degree work, he

opened in the first degree, and worked upwards.

For this reason also, they assert, he was unable to give the Secrets of a Master Mason, and invented the legend of the loss of them; and this is the explanation also why, although the Operatives have three Masters, the Speculatives have only one.

There are numerous other examples which could be quoted; but enough has been said to show that Dr. Anderson found the Operative Ritual very 'indigestible' fare, and this will explain the errors, anachronisms, and confusions, which occur in what may be termed the technical part of our present-day Speculative Ritual.

Let us, however, be thankful that those parts of Operative Masonry to which he had access have enabled him to transmit so much of it pure and unpolluted.

CHAPTER XXXIII

THE SUPREME COUNCIL OF THE ANCIENT AND ACCEPTED SCOTTISH RITE (33°)

'ON May 1, 1786, the Grand Constitution of the Thirty-third Degree, called the Supreme Council of Sovereign Grand Inspectors-General, was finally ratified by His Majesty the King of Prussia, who, as Grand Commander of the Order of Prince of the Royal Secret, possessed the sovereign Masonic power over all the Craft.'

'In the new Constitution this power was conferred on a Supreme Council of nine brethren, in each nation, who possess all the Masonic prerogatives in their own District that His Majesty individually possessed, and are Sovereigns of Masonry.'

'Every Supreme Council is composed of nine Inspectors-General, five of whom should profess the Christian religion' (Dalcho, 1802).

The English Supreme Council was established in 1845.

The following is a list of the thirty-three degrees:

407

Symbolic Lodges

1. Entered Apprentice.
2. Fellow Craft.
3. Master Mason (inc. Royal Arch*).

Lodges of Perfection

4. Secret Master.
5. Perfect Master.
6. Intimate Secretary.
7. Provost and Judge.
8. Intendant of the Buildings.
9. Elect of Nine.
10. Elect of Fifteen.
11. Sublime Elect.
12. Grand Master Architect.
13. Royal Arch of Enoch.
14. Scotch Knight of Perfection.

Council of Princes of Jerusalem

15. Knight of the Sword and of the East.
16. Prince of Jerusalem.

Chapter of Princes of R.C.

17. Knight of the East and West.
18. Knight of the Pelican and Eagle and Prince of the Order of Rose Croix of H. R. D. M.

* See definition of Pure Antient Masonry, Art I, Book of Constitutions.

Council of Kadosh

19. Grand Pontiff.
20. Grand Master of Symbolic Lodges.
21. Noachite, or Prussian Knight.
22. Knight of the Royal Axe, or Prince of Libanus.
23. Chief of the Tabernacle.
24. Prince of the Tabernacle.
25. Knight of the Brazen Serpent.
26. Prince of Mercy.
27. Knight Commander of the Temple.
28. Knight of the Sun, or Prince Adept.
29. Grand Scottish Knight of St. Andrew.
30. Knight Kadosh.

Consistory of Princes of R.S.

31. Inspector Inquisitor Commander.
32. Prince of the Royal Secret.

Supreme Council

33. Sovereign Grand Inspectors-General.

APPENDIX (A)

CRITICISM OF THE TRACING BOARDS

LITTLE needs to be remarked upon the Tracing Board of the First Degree. It is far from being all that can be desired, but it is not open to the strong objections which exist against the other two.

The Explanation of the Second Tracing Board, as given in the Ritual, is almost from the beginning to the end a series of statements having little or no foundation in fact; and in several of its details it is diametrically opposed to the descriptions in the Bible of the things alluded to. There is no Scriptural warrant for the assertion that 'the Entered Apprentices received a weekly allowance of corn, wine, and oil; the Fellow-Crafts were paid their wages in specie.' This, however, may be ranked among the *traditions*, and it is of small importance.

In the Ritual it is stated that 'after our Ancient Brethren had entered the Porch they arrived at the foot of the winding staircase, which led to the middle chamber.' This idea is partially embodied in the Tracing Board itself. There are depicted two columns under an arch, at the very entrance of the Temple, with a picturesque view of the open country, but *no Porch* at all. Almost from between the two columns springs a huge winding staircase, leading to a large and lofty vestibule, at the end of which is a doorway, with not a door, but a pair of curtains. The staircase clearly winds up to the *left side* of the building. The only description of the 'Chambers' is in I Kings vi 5, 6, and 8. Verse 8 runs thus: 'The *door* for the middle chamber was in the *right side* of the house.' It is clear, therefore, that the staircase, so far from facing the very entrance of the Temple, was not seen at all until the door at 'the right side of the house' was opened; consequently, all that is said about the Porch and the Pillars applies to the main entrance to the Temple, and not in any sense to the middle chamber.

It is clearly stated in the Volume of the Sacred Law that the three chambers were 'built against the wall'; and they measured, respectively, five, six, and seven cubits—that is, about nine feet, ten feet nine inches, and twelve feet six inches in breadth (length not stated); therefore the Porch and the

Pillars, etc., as applied to the middle chamber, are an absurdity. The two Pillars are asserted to have been 'formed hollow, the better to serve as archives to Masonry.' Now, supposing such Records to have been then in existence, and to have been deposited in the two Pillars, how could they have been made accessible?—how arranged for reference? The thing is too absurd for argument. The Pillars were formed hollow then, as they would be now, because solid Pillars would have involved a vast waste of metal, and, from their enormous weight, such difficulty in moving and rearing, as would have taxed the skill of the Craftsmen to the uttermost. It is said 'those Pillars were further adorned with two spherical balls, on which were delineated maps of the Celestial and Terrestrial Globes.' In 1 Kings vii 41, mention is made of 'the two *bowls* of the *chapiters*, that were on the top of the two pillars.' In verse 20 of the same chapter are these words, 'and the chapiters upon the two pillars had pomegranates also above, over against the *belly* which was by the network.' In these two extracts it would appear that '*bowl*' and '*belly*' both mean the swell of the capitals of the Pillars. These capitals were fixed at the tops of the shafts *in the usual way*; and the old compilers have here supposed that the *bowls* mentioned were identical with *spherical balls*, and those balls they have placed on the top of a square *above the chapiters*. The idea of these balls being covered with the delineations of the celestial and terrestrial Globes is sublime in its audacity. The first terrestrial Globe on record is that made by Anaximander of Miletus, 580 B.C.—that is, considerably over *four hundred years* after the date of the building of King Solomon's Temple; the celestial Globe would probably be of even later date. The height of those Pillars was seventeen cubits and a half each, and the chapiter five cubits, equal in the whole to forty-one feet (one account, 2 Chronicles iii 15, makes them, the Pillar thirty-five cubits, and the chapiter five cubits). Students of geography and astronomy must have had some difficulty in consulting globes placed at an elevation of from forty to fifty feet above the ground. The assertion about these globes is as wildly improbable as that the Pillars were 'formed hollow the better to serve as archives to Masonry.'

———

The meaning of the P. W. S. . . . is literally 'an ear of corn,' in some sentences in the Bible and a 'flowing stream' in others, and therefore correctly depicted in the Tracing Board. The *word* does not *mean* 'P. . . . y,' but its double signification may, when united, be said to denote 'P . . . . y.' Eminent Hebrew scholars have been consulted as to the interpretation of the word, and there exists no difference of opinion between them, except that one rather favours the 'stream of water,' inasmuch as the word was used as a *T . . . . beside a stream*. Nevertheless, a multitude of texts have been quoted in which the word is used in such connections that no other meaning *in those places* can be assigned to it than 'an Ear of Corn'; but no case can be cited in which the word alone can by any means be rendered 'P . . . . y.'

The remaining portion of the 'Explanation' needs little comment. The winding staircase may or may not have comprised flights of three, five, and seven steps. There is no mention of this in the Bible. The Tracing Board shows fifteen continuous steps, without a break, or any indication of these three flights. It is stated in the last clause of the Explanation of the Tracing Board that 'when our ancient Brethren were *in the M. C.* their attention was peculiarly drawn to certain Hebrew characters.' This is, of course, a pure invention. It is of little moment, but it does not agree with the Tracing Board, in which 'certain Hebrew characters' are shown *above the doorway* at the end of the vestibule and *outside* the M. C., while in the centre, at the top of the Tracing Board, is a letter 'G' in a radiated triangle. The Tracing Board shows a strongly marked Mosaic Pavement, whereas in 1 Kings v. 30 it is clearly *stated*, 'and the floor of the house he overlaid with gold, within and without,' meaning, probably, the Temple proper, the Holy of Holies, and the Porch. *Not one word* indicating a Mosaic Pavement can be found in either of the two accounts of the building of the Temple.

The Porch and the Mosaic Pavement were evidently in high favour with the old compilers of the Ritual. They have both of these in their explanation of the Sanctum Sanctorum.

They have given their fancy very free play, and have paid but scant attention to the clear descriptions of the Temple in the Kings and the Chronicles.

The following remarks embody all that needs to be said upon the Tracing Board of the Third Degree.

Perhaps the grossest absurdity of all in this connection is the statement 'he was not buried in the Sanctum Sanctorum, because nothing common or unclean,' etc. Evidently the old compiler considered it the height of *respectability* to be buried in the church, according to the bad old fashion existing in England some years ago, and he thought that H. A. B. would certainly be buried within the Temple, and he gives a reason (*in words borrowed from the New Testament*) why he was not buried in the Holy of Holies itself, being evidently ignorant of the fact that intra-mural interment was expressly forbidden by the Jewish Law. The Coffin is made a prominent object in this Degree. It is cited as one of the emblems of mortality, it is the most conspicuous (indeed, almost the only conspicuous thing on the older Tracing Boards. An actual Coffin, sometimes in miniature, sometime of full size, used to be (and in many places still is) brought into the Lodge, and actually used in the Third Degree. Many instances can be brought to prove that Coffins were not in use (then at least) in Judea. The Winding Sheet alone was used, and the body was

carried on a Bier. In 2 Kings xiii 21 it is
related that a man was hastily cast into the
'sepulchre of Elisha, and when he touched
the *bones* of Elisha, he revived and stood
on his feet.' Now it is clear from this that
neither the man nor Elisha could have been
in a Coffin, and Elisha was one to whom all
honour in burial would have been paid. In
the Christian era clear proofs are found of
the use solely of the Winding Sheet. Then,
again, the B. of our Master was found very
indecently i. . .d, and although it was afterwards re-. . . . . .d, it is as little likely that a
coffin was used as that it was ever contemplated that he should be buried in the Holy
of Holies, and was only prevented 'because
nothing common or unclean was allowed
to enter there.'

Equally absurd is the statement that 'the
same fifteen trusty Fellow-Crafts were
ordered to attend the funeral clothed in
white aprons and *gloves*.'

As to the Ornaments of a Master Mason's
Lodge. 'The Porch, Dormer, and Square
Pavement,' there is not in the Bible any foundation for supposing that they ever formed
part of King Solomon's Temple. There is
no room for doubt upon the subject; nothing
can be more clear than the description given
in the Bible of the whole internal arrange-

417

ment of the Temple; and the references given in the following remarks will show how entirely the Scripture accounts differ from the description in the Third Ceremony.

There could have been no 'Porch' to the entrance to the Sanctum Sanctorum. The only Porch was outside, at the entrance to the Temple, on either side of which the Two Great Pillars stood. The 'Dormer' is a pure invention. No such thing is mentioned (see 1 Kings vi and 2 Chron. iii). None was needed. The High Priest alone, and he only once a year, entered the Holy of Holies; and the Shekinah was there, the visible manifestation of the Divine Presence in the Pillar of Cloud and of Fire. In 1 Kings (vi 30) it is distinctly stated, 'the floor of the house he overlaid with gold, within and without'—that is, in every part—and certainly the Holy of Holies would not be less richly floored than the rest; consequently, 'the square pavement' is an error. As a matter of course, the High Priest must walk on the floor of the Holy of Holies, be it what it might, as he must go in at the door; but it would be absurd to say that the door was for the High Priest to enter by. The floor was just a necessary part of the structure, as were the walls and the ceiling, the whole being not simply or even primarily for the use of the High Priest, seeing that he entered it but once a year. The Holy of Holies was the receptacle for the Ark of the Covenant, and the Mercy Seat, with the Cherubim, etc. (see Exod. xxxvii). Then it is stated in the Ritual that the office of the High Priest was to burn incense once a year; that is true, but he had many other things to do on the Great Day of Atonement (see Levit. xvi). He had to offer a young bullock and two kids; then the Ceremony of the Scape-goat had to be gone through, and much in the way of 'Atonement.' The whole chapter is full of the various acts of 'Atonement,' but it has not one word to justify the assertion that the office of the High Priest on that day was 'to pray fervently that the Almighty . . . peace and tranquillity upon the Israelitish nation during the ensuing year.' He did nothing of the kind as a perusal of Leviticus xvi will clearly show. It may be mentioned that the words 'peace and tranquillity' are used twice in the Third Ceremony; such a conjunction occurs nowhere in the Bible.

APPENDIX (B)

'THE MASTER'S LIGHT'

'FREEMASONS' HALL,
'*December* 7, 1839.

'DEAR SIR AND BROTHER,

'In reply to your questions as to the propriety of extinguishing the Master's Light, and, if extinguished, of introducing a Lanthorn with a Star, etc., I feel no difficulty of stating that such extinguishment is not only improper, but positively in violation of a most maturely considered and unequivocal direction of the Grand Lodge, and that the introduction of a Lanthorn, etc., is equally against the order.

'In the Lodge of Reconciliation, the extinguishment had been proposed, and occasioned much dissatisfaction; in order, therefore, to settle that, and some other points, or, more properly speaking, to carry out the intention and direction of the Act of Union, that there should be a conformity of working etc., a Special Grand Lodge was convened on May 20, 1816, to witness the ceremonies

420

proposed by the Lodge of Reconciliation. These concluded, the several points were discussed—amongst others, the Lights in the Third Degree: and decisions were come to upon them. But to afford opportunity for the most mature consideration, and to leave the subject without a possibility of objection, another Special Grand Lodge was holden on June 5 following, to approve and confirm what had been done on May 20.

'At these Meetings, the M. W. G. Master presided, and the attendance of Members was larger than at any other I recollect (excepting the day of Union).

'The decision was, that the Master's Light was never to be extinguished while the Lodge was open, nor was it by any means to be shaded or obscured, and that no Lanthorn or other device was to be permitted as a substitute.

'One of the reasons is, that one of the Lights represents the Master, who is always present while the Lodge is open, if not actually in his own person, yet by a Brother who represents him (and without the Master or his representative the Lodge cannot be open), so his Light cannot be extinguished until the Lodge is closed; the two other lights figuratively represent luminaries, which, at periods, are visible—at other times, not so.

'As to the penalty with which the Grand Lodge might think fit to visit a Lodge acting in contravention of its positive order, I venture no opinion; you are as capable as myself to decide upon that point.

'I remain,

'Dear Sir and Brother,

'Yours fraternally,

(*Signed*)   'WILLIAM H. WHITE, G.S.'

APPENDIX (C)

The Entered Apprentice's Song

THIS ancient and very famous Masonic ditty was originally called 'The Freemason's Health.'

It is said to have been composed by Bro. Matthew Birkhead, who died on December 30, 1722, but it is quite possible that it was only 'arranged' by him, as it is said to have been in general use among Operative Masons about 1650, and that ancient Freemasons' jugs exist which have the song thereon, and which were made in the days of Matthew Birkhead the elder; not his son above referred to.

The earliest impression of it is taken from Read's 'Weekly Journal, or British Songster' (December 1, 1722), where it is printed in the following form:

423

The Freemason's Health

I

Come, let us prepare; We Brothers that are.
  Met together on merry Occasion;
Let's drink, laugh and sing; Our Wine has a
    Spring.
  'Tis a health to an accepted Mason.

II

The world is in pain Our secret to gain,
  But still let them wonder and gaze on;
Till they're shown the Light, They'll ne'er
    know the Right
  Word or Sign of an accepted Mason.

III

'Tis this and 'tis that, They cannot tell what,
  Why so many great Men of the Nation,
Should Aprons put on, To make themselves
    one
  With a Free or an accepted Mason.

IV

Great Kings, Dukes, and Lords Have laid
    by their swords,
  This our Mist'ry to put a good grace on;
And ne'er been ashamed To hear them-
    selves named
  With a Free or an accepted Mason.

V

Antiquity's pride We have on our side,
  It makes each man just in his station;
There's nought but what's good To be under-
    stood
  By a Free or an accepted Mason.

VI

Then joyn hand in hand, T'each other firm
    stand;
  Let's be merry and put a bright face on:
What mortal can boast So noble a toast
  As a Free or an accepted Mason.

☞ Note the use of the word 'or.'

*   *   *   *

In early days an accepted Mason was a sort of 'honorary' Free Mason. The phrase 'A Free or an Accepted Mason' embraces, therefore, either an (Operative) Free Mason or a (Speculative) Accepted Mason.

*   *   *   *

The words and music are given in the First Edition of the 'Book of Constitutions' issued in 1723.

Subsequently, about 1730, the following stanza was composed by Bro. Springett, Perm. Deputy Grand Master of Munster—

We're true and sincere, We're just to the
   Fair;
   They'll trust us on any occasion;
No mortal can more The Ladies adore
   Than a Free and an Accepted Mason.

The song appeared in the 1738 Edition of
the 'Book of Constitutions' with this stanza
added.

Various trifling and seemingly unnecessary
alterations have been made from time to
time by our irrepressible modernizers and
reformers until the following seems to be the
generally accepted present-day version of it.

(N.B.—Organists are respectfully reminded, that for the comfort of elderly voices
—and therefore the general good of the
occasion—it is advisable to play it in F.)

THE ENTERED APPRENTICE'S SONG

Come, let us prepare; We Brothers that are
   Assembled on merry occasion;
To drink, laugh and sing; Be he beggar* or
   King,
   Here's a health to an Accepted Mason.

* In the first section of the first Lecture we
read: 'Brother to a King, fellow to a Prince or
to a beggar, if a Mason and found worthy.'

The world is in pain Our secret to gain,
   And still let them wonder and gaze on;
They ne'er can divine the word or the
   sign
   Of a Free and an Accepted Mason.

'Tis this and 'tis that, They cannot tell
   what,
   Why so many great men of the Nation,
Should aprons put on, And make themselves
   one
   With a Free and an Accepted Mason.

Great Kings, Dukes, and Lords Have laid
   by their swords,
   Our Myst'ries to put a good grace on;
And ne'er been ashamed To hear them-
   selves named
   As a Free and an Accepted Mason.

Antiquity's pride We have on our side,
   To keep us upright in our station;
There's nought but what's good To be
   understood
   By a Free and an Accepted Mason.

(All rise and join hands.)

Then join hand in hand, By each brother
firm stand;
Let's be merry and put a bright face on:
What mortal can boast So noble a toast
As a Free and an Accepted Mason?

(*Repeat.*)

What mortal can boast So noble a toast
As a Free and an Accepted Mason?

APPENDIX (D)

PROPOSITION FORM

....LODGE, No.........

Form to be signed personally by the Candidate, as well as by his Proposer and Seconder, and then read by the Master or Secretary in open Lodge before the Ballot takes place.

1. Name (in full) of Candidate...................................

2. Full Postal Private Address...............................

3. Business Address...

4. Age...................... Occupation..........................

5. Has a proposal for Initiation been made before to any

Lodge ? ....

Signature of Candidate..................................

Date..........................., 19.........

We, the undersigned Members of the........................ Lodge, No..........., do hereby declare that we, from personal knowledge, believe that the Candidate who has signed above is a fit and proper person to be initiated as a Member of this Lodge.

Name of Proposer........................... Rank............

Name of Seconder........................... Rank............

Date........................, 19.........

I have had due inquiries made (Constitution 183), and the Candidate has been approved by the Standing Committee of the Lodge.

Signature...

W.M., Lodge No..........

Date..................................., 19.........

It is suggested that the proposed Candidate should be 'sounded' as to the answer he will be likely to give to that important question concerning 'the first and most important of the Antient Landmarks' (see p. 64), and that he should be made aware of the contents of the Declaration which he will be asked to sign (Const. 162); also that he should be given an opportunity of making himself acquainted with the By-laws of the Lodge of which he is to become a member, as his acceptance thereof at his Initiation is deemed to be a declaration of his submission to them. It is only fair, therefore, that he should see them beforehand.

APPENDIX (E)

INFORMATION FOR THE GUIDANCE OF ANY
LODGE OF INSTRUCTION WHICH MAY BE
DESIROUS OF OBTAINING THE OFFICIAL
RECOGNITION OF THE COMMITTEE OF
THE EMULATION LODGE OF IMPROVE-
MENT

1. The Lodge of Instruction must hold its meetings 'under the sanction of a Regular Warranted Lodge' (Const. 132).

2. Its By-laws must, *inter alia*, provide—

(*a*) That the Lodge of Instruction shall be governed by a Committee which 'shall be answerable for the proceedings, and responsible that the mode of working adopted has received the sanction of the Grand Lodge' (Const. 132).

(*b*) That of this Committee the Honorary Preceptor, and at least one other member, shall be approved in writing annually by the Committee of the Emulation Lodge of Improvement.

(*c*) That the mode of working shall be in complete conformity with:

(1) The Ancient Ceremonies of Initiation, Passing and Raising as approved, sanctioned and confirmed by the United Grand Lodge on June 5, 1816; and

(2) The Ceremony of Installation as agreed by the Board of Installed Masters, and sanctioned and approved by the Grand Master in 1827; and

(3) The Lectures corresponding with the said Ceremonies and the ancient usages and established customs of the Order;

that is to say, in complete conformity with the recognized system of the Emulation Lodge of Improvement.

(*d*) That no discussion on the Ritual or Working shall be permitted while the Lodge of Instruction is open for business.

(*e*) That neither smoking nor refreshment shall be permitted in the Lodge of Instruction during Masonic business.

(*f*) That the Lodge of Instruction shall furnish annually to the Committee of the Emulation Lodge of Improvement a report on the condition of the Lodge of Instruction and a summary of the past year's work.

(*g*) That any alteration of the By-laws affecting these requirements shall be forthwith communicated to the Committee of the Emulation Lodge of Improvement.

3. It is suggested that the Programme of Work should correspond as far as practicable with the work to be done at the Emulation Lodge of Improvement on the following Friday evening.